**DO NOT REMOVE
CARDS FROM POCKET**

YOU
CAN'T
HURRY
LOVE

LAURIE LEVIN AND LAURA GOLDEN BELLOTTI

YOU CAN'T HURRY LOVE

AN INTIMATE LOOK AT FIRST MARRIAGES AFTER 40

A DUTTON BOOK

DUTTON

Published by the Penguin Group
Penguin Books USA Inc., 375 Hudson Street, New York, New York 10014, U.S.A.
Penguin Books Ltd, 27 Wrights Lane, London W8 5TZ, England
Penguin Books Australia Ltd, Ringwood, Victoria, Australia
Penguin Books Canada Ltd, 10 Alcorn Avenue, Toronto, Ontario, Canada M4V 3B2
Penguin Books (N.Z.) Ltd, 182–190 Wairau Road, Auckland 10, New Zealand

Penguin Books Ltd, Registered Offices:
Harmondsworth, Middlesex, England

First published by Dutton, an imprint of New American Library,
a division of Penguin Books USA Inc.
Distributed in Canada by McClelland & Stewart Inc.

First Printing, February, 1992
10 9 8 7 6 5 4 3 2 1

LIBRARY OF CONGRESS CATALOGING IN PUBLICATION DATA:

Levin, Laurie.
You can't hurry love : an intimate look at first marriages after 40 / Laurie Levin and
Laura Golden Bellotti.
p.   cm.
Includes bibliographical references
ISBN (invalid) 0-452-93402-2
1. Mate selection—United States.   2. Marriage—United States.
3. Middle aged persons—United States   4. Single persons—United States.   I.
Bellotti, Laura Golden.   II. Title.
HQ801.L43   1992
646.7'7—dc20   91-24576
CIP

Printed in the United States of America
Set in Compano

Designed by Steven N. Stathakis

To the forty women and men who so openly shared their stories with us—and to the thousands of never-married and late-marrying men and women whose lives inspired us to write this book.

ACKNOWLEDGMENTS

First of all, a very special thanks to our agent, Susan Schulman, for her steadfast belief in us and this project; working with her has been a gift. We would also like to gratefully acknowledge:

- Richard Marek, former Editor-in-Chief at E.P. Dutton, who recognized the value of our topic, and Michaela Hamilton, our editor, who saw the book through to its completion.
- Psychiatrist Roger Gould, M.D., and psychologists Carl Faber, Ph.D. and Belinda Tucker, Ph.D., for their insights into mid-life marriage.
- Psychotherapists Nancy Golden, M.A., M.F.C.C., and Bill Rolfe, M.A., M.F.C.C., for facilitating group sessions with our interviewees. Nancy Golden for her professional critique of chapter 4.
- Attorney and mediator Kenneth Cloke for his expertise on the subject of prenuptial agreements.
- Publicist Kim Dower for all her good counsel.
- Lyndell Martin, our typist, for tirelessly transcribing countless hours of taped interviews.

And our families . . .

♥ Laurie's: my father, Daniel Levin; mother, Barrie Levy; stepfather, David Levy; and sister, Ariel; for the thousand and one ways they express their love and constancy.
♥ Laura's: my mother, Gladys Fabe; and my late father, Sanford Golden; for reading the manuscript and giving me their thoughtful comments; my sister, Deborah Begg, for her moral support; and, finally, my husband, Michael; and my son, Noah; for their patience and enthusiasm.

To Love, the Burning Point of Life.
—JOSEPH CAMPBELL

CONTENTS

xi

INTRODUCTION

YOU CAN'T HURRY LOVE challenges the widely held myth that if you don't meet the matrimonial deadline by a certain birthday, you'll be doomed to singledom forever. The lives of the women and men in this book prove that the "proper time" to find lasting love is *anytime*. Just because you haven't married *yet* doesn't mean you never will.

The idea for our book sprang from Laurie's experience as a never-married woman over forty. She, too, had suffered spells of hopelessness, fearing she'd never find someone to love and marry. But it wasn't until her friend Sylvie, 43, announced her engagement to be married for the first time that Laurie realized how cultural expectations about "timetables" had quietly undermined her own optimism. Many of Sylvie's friends and family carried on about how *miraculous* it was that Sylvie had finally beaten the odds. But Laurie started thinking: maybe Sylvie's midlife marriage wasn't such a rare exception after all.

As an anthropologist who had studied marriage patterns in a Mayan Indian village, Laurie decided to dig deeper. She had reason to believe that Sylvie's marriage was evidence of a growing trend among her peers: later first marriages. Now was the time to identify and give voice to these marital "mavericks." Hearing their life experiences would undoubtedly bolster her lagging spirits, so why not share the encouragement with a generation of other never-marrieds?

She teamed up with her friend Laura, a book editor who specialized in women's issues. Laura had a personal interest in why so many in our generation had deferred certain conventional life experiences—including having babies. She'd just had her first at age thirty-nine.

Our objective was to interview as many first-time-marrieds over forty as possible, using that as our sole criterion. We put the word out to everyone we knew, placed ads in newspapers, magazines, and organization newsletters. To our surprise we received a flood of responses from such people eager to tell their stories. We limited our sample to twenty men and twenty women to insure that we would come away with in-depth interviews. Even though our subjects were not randomly selected and don't constitute a scientific sampling, we believe their experiences illuminate many values and attitudes that are shared by this special population.

Our interviewees hail from all parts of the United States. They range in occupation from building contractor to physician to graphic artist to insurance adjuster. They're as young as forty and as old as eighty-five. Some are newlyweds, and some have been married as long as thirty-seven years. To protect their anonymity we have changed their names and occupations, but have preserved all the other elements of their stories.

With so little written on the subject of delayed marriages, we had to start from scratch. So we relied directly on the experts: first-time-marrieds over forty themselves. Our questions fell into two basic categories: first, why didn't they marry sooner and what turned them around? Second, what are their midlife marriages like? *You Can't Hurry Love* is divided into these two parts accordingly.

During the course of individual interviews and two group sessions, these women and men openly shared the details of their unique personal histories—enthusiastic that the special circumstances of their marriages were finally getting the attention they deserved. Although no two stories were the same, there *were* common themes. *You Can't Hurry Love* presents these intimate portraits and explores the many reasons why marriage happens later for some people than for others. Some lived together instead of marrying. Some had "psychic baggage" to sort out. Some were anti-marriage. Others simply never met the right person. Until something happened to change *everything*.

You Can't Hurry Love zeroes in on how midlife marriers met their mates and made the transition from "me" to "we" after twenty-odd years of uninterrupted singlehood. Husbands and wives talk about how marrying later directly affects their marital conflicts, sex lives, finances, careers, and parenting. How are their marriages unique? Are they more mature when they argue, or are they "set in their ways"? Do they miss sexual freedom, or is monogamy easier because they've already "sown their wild oats"? How do they feel about sharing money after being financially independent for so long? What kind of parents do they make—wiser or wearier?

You Can't Hurry Love is for midlife marriers who will want to compare their own experiences with those of the people we interviewed. It will also speak to never-marrieds who want to learn what might be in store for *them* if they delay matrimony. Additionally, it provides valuable insights to those who have *remarried* in midlife.

For all who read *You Can't Hurry Love*, the message is the same: It's never too late. Sometimes it is difficult to believe this, and we lose heart. We're constantly bombarded by dismal predictions and outdated notions about "old maids" and "confirmed bachelors." But times have changed. Not only is it okay to remain single, it's also okay to take as long as you want to find a mate. The women and men in our book prove that everyone's life unfolds according to its own sequence, that at every age there are unexpected gifts, and that you can't *hurry* love.

Roster of
First-Marrieds Over Forty

Women

	AGE	YEARS MARRIED
Alice	58	18
Bonnie	42	2
Cheryl	47	7
Deborah	52	9
Diana	43	1
Edna	77	37
Faith	41	1
Helen	47	1
Jackie	42	2
Kate	51	9
Lilly	44	2
Marylin	51	6
Maxine	47	6 mos.
Nancy	41	1
Nora	85	1
Rita	47	7
Simone	59	18
Tess	46	2
Toby	45	3
Vicki	45	5

Roster of First-Marrieds Over Forty

Men

	AGE	YEARS MARRIED
Andreas	41	3 mos.
Andy	42	2
Ben	77	37
Chris	42	1
Derek	43	2
Duncan	50	6
Ed	45	2
Eric	53	7
Glen	46	1
Greg	60	18
Henry	42	2
Ivan	61	3
Luke	46	1½
Ned	45	1
Oliver	52	5
Ray	46	2
Robert	47	4 mos.
Stuart	59	18
Todd	48	8
Victor	44	3

PART

I

WHY THEY DIDN'T MARRY SOONER AND WHAT TURNED THEM AROUND

CHOICE VS. CHANCE

"The soul cannot exist in peace, until it has found its other."

—CARL JUNG

The first words out of Bonnie's mouth were, "I never believed it would happen to me—never in a million years!" Even after two years of marriage, she was still the blushing bride—blushing but not the least bit shy. We settled in around the table in the sunny breakfast room of her duplex apartment. And before we could ask our first question, Bonnie began reminiscing about the magical moment that had led to her first marriage, at the age of forty. Her dark blue eyes danced between us as she recreated the scene.

> *I would have chosen marriage years earlier, had I been given the choice. But I didn't meet Bill until I was thirty-nine. After years of fantasizing about "the proposal," his came very close: dark restaurant, candlelight, my hand in his under the table. Still, I thought I was just on another romantic date with the guy I had grown to love in a very short time.*

3

We were sitting there and suddenly he looked at me long and hard without speaking. Finally he said, "I have something to give you." I got so nervous I started saying, "No, no, I'm too scared." But he clasped my hand in his anyway and whispered, "Will you marry me?" And I said, "Yes!"

I could barely finish my meal, I was trembling so. After all this time, after all my doubts, I had finally gotten engaged. I was so excited that as we drove downtown to the concert hall, I rolled down my window, stuck my head out, and shouted, "I'm going to get married!" I thought, even if, God forbid, we ever broke up, at least I got engaged.

If we are honest with ourselves, there is a little bit of Bonnie in most of us who have never been married by the time we reach midlife. That is because, in the deepest recesses of our hearts, a strong pulse beats toward relationship. We are programmed to bond with another human being; something inside of us longs to recognize our soul's counterpart in another's. Through a loving union we attempt to bridge our human separateness and soothe our sense of isolation. But these days the search seems exhausting and, often, unending. Many of us fear we will never find love. With wavering hope we look forward to a time when we can actively care for the life and growth of our chosen mate, and they for ours. And when we finally do find love, we are elated and not a little relieved.

By midlife we have considerable life experience to help us in making an intimate relationship work. We are more "ready" than ever. Our own identity is firmly established. We know our own frailties and limitations and are in a better position to love someone for who he or she *really* is as a human being, independent of our own expectations and fantasies. We also know that we are responsible for our own happiness or unhappiness. With these understandings under our belt, we have the potential to love in a mature way. Once the ability for mature love is developed, it is finally possible to build a "true marriage." According to the mythologist Joseph Campbell, marriage in this highest sense is a lifelong bond,

a commitment to that which you are [and to the understanding] that that person is literally your other half—you and the other

*are one. A love affair isn't that. That is a relationship for
pleasure, and when it gets to be unpleasurable, it's off. But a
marriage is a life commitment, and a life commitment means the
prime concern of your life.*[1]

But, for many never-married men and women in the United
States, finding a true marriage, committing oneself to it, and keeping
it alive often seems more an impossible dream than a realistic pros-
pect. How many of us are battling "singles' gridlock" and "hope
burnout"? It is true that there are more single people now than ever
before; 42 percent of all adults over eighteen are single; and nearly 20
percent of these have never married.[2] But that doesn't necessarily
mean never-marrieds are at any more of a marrying disadvantage than
anyone else, or that they will remain unwed forever. Quite the
contrary—it's estimated that approximately 90 to 95 percent of *all*
adults will eventually marry at least once in their lifetimes.[3]

Women and men who marry for the first time later in life aren't
social misfits or unlovable leftovers, but represent a fast-growing and
relatively new marriage phenomenon. Just twenty years ago, only 12
percent of men and women between the ages of thirty-five and
thirty-nine had yet to be married for the first time.[4] Today that figure
has almost doubled. What do first-marrieds over forty *themselves* say
about why they were single for so long and what led them to meeting
their mates and finally marrying? How are their marriages different as
a result of having delayed a rite of passage traditionally completed in
one's twenties?

As you read this book, you may discover, as we did, aspects of
your own personal history in the many stories we were told. What
becomes clear is that there is no *one* reason why men and women
delay marriage, and no *one* formula that transforms destinies. Perhaps
you will identify with one aspect of Bonnie's story, or find an uncanny
parallel with Helen's or Eric's. We hope you will also come to appreciate how our generation was influenced by the cultural changes of the
1960s and 1970s and how those changes played out in the lives of
late marriers.

If you are worried that you will never marry because your luck
is bad and the odds against it are gargantuan, take heart! *None* of the
disheartening, highly publicized studies on the dismal marriage proba-

bilities of never-married women were designed to take into account an individual's purpose or plan. Nor did the studies distinguish between women who were interested in getting married, those who had declined offers, those who didn't care or had never met the right person, or those who favored living together instead. In many cases, as we found out, deciding to remain single is more a matter of *choice and chance* than just about anything else.

CHOICE: MARRIAGE ON HOLD

Choice became the byword for our generation during the sixties and seventies when both men and women began defining their futures in broader terms than marriage and parenthood. For women, in particular, it was a heady time. Suddenly, *housewife* became a dirty word. Women whose resources permitted them the choice now had and took advantage of more options than ever before.

In a survey conducted from 1969 to 1973, the percentage of college-educated twenty-two- and twenty-three-year-old white women who said they planned to be housewives by age thirty-five declined from 53 percent to 17 percent.[5] Back then, many of these women, whose education ostensibly made them the most desirable marriage partners, became, at least for that time, the least desirous of marrying. A sizable number, many of whom are now in their forties, were not necessarily rejecting marriage over education, but rather revving up for lifelong careers and placing marriage and family responsibilities on hold. But who are the *real* women beneath these hefty statistics?

When we considered interviewing women who chose to defer marriage temporarily in order to nurture a career, we couldn't think of a better place to find one than New York City—the spawning ground of the mythical high-powered career woman. Deborah, a fifty-two-year-old publishing executive, fit our profile perfectly.

On short notice, she generously sandwiched our meeting between a breakfast appointment with an upcoming author and an editorial conference. We were ushered into her buzzing office on Manhattan's East 48th Street while she was concluding a phone conversation. She sat behind a large desk in a well-tailored beige suit and was doodling on an elbow-high stack of sales printouts. Once off the phone, Deborah welcomed us. She is a distinguished-looking woman with a direct, self-assured voice. For the next forty-five minutes she openly shared her story with us.

It is not unusual to hear today's professional women say that they want it all—a career, a husband, a home, a child. But when Deborah decided to postpone her marriage, women's choices were defined far more sharply than they are now. It was one or the other: marriage or career. For Deborah, who believed that freedom was something one had only outside of marriage, marrying seemed like a form of "retreating," and that was the last thing she wanted to do. A smile came to her face when she recollected her thinking at the time:

> *The career part was the "fun" part that would come first, and then I would eventually marry and have children. I never intended not to settle down, just to delay it. My goals were very short-term then—in business and in my life. I loved the spontaneity of being single—picking up and going whenever I wanted to. I had no pets and lived in a doorman building. I had the most freedom that you can have as a single woman in this society. I enjoyed it immensely.*

Deborah was riding the same wave of possibility that swept through many women. With expanding priorities and a new found independence from a marriage-centered value system, men and women began to reevaluate the merits of marriage. Not only did singlehood emphasize autonomy and self-sufficiency, but it offered the opportunity for introspection and experimentation that nurtured a personal and professional identity. Staying single began to be viewed as a valuable path to self-actualization: by remaining unattached, one could buy time from the distracting snags and snarls characteristic of married life.

Deborah, like many of us, was exercising her prerogatives and working her way up the corporate ladder. Since she never had a compelling desire to have children, marriage wasn't a priority and its timing wasn't a problem. She had a New York "everything is possible" attitude, and figured that when she wanted a husband she'd find one; Deborah never panicked. Her life was filled with lots of terrific times and great friendships with men she knew she wouldn't marry. Deborah was using her "single time" to mature as a person.

> *Those were wonderful growth years, ones I would never have had if I had gotten married. I wasn't running my life in a way that was going to make it possible for me to find someone to marry. It's funny because I had been very successful in business, nurturing contacts, addressing clients' needs, knowing what your customer wants, but I didn't do that with the men I was involved with. I was not tending to relationships in the way you need to if you want them to lead to marriage.*

Deborah's attention was channeled toward her professional success. She was able to manage her life under her own steam, and did not feel an urgency to marry for survival. Traditionally, women have gained financially from marriage, but have had to pay dearly for it. Wives were generally expected to take care of their families, surrender their own privacy, limit contact with friends, and preempt their own schedules in order to run a household.[6] But, today, women are much more wary of marriage in light of their increased ability to support themselves outside of it. With more women spending full-time in the workplace and facing a second shift at home, there is a growing realization that they may be coming up short in the bargain. They can now afford to think twice before taking matrimonial vows, setting higher standards, and taking their time to *choose* an acceptable match.[7]

CHANCE: "I WAS THERE, WHERE WERE YOU?"

But what about all those quirky, ill-timed factors that play just as great a part in staying single as conscious choice? Many men and women found themselves *wanting* to marry all along, but now claim that the vagaries of chance got in the way of finding the right person. Luck *is* a big part of finding love, and too many unmarried women complain they don't have enough of it. Many believe there is a shortage of available men who are old enough and interested enough to settle down. How often have we all heard (or started believing) the common laments, "All the good ones are taken," or "The ones that are left aren't cute, healthy, straight, or sane"? Trust your instincts, for they may be telling you something that demographers have been debating for years.

Demographic evidence suggests that we may be in the middle of a "marriage squeeze," one that has specifically affected women born during the first wave of the baby boom, from 1946 to 1954. The assumption behind this theory is that women, in keeping with the preferred marriage pattern in the United States, usually look to wed men slightly older than themselves. As a group, the total number of female baby boomers far exceeds the total number of males born five to ten years earlier, when the birth rate was considerably lower.[8] Therefore, there is more competition among women for fewer men.

Theoretically, this short supply of eligible grooms would affect the marriage chances of women who would be looking to choose a man now in his late forties. It is probably little consolation to older unmarried women, but since men tend to marry women a few years younger, the men born during the second wave of the baby boom, from 1954 to 1964, are expected to experience a similar difficulty by the early 1990s, when younger marriageable females become less plentiful.[9]

But, in all fairness, men and women alike have difficulties dating and keeping their failing spirits up. For never-marrieds in midlife, looking for one's life partner doesn't necessarily get easier with years of practice—and neither does dealing with the cumulative disappointment each time a potential commitment falls apart. Chronic dating fatigue may actually begin to undermine our self-esteem, especially if we believe that we are doomed to date forever. We get stuck in a vicious cycle: the more we date and fail to find what we are looking for, the worse we feel about ourselves; the worse we feel about ourselves, the less we will want to date; the less we date, the less likely it is that we will meet the right person; and 'round and 'round we go. Diana, forty-three, was one of several delayed marrieds who felt as though she had been hitting the wall on the dating marathon for as long as she could remember. Now happily married, she lives with her husband of two years in a house that is a replica of an antebellum mansion: stately pillars, white shuttered windows, a veranda dripping with lilacs—everything but the Mississippi.

Our interview took place in her cavernous living room overlooking a pool and tennis court. Diana's casual demeanor put us at ease immediately. She plopped onto one of the two large floral couches, kicked off her shoes, and tucked her feet snugly under her peasant skirt, urging us to do the same.

"Deep down," Diana began, "I *always* wanted to wear a wedding band, I wanted my husband to wear a wedding band, but I never found him until recently. After twenty unwedded years, I heard myself saying that if I didn't marry it would be okay, but that wasn't how I *really* felt. It was at those times that I wondered if my luck really *had* run out when I was twenty-five."

In her mid-twenties, she had been convinced she was heading for marriage with a man who, despite his difficult mood swings that went from euphoric highs to crashing lows, seemed to be "the guy." After five and a half years of on-again, off-again marriage proposals, it became increasingly clear that her boyfriend's painful and deepening indecision had little if anything to do with Diana and even less to do with fear of marriage. When he was finally diagnosed as suffering from clinical depression, Diana, a loyal and caring person, joined him in therapy in hopes of salvaging the relationship. Through counseling she came to realize if she was to marry this man, it would mean marrying his chronic depression. Diana wrestled with her guilt about leaving, but became aware that even her devoted love couldn't rescue him from himself. She decided to move on with her own life.

Diana began dating again nine months later, but her heart really wasn't in it. Her emotional reserves were depleted, and she decided it was time to find out what she really wanted for herself. She decided to take a three-week vacation by herself, something she'd never done before. The success of her solo adventure in Brazil boosted her confidence. She discovered she was a lot more resourceful, independent, and resilient than she had ever expected. She returned reenergized and started tackling the dating world with an attitude of "Here I am—what you see is what you get."

This renewed sense of self-worth helped her to deal with the insidious and not-so-subtle stigma that never-marrieds face after a certain age when one is asked the seemingly innocent question: "And why has a person like you never been married?" Translated, this often means, "Okay, what's wrong with you?" The question arises from the misguided assumption that even if someone has been married unhappily, at least he or she has been chosen once and is more desirable than someone who's never been picked. Diana resisted this persistent implication that she had been left on the shelf, and forced herself to stay in the dating fray.

I'd get so fed up with dating and that same old question more times than I can tell you. After a while I just wanted to video myself and send it to the guy so that I wouldn't have to go through the whole song and dance each time I went out with a new fellow. I remember complaining to a friend, who said, "Okay, I'll go out on your first dates for you!"

After a slew of "first dates" I'd swear I would never do it again; then three weeks would go by and I'd say, "Maybe I can do it just one more time." I had to go through it to get to the other side.

Diana was determined to marry for love—not just for the sake of being married. Her mother had always told her, "Marriage is a twenty-four-hour job that you do for the rest of your life because you love it." It was counsel that Diana took very seriously, but despite her strong determination to resist "settling," she was beginning to wonder if she would ever meet a man with the qualities she was looking for.

People began to say that I shouldn't look for love, that I should look for a compatible relationship instead. There were times when I thought maybe they were right. But then another part of me kept saying, "I don't want that! I am okay the way I am—single."

My brother, who had been single for a long time, said to me, "Don't give in—hold out!" I trusted him because he had just met someone he was crazy about. He fortified what I believed deep down.

According to the sociologist Jesse Bernard, if Diana had been limiting her search to never-married men, she might rightfully have had cause for concern. Bernard's controversial research describes the pool of never-married men and women as being at opposite ends of the marriage gradient; that is, the men are "the bottom of the barrel" while the women are "the cream of the crop."[10] This study concluded that older single women, as a group, tended to be superior to single men in terms of education, occupation, and income, and were often more upwardly mobile than their married sisters, both educationally and professionally. Following this logic, Bernard claims that these women have preferred to remain unmarried rather than "marry down."

However, we didn't find this to be true of the late marriages in our survey. With only a few exceptions, our interviewees and their spouses were on a par socially, financially, professionally, and educationally. The couples themselves thought so too; they used words such as "my peer," "my equal," or "my match" to express how well they fit with their mates. While not everyone was absolutely, perfectly happy, not one late marrier complained that his or her marital problems were a result of having "married down." We conclude that marrying later does not mean marrying less!

BETTING ON YOURSELF: CREATING YOUR OWN INDIVIDUAL ODDS

Most of us remember the widely publicized Bennet, Bloom, Craig study in 1986 that declared dismal marriage prospects for never-married white women thirty years of age and older. The study results, now widely disputed, stated that the marriage probability of a thirty-five-year-old never-married woman dropped to 5 percent, and plummeted to 1 percent by age forty.[11] The probabilities for black women in the same groups were even smaller, according to the researchers. Jeanne E. Moorman, a demographer at the United States Census Bureau, using a different set of data and an alternative statistical method, arrived at more encouraging projections. Moorman concluded that never-married, college-educated, thirty-five-year-old women had a 32–41 percent chance of marrying; forty-year-old women had a 17–23 percent chance; and forty-five-year-old women had an 8–11 percent chance.[12]

Even more recent figures indicate that increasing numbers of both men and women are marrying later for the first time. First-marriage rates have actually improved by 3 to 4 percent for women aged thirty to thirty-nine, and by 11 percent for never-married men aged forty to forty-four—the highest increase since 1974.[13] And if you are looking to marry a never-married man, by age forty to forty-four there are actually 148 never-married men to every hundred never-married women, and more never-married men to never-married women in every group to age 65![14]

Keep in mind, however, that scientific probabilities *are not* predictions but, rather, educated guesses based on what has happened in the past and projected onto the capricious, unknowable future. Even more critical to remember is that there is a world of difference between statistical averages of groups and your own personal odds. And, most important, all of us bring our own special limitations and strengths to the process of creating solutions for ourselves.

When we bring the odds down to an individual level, finding love and intimacy are subject to many complex and interconnected influences: what we do; who we are; where we live; what we believe. In the following chapters we will hear the firsthand stories of forty midlife marriers who transformed their lives in a variety of ways: Kate, for example, gave up hope and moved to the country after loving men who were either too wild, too young, or too married—only to meet her future husband in a small-town church choir. Tess believed that marriage was a repressive institution designed to subjugate women, and vowed never to take a relationship beyond living together. Yet she found herself saying "I do" on April Fool's Day to a man ten years her junior. And Andy, having lost two mothers—his birth mother, who gave him up for adoption, and his adoptive mother, who died when he was twelve—had a hard time trusting women until a dramatic catharsis turned him around.

Each of the men and women in our survey has been where many of us still are—single and concerned we're going to stay that way from here on in. They, too, had listened to the well-meaning counsel of countless others and had worn out ways of meeting the right person. They, too, have done exactly what we all do—wallowed in self-pity, trashed the opposite sex, longed for lost loves—anything and everything before bracing themselves to go out and try again.

We asked our first-time marrieds over forty to reach back into their storehouses of experience and share what had encouraged *them* so that they could, in turn, encourage *us*.

ADVICE FROM THE LOVE-WORN

Even though no two people are alike, and meeting one's mate never happens the same way twice, we tried to reconstruct the common themes that echoed throughout the diverse personal stories older first-marriers told us. It is true: there is no one "quick fix" for terminal singlehood, but what follows is a summary of their collective wisdom—wisdom that worked! Throughout this book we will explore how these themes relate specifically to their lives, in hopes that what they learned may benefit us all.

1. TAKE RISKS: KEEP ON DATING

Sometimes it feels as though it is easier to give up on an unsatisfying social life than to keep fighting for one we want. This is particularly true of dating, especially when, like Diana, we'd rather have root-canal therapy than go out on one more dippy date. But remember that dating to find a partner is simply a means to an end, and that is where risk-taking comes in. Risk the possibility that the next date, and the next date after that, may not deliver on your expectations, and then risk the next date. According to Eric, a fifty-three-year-old real-estate agent who met his wife at a Dallas pool party, finding love is like betting on any other sport; in order to succeed, you have to risk failure. "I maximized my chances and created my own point spread," Eric asserts, "when I developed the attitude that dating is a game where either way—heads or tails—I win."

If you are paralyzed by the thought of rejection, then you may end up cutting your chances down to nothing. Carl Faber, a Los Angeles psychotherapist in private practice, counsels his older, more cynical single patients to gamble a little with life. "The most you're going to experience is the limit of your bet," he says, "and if you're hedging your bet, holding back 10 percent, the best you're going to get is 90 percent. You're never going to get it all unless you put it

all on the table! Even then there are no guarantees, so go for the big stuff anyway, go for it all and put your heart out there!"

2. LIVE YOUR OWN LIFE TO THE FULLEST—REGARDLESS!

Be committed to making yourself as happy as you can so you are not looking to marriage to make up for what you can't make happen for yourself. If you are involved in the kinds of things you want and need to do, the chances increase that you will meet someone compatible— that is where your stable of potential mates comes from. Cheryl, a part-time songwriter, now forty-seven, who met her husband back-stage at a local jazz club, spent years focusing more on getting married than on simply living to the fullest. "A good life," she told us, "is just as valuable as a marriage. When I finally got busy living *my* life, I met my husband. In my mind, there's no question that the more fun you are having, the more likely you'll get what you want— whatever that is!"

3. THERE IS NOTHING WRONG WITH YOU IF YOU ARE SINGLE!

Take yourself off the hook: you are not necessarily incapable of having a relationship just because you currently don't have the love of your life *in* your life. Being single is not a confirmation that your personality is defective or that you are socially deformed! Yet too many of us believe otherwise, and the self-hatred shows; it not only handicaps our own growth and happiness, but also hinders our chances to attract a suitable partner. Lilly, forty-four, met and married her husband Kevin shortly after she *stopped* telling herself, "If I haven't had a committed relationship by now, I'm probably not worthy of one."

A sense of low self-esteem is often compounded by the profound loneliness we feel in the absence of a supportive, intimate relationship. It is often difficult to determine whether our low self-esteem stems from unresolved personal issues or whether we're crumbling under the pressure of our couple-oriented society. But try to figure out the difference, and take responsibility for getting to know yourself better and removing the personal obstacles that prevent you from having more successful relationships. Most of all, be gentle on yourself.

4. RESIST BELIEVING THAT AGE IS A LIABILITY

We live in a society riddled with ageism, which would have us believe that once we're over thirty our options start snapping shut like mousetraps. We are culturally programmed to consider age forty as the beginning of the end; many of us at that age start to behave as though we were really "over the hill." It is undeniable that our options *change.* But the great thing about life is that it is constantly renewing itself: the same options that we had at twenty-three we wouldn't want at forty-four, and vice versa. What doesn't diminish is our capacity for feelings. In fact, feelings can be "forever young" and loving feelings can be timeless. So don't let the idea that you are "getting old" bury you alive and alone.

Our most striking example of the perpetual possibility of finding love is Nora, an eighty-five-year-old physician from Maine who married for the first time a year ago. Nora would have been very happy to find a mate earlier in life, but she didn't want to marry just anyone for the sake of being married. Despite the passage of so many years, she stayed open, kept going out, and didn't cave in under the pressure. "I never really clicked with anyone until Alex," she began:

> *As I got older, a part of me felt that there was less likelihood of meeting the right person, but I never closed my mind to it. From the very first time we met, I knew that Alex was someone with whom I wanted to develop something right away　but neither of us ever mentioned the word* marriage *for the first six months.*
>
> *One day we were sitting at my dining room table. He looked at me and we didn't exchange a word. I knew what he was saying, but I couldn't believe that was what he meant. It was all through his eyes, and that closed the deal.*

These words could as easily have been spoken by a thirty-five-year-old woman as by an eighty-five-year-old one. The lesson in Nora's story is a simple and direct one: listen to your inner voice, don't look desperately, and never think it's too late.

5. CLARIFY YOUR PRIORITIES AND INTENTIONS

Individuals *can* boost their personal odds if they harness their desires, get more sure about what they want, and act on their convictions. Our intentions can be defined as those things a person hopes to achieve or attain—the active component of our wishes and dreams, whether they are formally expressed or not. Intentions drive the attitudes we hold and underlie the decisions we make, decisions that bring us closer to achieving our aims. It is surprising how few of us actually sit down and formally articulate what we want and our plan of action to achieve it.

Rollo May, the distinguished psychologist and author of *Love and Will*, states that by bringing our intentions out of the imagination and trying them in actuality, we can participate in forming our own future.[15] As we conceive of and experiment with new possibilities, we move outside of our self-imposed limitations to form the foundation of what is to come. Making choices in our lives, especially choices about how we go about selecting a mate, can tell us a great deal about the depth and clarity of our convictions and the risks we're willing to take.

Remember Kate, the woman who moved to the country and met her husband singing in a church choir? She strongly believes, like others, that there is a distinct difference between knowing that you *don't want* to be single anymore and knowing you *want* to get married, and that this greatly influences how you go about finding love. "Decide what you want and make a plan to get it," she advises. "You have to make a physical movement—a step, an actual outright step! You can't just sit back and say, 'Okay, now I've decided I don't want to be single, so I'll wait for him to come to me.' That is not enough!"

So don't be too proud to ask people you trust to introduce you to available friends, and don't waste time dating people who are not right for you. Helen, who could have married any number of men over the course of her single life, is another late marrier who stuck it out. Until she met her husband, Dan, while ballroom dancing on the night of Los Angeles's last major earthquake, none was right for her. "People would say, 'You're too particular,' " she recalled, "and I would say, 'Yes! I don't want to settle for something that is less than I should have.' When I finally met my husband, I knew *he* was someone I could marry."

If people start calling you "too picky" and begin suggesting that you be more "realistic" and "reasonable," be careful how you interpret this message. On the one hand, you might consider whether or not you *are* setting your standards too high or looking too hard for fairy-tale love in order actually to avoid an intimate relationship. On the other hand, if you've taken thorough stock of yourself and consider your wish-list findable, then resist the other interpretation of this message: that it might be better just to get married than to risk never getting married at all. None of the men and women we interviewed shared this sentiment, and none had been prepared to sacrifice their single lives simply to marry for marrying's sake. Instead, they resolved to share their lives with someone who would enhance them, and they believed that a marriage based on the fear of remaining alone would be unworkable.

Getting back to Deborah and Diana, each took risk-taking and intentionality to heart in order to meet their life partners. First, Deborah's story:

By the time she was in her mid-thirties, Deborah's career was firmly rooted and she enjoyed her unmarried life, supported by a close network of friends and family. Had she lived never-married in her native Detroit, she might have felt more pressure to marry, but being single in a large city like New York was easier: she had wider freedom to move socially as an unmarried woman, and there was a larger pool of unmarried men to choose from. Both of these aspects became important as Deborah's needs for a sustained relationship began to shift. She found herself wanting something more permanent, more committed. So, based on her new objectives, Deborah set about redirecting herself with the same concerted effort that she had previously applied to her career:

When I decided I wanted to get married, I knew that it had to be one of the foremost decisions of my life, not unlike how I went about developing my career. It meant that I had to stay on course and not let myself be diverted too much. I had to give myself a shot, so I started doing things that I'd never done before.

Deborah realized that if she wanted things to change in her life, *she* had to change. With the same analytical eye that guided her professional success, she examined how she had been behaving in her relationships, discovered that her actions were thwarting her goals, and revised her approach. But first she did some experimenting and practicing:

> *I was seeking in a way that I had never sought before. I had always made it very difficult for people to introduce me, let alone line me up for a blind date. I had my rules: first they had to make a dinner party, and then they had to sit me next to the person, and then, if they were lucky, I would show up!*
>
> *I also began accepting invitations to places where I wouldn't ordinarily have gone for the purpose of seeing if there were any men that I might be interested in. In the past, I'd always gone to a lot of business parties, but instead of checking the room for an eligible male, I'd make a beeline for the editor of* The New York Times. *Now I started doing it another way.*
>
> *I'd see if there was anyone who appealed to me and then, in the old-fashioned way, I'd ask three or four questions to see if he was married. If he was, I'd stay away. If he wasn't, then I'd just talk and flirt. Men find meetings as difficult as women; they need to feel you're interested in them before they risk getting rejected.*

Deborah eased up on her restrictions. She even broke tradition and asked friends to fix her up, with one proviso: that they knew the prospective date firsthand. Deborah was also ready to redefine Mr. Right. At first she was so busy enjoying herself—flirting at parties, asking open-ended questions instead of always talking about her high-power job—that when she met Irv, her husband-to-be, she almost passed him over:

> *I used to think men like my husband were dull and boring. He is no way, in appearance or temperament, like anyone I had dated in the last fifteen years. I was looking at him sideways,*

saying to myself, "Who is this guy?" But somehow one date led to another.

Our fourth date coincided with a crisis I had at work. For the first time I found myself opening up to him, and I began to appreciate his concern and understanding. The whole idea of wanting someone who cared about me finally sunk in.

Although many of us might not plot our love trajectory with the same kind of boardroom precision that Deborah used, her story is a valuable example of what can happen when we step back, rethink what we want and how we want to get it, and point ourselves in a more productive direction. Predictably, when we do take the initiative, we find ourselves in uncomfortable, unfamiliar territory. But if we can tolerate our temporary discomfort, we are just as often rewarded: not only can we learn something about ourselves in the process; we can even create a positive factor that directly influences the vagaries of chance.

Diana, too, was at a crossroads in her life when she hit her mid-thirties. Five years after recovering from the traumatic breakup with her fiancé, she was still dating as usual, with no one special on the horizon. One of her friends made the friendly suggestion that Diana join a video dating service. She told Diana the service was like a supermarket of men, and that *she* could be doing the picking instead of waiting to be picked. At first Diana wouldn't hear of it. But a year and a half later she signed up. To her surprise, nearly fifty men requested dates during the time she was active. She pre-screened all of them, chose to say yes only to the ones that interested her, and received an unexpected but very valuable dividend: a bird's-eye view of how her previous preferences were limiting her socially.

I learned how to date someone who didn't necessarily fit my "perfect picture": financial background, education, specific looks, certain interests in the arts and culture—all the things that would read nicely in the nuptial columns. It is funny because some of the guys who would "read" like that would have been boring as husbands. I met men I knew wouldn't necessarily be life mates. Instead, I was discovering more about what I really wanted from a man, and what I could live with. Once I filtered

*out all the junk I had in my head in terms of expectations, the
most important trait left was someone who was a nice guy who
could make me laugh and feel happy.*

One day, when Diana was in the dating service's video library,
flipping through the volumes of eligible men, she met a woman
named Margo. They got to know each other well through the course
of the next year. One day Margo said she had briefly dated a fellow
she'd met through the video service who she thought would be
perfect for Diana. When Margo located his picture and bio in the
registry, Diana couldn't help but feel encouraged. By coincidence, she
herself had chosen the same man just a week before. She bypassed the
"official channels" and gave Margo the go-ahead to fix her up.

When Jim and Diana met, it was "lust at first sight." They
laughed and giggled over lunch. From the moment of their first
good-bye kiss, things got serious and complicated very quickly. By
the second date, Jim told Diana he had two children but wasn't able
to have more. It gave her pause, since she thought she still wanted
to have children with a husband. Instead of rejecting Jim on the basis
of his vasectomy, however, she told herself, "Don't be a jerk, find out
about this guy first!"

Once Diana had decided to give Jim a chance, they were inseparable. But there was another problem. Early into their courtship, Jim
told her that he had unfinished business to attend to: a woman he'd
been seeing off and on for the previous six years. Diana was utterly
devastated. With all the courage she could muster, Diana refused to
become the "other woman."

*I said to him, "I came to you freely and thought you came to me
that way. I am not going to hang around while you make a
decision about someone you've had years of experience with. If
you are going to take care of business, you have a right to do
that, but know that I am not going to be here while you do."*

Diana immediately left town for a week with a friend, and told
Jim that when he was finished working out his life, he could call her.
She insisted that until he knew one way or the other what he wanted
to do, she didn't want any letters or phone calls—not because she

wanted to hurt him, but because she needed to protect herself. Her resolve was firm and sincere.

Diana didn't have to hold her ground for long. By the time she got home from her trip, Jim had left a series of phone messages telling her that things were over with his ex-girlfriend and asking to see her as soon as possible to explain. They planned to see each other the next day, and they've been together ever since. That was September, and Jim asked Diana to marry him on Valentine's Day of the following year.

TAKING A CHANCE ON LOVE

Once you have clarified your intentions and are acting on them, inevitably, like Deborah and Diana, you will run into a kind of cosmic "super glue" that binds *unlikely* occurrences and *likely* people together into a series of critical moments. The pioneering psychoanalyst Carl Jung first named this process *synchronicity*. The concept challenges the common notion that we are simply isolated objects that bump into each other like so many billiard balls, and suggests, instead, that we all participate in a profound interconnectedness in which we are continually influencing one another and of which we are largely unaware. Synchronicity describes those links between events that cannot be explained by cause and effect or total coincidence—connections that lie somewhere between the realms of fate, logic, and randomness.

Usually these meetings come when we least expect them, aren't prepared, and were ready to throw in the towel altogether. In particular, the moments in which we meet and recognize our potential mates contain all the elements we wish we could control, design, and ordain, but can't. When two people *do* experience spontaneous chemistry, some interpret these chance meetings as destined, or as meaningful coincidences. But as the psychiatrist and Jungian analyst Jean Shinoda Bolen explains in her book *The Tao of Psychology*, "When inner timing and outer meeting show a precise fit, when a meeting seems uncannily tailored and impossible to have arranged deliberately, then synchronicity may be the matchmaker at work."[16]

Intention and synchronicity play a kind of tag in our lives, and the give and take between them shape and form the potential of our relationships. So, for example, when Deborah chose to see Irv another time and decided to open up and voice her concern about an unexpected crisis, an opportunity was created wherein she was able to recognize and appreciate aspects of his character that might not have been apparent to her otherwise. When Diana was faced with Jim's "unfinished business," she was forced to take a stand about what she *didn't* want, which in turn led to their reconciliation. In both instances, external random circumstances prompted Deborah and Diana to crystallize their intentions and moved them closer to realizing the potential of their relationships.

Each life is a unique product of choice and chance, full of uncertainty and some measure of chaos. What often appears as a tangle of paradoxical and haphazard events while we are in the midst of living them inevitably makes a kind of sense when we look back. If we acknowledge and become more comfortable with the fact that we are not in total control, then we can allow the invisible and uncalculated to take place, and synchronicity, the hidden matchmaker, can do its work. This may mean we will need to release our preconceived notions of when or how "it" will happen, and who will fit the bill. And it may mean easing up on the desperate feelings that drive us to make unwise moves.

Finding one's mate is the process by which we commingle our hearts, our luck, and our choices with those of another. Ultimately the formula is elusive and unknowable. Even so, we are like "love alchemists" who tirelessly seek to transmute the base metals of our lives into the gold of relationship. And many of us succeed.

2

Marriage Meant Growing Up, and Growing Up Meant Dying

I never wanted to grow up because growing up meant dying. Maybe that's part of the reason why I waited so long to get married. I felt that would be the beginning of the end of me. If I got married, then I would really be losing it.

—CHRIS, age forty-two, married one year

When I was eighteen, I was against the war, against spending my time at some boring job, and, most of all, against getting stuck in a passionless marriage. Following in my parents' footsteps, putting myself on automatic pilot, was the last thing I wanted to do. Getting married and settling down was part of the old guard, and that's what I was striking out against.

—LILLY, age forty-four, married two years

THE ANTI-MARRIAGE GENERATION

Today's forty-somethings were in their late teens and early twenties during the cultural upheaval of the 1960s and early 1970s. It was then that marriage, the most time-honored sign of adulthood, was pronounced outdated by a sizable portion of the younger generation. Although it has always been standard for young adults to question their parents' values, young people in the sixties possessed a heightened spirit of rebellion that had a lasting effect on our culture. The antiwar movement galvanized that spirit, but there were numerous other forces that challenged the status quo and contributed to the backlash against the institution of marriage.

As early as the 1950s—at least a decade before women started protesting their limited lives as housewives—American men were quietly signaling that they resented their lot in life, their obligation to "settle down" and support wives and children. In her book *The Hearts of Men*, Barbara Ehrenreich describes what she terms "the male revolt" against the traditional breadwinner role. Middle-class men were suffering from "white-collar blues" and white-collar heart attacks, and wanted more from life than a station wagon in which to drive to and from the daily rat race.

One of the first forums for male dissatisfaction with marriage was *Playboy* magazine, initially published in 1953. It irreverently rejected husbandhood and urged men to relive their adolescence. At a time when American culture extolled the virtues of conformity and maturity, *Playboy* celebrated the fantasy that men could keep company with young, sexy playmates who wouldn't entrap them with kids or demand financial support until death. Its name said it all: *play boy*.

"Beat" writers from the fifties also gave voice to an antimarriage ideology, although in their case the voice was distinctly non-middle class. They shunned "straight" jobs, sought to abandon the straitjacket of responsibility and convention, and escaped to freedom—even if that freedom condemned them to an economic underclass. When Dean, the protagonist in Jack Kerouac's *On the Road*, played out the male escape fantasy by walking out on his wife and baby to travel, he looked forward to "the ragged and ecstatic joy of pure being."[1]

If Kerouac and others didn't always appeal to the masses, such fifties media rebels as James Dean, Marlon Brando, and Elvis Presley did. What these defiant young men embodied was the possibility of avoiding the predictability and boredom of middle-class life. Disdaining the world of white picket fences and happily-ever-after, they ignited the restless yearnings of Eisenhower-era youth.[2]

The *Playboy* ethic, the Beats, and the bad boys of the fifties laid the foundation for rebellion against traditional family life. What came next, in the form of sixties popular ideology, was an all-out assault. Young people told their parents point-blank that they didn't intend to sign up for the same mainstream existence that tolerated war, bigotry, and meaningless employment simply in order to provide for their families. This new outspoken generation rejected the whole notion of the nuclear family as being too insular, too cut off from the conflicts and realities of a changing society. Marriage inhibited both contact with the world and contact with oneself; so, in the interest of personal development as well as social involvement, matrimony was to be avoided. Many baby boomers—the younger brothers and sisters of the quietly dissatisfied fifties generation—baldly declared to their elders that they weren't buying into anything the "straight" world had to offer, and that included getting married.

Victor began rejecting the establishment after his stint as a GI in Vietnam. He told us how his army experiences made his parents' moral and religious values appear hypocritical, and how they ultimately made him distrust all authority, including that represented by the institution of marriage. Although Victor eventually married, at forty-one, he emphasized the insignificance of "the piece of paper" as compared with the weight of his feelings for his wife:

> *The message my parents gave me was that I should marry someone of the same faith and live near home. If they had had their way, everything would have been the straight Church party line. Virgins marrying virgins, having a lot of kids, who they would then raise within the Church. I rejected all of that by my twenties, when I was a chaplain's assistant in Vietnam and had a lot of conflict about what my government was doing and how my church was supporting it.*
>
> *If I look back, [I see that] my disdain for authority began with Vietnam. When I finally married, it was more my wife's decision, because as far as I was concerned, I didn't need any outside authority sanctioning my commitment to the woman I loved.*

The rejection of middle-class values, the accessibility of birth control, women's increasing ability to support themselves, and an economy healthy enough to allow baby boomers to take their time choosing a career contributed to many young people's decisions not to marry in the late 1960s and the 1970s. The combination of these factors simply hadn't existed a generation, or even ten years, earlier. The marriage boom of the 1940s and 1950s, which had swelled wedding chapels with the youngest group of newlyweds on record, gave way to the "marriage bust" of the 1970s, during which marital rates plummeted. Marriage was no longer "hip," sexual freedom was, and the average age at first marriage for both men and women began its upward swing from its 1947–62 all-time low of 20.3 years for women and 22.6 years for men[3] to 24.3 years for women and 26.2 years for men in 1986.[4]

Vicki was one young woman who opted for a single life throughout her twenties and thirties. Since she's always been serious about her career, it would be easy to draw the conclusion that she must have been too focused on success to think about marriage. Actually, Vicki's explanation of why she waited until forty to marry has much more to do with the new sexual choices ushered in by the 1960s:

> *I spent a lot of time developing my career in the sixties and seventies; it was important to me, but it wasn't the reason I didn't get married. It was the fact that the sixties allowed me the freedom to experience different partners. If I had had to choose between having a sexual life and getting married, I would have felt more compelled to marry. But with birth control and the fact that nobody cared who you slept with, I could do a bit of looking around and put off marriage till later. I feel lucky to have had all that fun before the onslaught of AIDS and sexual paranoia.*

MARRIAGE: A GOOFBALL IDEA

The 1960s gave young people many choices when it came to relationships. They could live together casually or as "trial" marriage partners. They could have sexual relationships without commitment, or commitment without living together. They could be "serially monogamous"—faithful to one partner at a time—or they could even get married.

Getting married did cross Chris's mind during the sixties, but it was only a passing thought. Like many of his peers, he considered marriage irrelevant and unfashionable, and preferred to be involved with a series of women. Still, having been raised with more or less traditional Catholic values, Chris acknowledges the influence his mother's fierce belief in monogamy had on his life. Now forty-two, Chris has been married about a year. The afternoon we interviewed him, he rode up to our office on his motorcycle, dressed in jeans and leather. Exuding a youthful energy and warmth, he answered our questions with both openness and intensity:

> *I went to college in the sixties, and I really bought into all that stuff about not selling out, not joining the establishment, not doing what you're supposed to do. That's why I gravitated to the arts instead of business. As for relationships, I embraced the free-love ethic, but was never the kind of guy who could have more than one girlfriend at a time—or be sleeping with more than one woman at a time.*
>
> *On the other hand, sex was like a way to get high, like dope. It really didn't have a lot to do with love. But because my parents had taught me that you didn't have sex with someone unless you were in love with them, I convinced myself that if I had sex with someone, that meant I cared about them. So it wasn't unusual for me to meet somebody, sleep with them, and then tell myself there was a relationship there. I was involved with a lot of women during that period.*

Had Chris been born a generation earlier, perhaps his self-described sexual addiction during his twenties would have been played out in the context of marriage and infidelity. One need not be single, after all, to avail oneself of serial love affairs. But twenty years ago, marriage wasn't on the agenda for either Chris or for many of his peers:

Looking back, [I see] there were two women I would have married, had it not been for the sixties. The first girl I got really emotionally involved with was when I was in college—and marriage did cross my mind 'cause we were very happy and really loved each other. We didn't do it 'cause it was such a goofball idea to get married. None of our friends were getting married, and people I knew who did were miserable. None of them had relationships I was at all envious of.

So I never had a model, never heard of a good model for marriage. I knew people who had "stable" marriages, but that usually meant the woman was firmly in control or the guy had her under his thumb. That didn't really look very good to me.

Chris's notion of marriage being a "goofball idea" and his assessment that most marriages he knew about were "miserable" were ideas shared by many of the people with whom we spoke. Not only was marriage considered old-fashioned among young people during the sixties and early seventies, but unmarried people often had difficulty finding positive role models to counter their negative assumptions. Why give up your freedom, they reasoned, if all that lay in store for you was marital discord, sexual stagnation, and isolation from your more adventurous, experimental comrades? Why trust anyone over thirty who was trying to persuade you to "give in" and "settle down" when there were so many more exciting options?

The world was being shaped anew, and relationships were included in this grand restructuring. Experimenting with different romantic and sexual partners was not only a way to find out about yourself, but also a way to participate in the creation of a new order—one that was more natural, more liberating. Possessiveness, jealousy, structure, rules of any sort were criticized as being destructive of the human spirit, whose natural inclination was toward spontaneity and pleasure. The dream was that this new "love generation" would share love openly and freely and, by so doing, become more honest, peaceful members of humankind.

Of course, there were those "counterculture" baby boomers who shared in that dream and *did* get married in their twenties and early thirties—believing that they could change the meaning of committed love within the context of marriage. But they didn't have an easy time of it. Raised with their parents' traditional values, which placed loyalty above all else, yet committed to the more radical ideals of honesty, equality, and personal fulfillment, baby boomers had no formula for synthesizing such disparate value systems. It's not difficult to understand why three-fourths of the divorces in the seventies were among the sixties generation.[5]

PROTESTING OUR PARENTS' MARRIAGES

The growth of the divorce rate was just one more reason never-marrieds had for justifying their uncommitted status. Watching their friends' relationships dissolve after only a few years of marriage—even when those marriages were intended to be open and liberated—convinced them the institution was virtually unworkable. Just as some sixties radicals believed that egalitarian values couldn't possibly be practiced within the context of corporate America, so others were certain that an ideal relationship couldn't be had within the confines of marriage. And if their friends' broken or joyless marriages didn't provide enough evidence to convict the institution of marriage, their parents' unhappy marriages did. Again, Chris talked about how he came by his anti-marriage bias:

> I didn't get a very positive message about marriage from my parents. They never seemed very happy, even though my mother claims that what initially brought them together was passion. But it was sure hard to believe when I was growing up, because my dad was so hard on her. He was a terror. I'm still coming to terms with my anger about the way he treated my mother— not physically abusive, just always upset with her.
>
> As for my mom, she made up her mind she was going to make the marriage work, no matter what. In fact, they both seemed to have a very strong sense that they had to stay married, 'cause I guess that's the way they were raised. And I have no idea if it would have been better for them to split up—better for them and better for me and my sister. But marriage didn't look like a very pleasant thing, judging by how theirs was.

Faith's parents have been married nearly forty-five years, but the longevity of their marriage doesn't impress Faith any more favorably than Chris's parents' thirty-seven-year marriage impressed him. She talked about the impact her parents' relationship had on her lack of desire to marry. Faith is now forty-one and has been married a little over a year.

All I can say is that the things I don't like about my parents' marriage caused me to put the idea of marriage or having a lifelong relationship out of my mind. My mom is real critical of my dad, and my dad is off in his own world. There's a lack of closeness, a day-to-day disharmony, a lack of appreciation for each other. On my mom's part, she will take her own misery and expect my dad to fix it for her rather than taking responsibility for it herself. To avoid that, my dad escapes into his golf game, and they both end up being real lonely. Growing up, I didn't know what else I wanted, but I sure didn't want what I saw them experiencing.

We heard from quite a number of first-marrieds over forty whose decision to avoid marriage stemmed from their parents' unhappy relationships. Even when there were no serious problems or overt abuse, the lack of joy in their parents' marriages left a very negative impression on those we interviewed. One late marrier commented that although his parents were married fifty years, he had never seen his father *enjoy* his relationship with his mother. Marriage was something they merely "got through."

Our critiques of our parents' marriages may have been poor excuses not to become committed ourselves. On the other hand, perhaps we were wise to avoid marriage rather than make the same mistakes that had made our parents so miserable. In either case, many of our generation thought we could sidestep unhappiness and conflict by taking our time and demanding much more from a relationship than our parents had. We felt ourselves to be more discerning, more thoughtful about the momentous decision of choosing a mate. One midlife marrier summed up the mistakes she felt our parents' generation made by revealing what had originally brought her own parents together: "My mom admits that she married my dad solely because he was a good dancer and looked handsome in his uniform. No wonder they were at each other's throats for forty years!"

FOREVER YOUNG

While unhappy marriages may be more the norm than happy ones, and while children whose parents are at odds may be just as likely to marry earlier as later, many post-forty marriers with whom we spoke talked about a fear of replicating their parents' unhappy relationships. Some linked this fear to their desire to escape adulthood altogether. If they didn't get married, they reasoned, not only would they avoid the pain and conflict they had witnessed in their families, but they would also avoid entry into the stagnant world of grown-ups. As one older first-married put it, "By not becoming like my parents, I was younger at forty-five than they were at twenty-five."

Our generation seems obsessed not only with youth but with the need to prove we're not like our parents, and the two are closely connected. We joke about how, when our parents were forty-something, they never would have been caught dead doing the juvenile things we still enjoy doing, or being as open as we are, or as daring or spontaneous. Our rebellious jabs at our elders mask the fear that we now have one essential thing in common with the way they were thirty years ago: middle age. When we demand more from life and from our relationships than they did, we hope it will set us apart from them, keep us more aware, more vital. We hope that by steering clear of the conventions that deadened our parents, not only will we not die, we will not age either.

Yet striving for a richer, more fulfilling life than we believe our parents had also has its negative consequences. While we know what kind of relationship we *don't* want, we're not always so certain about what we *do* want. Or, if we are certain, we get impatient when we can't find it. Or, if we do find it, we're not sure there isn't something slightly better if we just hold out a little longer. This attitude holds true whether we're looking for the perfect job, house, or relationship.

Our generation's definition of love differs dramatically from the one accepted by our parents. Most of us believe that married love involves both partners fulfilling each other's needs; our parents thought marriage had more to do with obligation. And although baby boomers have the higher divorce rate, it's impossible to assess which generation is actually happier in matters of the heart. Our focus on self-fulfillment makes finding and sustaining an intimate relationship extremely difficult. But our parents' reverence for the institution of marriage made a lot of incompatible couples stay together unhappily ever after.

While our parents didn't necessarily have all the answers, at least they didn't seem to expect things to be so perfect, so they weren't as disappointed. We baby boomers, on the other hand, can't understand why love and marriage are so difficult when all we want from a relationship is the harmonious blending of personal growth (perfecting ourselves) and romantic love (losing ourselves in our perfect lover)—not to mention equal division of the breadwinner and homemaker roles and the freedom to do our own things, even if that means opting out of the relationship somewhere down the line! We want to be free to develop our interests, to pursue our dreams, to explore who we are by experimenting with whatever captures our curiosity—and those goals are admirable. But focusing on our own growth often conflicts with preserving our commitment to our mate. When we can't satisfy our own needs and be happily married at the same time, we get resentful or disappointed or depressed—or divorced!

No wonder so many of us are terrified of making commitments; we've set ourselves up for failure by creating impossibly high standards for success! In our rush to reject the self-sacrificing, sexless, sexist marriages in which we believe our parents were trapped, we redefined relationships only to become disillusioned, pronounce ourselves or our mates failures, and move on to the next partner. For some, the only alternative to divorce was to avoid marriage altogether, and in so doing, many felt they had condemned themselves to an extended sentence of adolescence.

Chris prolonged his youth for so long that even *he* began to worry in his mid-thirties. Until then, he clung ferociously to his desire for freedom and his addiction to the "high" of new lovers. Both seemed to be connected to a fundamental wish to avoid a kind of death he felt was inherent in growing up. For many years he meandered from job to job, wondering what to do with his life. The same discontinuity held true for his relationships with women; he found himself involved again and again with unpredictable women who provided adventure but never threatened to become part of his future.

I had no sense of a future up until a year or so ago. I used to read science fiction and thought by the time it got to be 1980 the world would have blown up. Maybe I figured I didn't have to worry about planning for anything.

At thirty I took a look at myself—I had never been married, never bought a house, never bought a car on time. I hadn't established a career. And I realized that a lot of these issues had to do with my fear of growing up.

I never wanted to grow up because growing up meant dying. I remember as a child being struck by the fact that grown-ups would rather sit on the couch than go out and play with you. I told myself then, "When I'm grown up, I'll go play with the kids." I still feel that way and don't really intend for that to change. Maybe that's part of the reason why I waited so long to get married. I just felt that would be the beginning of the end of me. If I got married, then I would really be losing it.

Nevertheless, marriage had always been in the back of Chris's mind—and so had marrying at an older age. Early on he planned to put it off as long as he could. But eventually his attraction to the struggle and drama of transient love affairs—the cycle of splitting off with one lover and starting up with another—began to wear him down. Breaking up became so emotionally draining that he thought it might almost be better not to get involved at all rather than face going through the trauma again and again.

When I hit thirty-six, each relationship started getting a little more depressing. I got involved with a high-powered career woman—as a way to prove to myself that I could be with someone respectable. When she cut me loose, I realized the whole affair had been a big gag for her. She was in a stuffy profession, so having a boyfriend like me who was a bit on the wild side was a kick.

It almost seemed like the sexual revolution had backfired on me. In my early twenties I couldn't figure out why girls didn't want to have sex with everybody, like guys did. But in my late thirties it had gotten to the point where some girls wanted to have sex with me even when they didn't like me that much. It was like I was getting ripped off sexually.

Finally I was on the verge of saying, "Well, I'm a single guy, I'll just be a single guy forever," but that was scary. It meant never settling down, 'cause you can't really buy a house if you're alone. It meant not having a family. It meant always being this oddball guy. It meant getting eternally fixed up. It meant my life was still up in the air.

SOMEONE TO NEVER GROW OLD WITH

Although Chris was nearing forty and tiring of the chaos in his life, he was still uncertain about giving up his unbridled lifestyle. What turned him around? What made him decide to get married when for so many years he equated marriage with "losing it"—losing his freedom, his joy, his spontaneity, his youth, losing himself? His love life had always been fueled by unpredictability. The few times he had tried stable relationships, he wound up being bored and moving on to another fiery yet disastrous affair.

How was Chris going to be able to give up all that drama for marriage? We were curious to know exactly what it was about Kelly that convinced him he wouldn't be losing anything by marrying her.

I met Kelly by accident. I was going to have dinner at [the home of] a woman friend of hers, and Kelly happened to be there. I got talking to her, and there was an immediate attraction. At the end of the evening, after Kelly left, I said to my friend, "How come you never introduced me to her? She's the perfect woman for me!" She said, "Oh, you're crazy. She's with another guy." Then I said, "Let me know when they break up, which I know will be very soon." And my friend just said, "Dream on."

Part of what was so exciting about meeting Kelly was that she was a combination of the two kinds of women I had always been attracted to: the sweet women—who I've loved in a child-

ish, tender way—and the more intelligent, dangerous ones with
whom I have more in common.

But almost more important than either Kelly's sweetness or her intelligence were her youthful outlook and appearance. By joining forces with someone who personified the energy, spontaneity, and fire Chris associated with youth, he could have his cake and eat it too. He could preserve his own sense of *joie de vivre* and, at the same time, break the cycle of endlessly starting and cutting off intimate involvements.

I really waited for a marriage where I thought I wouldn't have
to give up my youth. With some of the women I dated, there was
a real sense of age and decay, which really frightens me—maybe
because I connect getting married to getting old and losing
things. That's part of what attracted me to Kelly. She's thirty-
four, but people think she's five to ten years younger than that.
I felt like we could be together for many years and never grow
old. A lot of it has to do with Kelly's attitude. She has no fears.
She takes risks. When I met her, she was living in this great
place by the beach which she could barely afford. But she wasn't
the least bit worried about it. If she had the money, fine. If she
didn't, she figured the worst that would happen was she'd move.
She doesn't let fear stand in her way, and I find that incredibly
attractive. I don't ever want to get so old that I can't feel my life
is an adventure. Kelly's fearlessness is a youthful quality, and it
makes our life together very exciting.

Just as Chris had delayed marriage as a way to stay young, and then chosen a mate who he felt would help keep him youthful, he also talked about having children as a way to delay growing old. While he is aware of the drawbacks of becoming a parent at his age, he seems fairly certain he will be able to gain some control over his own aging process, even to the point of deciding how he would like to die.

Some people who had their kids early seem to have given up their
youth to their children. They seem really beaten. If I had had a
child in my twenties, I think I might have flipped out. But my

feeling is kids will keep me young. Right now, at forty-two, if I had a kid tomorrow I would be sixty when he was in college. But in a way that's okay, because it's a good reason for me to stay fit until I kick. My idea is to die of a massive stroke at eighty or ninety, and just stay in good shape until then.

AM I AN ADULT YET?

While his obsession with holding on to his youth is certainly not shared by all baby boomers, Chris's sense of himself as not being quite an adult—his perception that the major events in his life seem to be occurring "out of turn"—is very common among his peers.

There is an entire generation of Chrises who have difficulty defining themselves as full-fledged adults, since the standards of adulthood have changed so drastically over the last twenty years. Career, marriage, children, and one's own home don't necessarily materialize in the systematic fashion they once did. In fact, for some of us, the milestones that previously defined middle-class adult existence may be permanently unattainable. Some of us may never marry; some may never have children or own our own homes.

But while many of us feel less "adult" than our parents because our lives don't resemble theirs, the fact is that *their* generation was the anomaly, not ours. The parents of baby boomers got married earlier than any other generation in history. The 96 percent of American adults who married in the forties and fifties had children earlier and in greater numbers than *their* parents had, and more of them owned their own houses than any previous generation.[6]

There were some very concrete reasons for such early marriage, parenting, and home-ownership frenzy: it was all very strongly encouraged and supported by unprecedented government funding after World War II. The GI Bill's offer—free tuition, cheap mortgages, insurance, loans to start businesses, and allowances for wives and kids—was one our parents' generation simply couldn't refuse. In contrast, when baby-boom children reached their twenties and thirties and found the economic picture pale by comparison, the material trappings of their parents' adulthood were simply out of reach.

Like Chris, many baby boomers are unable to accumulate the resources to begin a "proper" adult life, and that sense of financial insecurity—rooted in some very startling economic realities—often influences their decision to delay marriage. Inflation and out-of-reach housing prices have led to the claim that the postwar generation has become "downwardly mobile." Chris isn't the only forty-two-year-old panicking about being able to buy his own house.

If one looks at the facts, "yuppies" are a figment of Madison Avenue's imagination. Only 5 percent of all baby boomers qualify as yuppies. The sobering truth about our generation's economic status reveals that in 1985, four out of ten baby boomers made less than $10,000 a year, making them roughly eight times as numerous as yuppies. And there are four baby boomers at or below the poverty line for every yuppie far above it.[7]

LEARNING TO APPRECIATE MARRIAGE

Whether or not we can claim that post-forty marriers come to marriage late as a consequence of shifting economics, rebellion against their parents' lifestyles, or a desire to stave off middle age for as long as possible, many of them credit the success of their marriages to qualities that have a distinct connection to 1960s values. Chris views his marriage as a means to secure his vitality. Such a notion is most likely quite foreign to his parents and their peers, whose measure of a successful marriage is simply its longevity. In summing up his thoughts on his one-year marriage, Chris commented:

> Kelly seems like the kind of person who will not stop being interesting, who will continue to learn. There was a point where my father stopped learning and being curious about the world, whereas my mother never stopped. I think Kelly and I are both people who won't stop.
>
> Getting old means giving up, letting the arteries harden, gaining weight, losing limberness, forgetting your stretch. But you don't have to. After I turned forty and got married, I realized the sky didn't fall. I didn't get old. I didn't lose it.

Chris now admits that he has come to appreciate some of the more traditional aspects of marriage that he used to criticize twenty years ago. Perhaps there's no getting around the reality that we all gradually take on aspects of our parents' values. We all yearn for intimacy and constancy. And most of us reach a point where those things are worth sacrificing some of the freedom we clung to so desperately in our youth. Here is what Chris had to say about his own development over the years:

> Being married makes my dealings with the world a lot easier; there are boundaries. That was part of the problem in the sixties; everyone was getting it on with everyone else. If you didn't, it was like, "What's wrong with you?" I realize, now, that I like the structure of marriage. Knowing that there is somebody there for me is a great comfort. I have someone to bounce ideas off of.
>
> We're still in the apartment I have lived in for ten years, only now there's Kelly and all the stuff she brought with her, including her cats. All this life in my apartment, which never was there before. That's really what it's all about.
>
> I talked with a friend recently, and he said, "If you look at the whole history of the species, there's a reason why human beings bond for life." I guess evolution finally caught up with me.

EXPLORING OURSELVES

Lilly's story shares many of the same elements of Chris's. Forty-four and married for the first time two years ago, Lilly caught the 1960s fever of revolt in her early twenties, promising herself then that she would never become like her parents. She rejected their symbols of adulthood—marriage, kids, upward mobility. Unlike Chris, however, the undercurrent beneath her life's decisions was not so much a fear of growing up as a need to explore who she was and what her place was in the world. While the critique of people like Lilly has often been severe—with everyone from Christopher Lasch, the author of *The Culture of Narcissism*, to TV's Archie Bunker decrying the self-indulgence of self-development—Lilly's involvements and experiences reflect a sensitivity to more than just herself and her own desires.

Lilly has always had a keen interest in connecting her life to the community and the world at large. She has a degree in public health, and her profession has required her to travel and live throughout the country and abroad. Over the last two decades she has grappled with the problem of how to include intimate relationships in her life without giving up her livelihood or her identity.

When we met Lilly in her cramped but cheery office at the university where she teaches, she was busy finishing off yet another grant application that she hoped would keep her current project afloat. Her undiminished enthusiasm for her work was as appealing as her unaffected appearance. She wore little makeup, yet her dark, naturally curly hair and simple Indian jewelry framed a face no less lovely for its forty-four years. Lilly reflected for several moments before beginning her story of why it had taken her so long to marry.

One of the things I disliked most about married couples of my parents' generation was their insularity—they didn't seem to give a damn about the outside world. The women were only concerned about their own families, and the men cared only about making money. I didn't want to end up like my mom. Although she seemed happy and loved my father, being a homemaker wasn't very appealing to me. But neither was my father's life. I remember asking him when I was about thirteen— and took these matters very seriously—just what it was about his job that he found satisfying. He kind of smirked back at me and said that he made a good living so that he could give me and my brother all the things we wanted.

I couldn't fathom going to work day in and day out just to earn a lot of money. With so many problems in the world, so many things to accomplish, I wanted to make a difference somehow. Of course now I realize my naïveté, and how it would have been difficult for me to fulfill those lofty aspirations had I not been given economic security. But at the time I was critical of my father's priorities. And I blamed marriage for the isolated, predictable roles both my parents played.

As a teenager, Lilly didn't envision getting married as much as finding a man with whom to share a new kind of life. They'd be together, committed to social causes, and deeply in love. But their union wouldn't include marriage. Or kids. Or worrying about money, health insurance, or buying a house.

In my early twenties, my boyfriend and I joined the Peace Corps and were sent to Ecuador to oversee a weaving cooperative. Jeff and I were going to "change the world," and we shared a commitment to the Indian people and the village where we set up housekeeping. At first I was quite taken with Jeff, but then he began to treat me like a wife. He had a whole list of dos and don'ts which seemed to be designed to domesticate me. Just because the women there did their men's laundry and were the only ones to cook, he thought that was what I should do too. When he insisted I start wearing a wedding ring so the villagers would know I was "his woman," I drew the line. Four months into my stay I requested a transfer to a neighboring town. I left Jeff, I left our dream, but at least I no longer had to feel like someone's property.

After that experience, Lilly made certain that the men she got involved with weren't out to mold her into a premature *hausfrau*. She still had no interest in marriage, preferring to think of her life as "an adventure that had just begun." Continuing to combine work and travel, Lilly had several relationships that lasted three months or so, slept with a lot of men, and enjoyed feeling unattached. Even when her romantic entanglements led to painful breakups or heartache, she figured it was all part of the kind of life she had chosen for herself.

I wanted to learn about myself and to experience whatever I could. Foreign cultures intrigued me, as did the men, and I got a good deal of my education through my relationships. Exotica erotica. Many lovers in as many circumstances—from a stilt house overlooking the railroad tracks in East L.A. to thirty feet deep in a Caribbean Sea coral cave.

Not that there weren't many long periods of celibacy—as well as some relationships that ended unhappily—but I didn't worry. I had all the time in the world to explore. I was quietly detached and kept reminding myself that not only had I not met the "right man," I wasn't even seriously looking yet.

Like many of her peers, Lilly spent her twenties and early thirties with a variety of partners. While she never considered herself promiscuous, she told us that there came a time when she began to question whether being sexually intimate with so many different men had any real meaning.

I once tried to make a list of all the men I had slept with. What surprised me was how many I had totally forgotten. I'd bump into a man and realize that once, just once, we had slept together—or had we? That bothered me. The not-remembering part began to feel like sexual Alzheimer's. I couldn't remember because there probably wasn't anything worth remembering. It had been as easy to sleep with someone as not; I felt neither guilt nor obligation with sex. But as time went on, I didn't feel much of anything else either.

Her life of sexual adventure, once so thrilling, ultimately failed to fulfill the need for intimacy that Lilly had only begun to acknowledge. Although gratified by her accomplishments and her free-spirited existence, she began to wonder if she had become stymied by her own self-sufficiency.

I had my work, I had my friends, I had my lovers. But I became concerned that I might not be able to have a deeper connection to a man—or, worse still, that I had lost the need to. Maybe I was so good at being my own person, I'd have to be my own person forever—alone.

Other late marriers echoed Lilly's fear that being so accustomed to living on their own may have diminished their need to become part of a couple. They wondered if taking care of themselves for so long made it more difficult to reach out to a potential partner—or if making their friends a substitute immediate family had impeded their ability to create one of their own.

Lilly enjoyed the life she had created for herself, and was glad she didn't need a husband in the way her mother had, but had she taken it one step too far? Now that she *wanted* a deeper connection with a man, to what extent did her self-sufficiency stand in her way?

It was true she had no economic need for a husband, but other financially independent women seemed to naturally gravitate to commitment and matrimony in a way that eluded Lilly.

Matrimony was the key word. There was still something slightly repugnant to Lilly about the thought of marriage and all the old images it conjured up: being isolated, cut off, "grown up and sewn up" as one older first-time-married put it. Lilly continued her story:

> *As much as I wanted a meaningful and continuous relationship with a man, being married still didn't appeal to me much. When I used to read fairy tales, they'd always end with the princess and prince finally marrying and living "happily ever after." I took that to mean their lives were over. And I still thought of getting married as being "the end," not the beginning of anything. The end of my life as I had grown to love it. The end of all the exciting parts and the dreary initiation into adulthood.*

It wasn't that Lilly didn't consider herself an adult, but that she felt that remaining single had kept her more alive and more involved than most adults who are hemmed in by the exigencies of wives, husbands, children. Certainly there was a good deal of truth to her opinion, and yet perhaps Lilly hadn't considered the changing face of both marriage and adulthood. Perhaps marriage and self-discovery didn't have to be mutually exclusive.

THE NEW ADULTHOOD

Just as our culture has outgrown sex-role stereotypes, we have also begun to shed marital and age-role stereotypes as well. What it means to be a marriage partner and an adult has changed radically over the past twenty-five years. Those of us who were born after World War II have many more options than our parents ever did. We can wait until we're sixty to go to college. We can give up one career and begin a new one. We can get married for the first time later in life. And enjoy the kind of mutually satisfying relationships we struggled to invent through the women's and consciousness movements.

Although marriage and adulthood used to signify a time of

predictability and routine, they can now mean a period of continued change, discovery and growth. In other words, it isn't necessarily all over once we say "I do." While the courtly tradition of love heralded moral obligation, self-sacrifice, and self-discipline, contemporary culture makes love and marriage part of our quest to know and be known by another person and, in doing so, to come to know ourselves.

Until recently, most psychologists considered "normal maturation" as a series of stages. To achieve adulthood successfully, it was necessary to complete certain "tasks," marriage and family being two essentials in a prescribed sequence of many.

In her popular book *Passages*, which drew on material from experts in the field of adult development (most notably Erik Erikson, Else Frenkel-Brunswick, Daniel Levinson, and Roger Gould), author Gail Sheehy asserted that in our twenties we prepare for our lifework—men for their careers, women for their families—and form the capacity for intimacy. Before we reach thirty, if we're still single, we feel the push to find a partner. If we're married, we decide to have kids—or more kids. In our early thirties, men concern themselves with "making it," while women focus on raising children. During our mid-thirties to mid-forties, we reassess our progress and accomplishments, and some of us go through what is popularly known as "midlife crisis." By our mid-forties, men discover a new stability and emotional awareness while women let go of their grown children and perhaps find renewal in involvements outside the home.

If this "normal" sequence of events doesn't fit your experience, you're not alone. A lot has changed since 1976, when Sheehy's book was first published. Her "stages" apply almost exclusively to the *parents* of baby boomers, those who preceded the advent of feminism, counterculture, and the economic squeeze of the 1970s. The psychiatrist and life-stage theorist Roger Gould has rethought these issues and now says that given today's life options, our continuing development as adult human beings who work, love, and nurture need not be dependent on our marital or parental status. He told us, "I don't think there is this 'thing' called adulthood. There's no one standard. A person's ability to love doesn't necessarily have to be demonstrated within a marriage. You can be nurturing or giving with your friends. And you don't have to marry and have children in order to grow and develop."

Rather than seeing adult development as a straight line, many sociologists now propose that adults reach maturity via a number of alternative routes. They argue that life is much more haphazard, that developmental "tasks" don't happen to everyone on cue. Therefore, when and how each of us resolves conflicts and needs related to work, intimacy, and community depends upon our own particular lives, not on some predetermined order.

Lilly began to realize, too, that adult life need not be as conventional as she had once presumed. She started to believe she could commit herself to a man without being confined by the rigid forms of marriage and adulthood embraced by her parents. She could create her own patterns and live out her own values, and maybe it would work. She attributes her change of heart to two very special people:

One of the experiences that wiped out a lot of my preconceptions about marriage was getting to know my friends Howard and Gail. They'd been married about twenty years and yet couldn't have been further from the traditional image of "old marrieds" I carried in my head. They were wonderful! Howard had had as big a part in raising their two kids as Gail—and he did most of the cooking. They both worked free-lance and didn't have a great deal of money, but they really seemed to enjoy life. When their kids went away to college, they made a decision to move to an old farmhouse in Italy, and that's where I ran into them. They travel a lot, laugh a lot, and still seem to have a real spark between them. What an inspiration!

TRYING MARRIAGE

Lilly never had any regrets when she looked back at the relationships she'd had over the previous unmarried twenty years. She felt that getting to know a number of men intimately, testing herself against a variety of temporary mates, was the natural course her life needed to take. As painful as some of those alliances were, she says she learned from each one. But as she reached her middle to late thirties, she was ready to consider marriage—to "try something new."

I began to actively want to be married. I finally felt confident that I could have a marriage on my own terms, that having a husband didn't have to mean closing off to the outside world or being trapped. I understood and knew every nook and cranny of my being and now wanted to share this "whole person" that I had become with someone else. Also, I yearned for the constancy of one relationship, and maybe some of that had to do with fears about growing old alone—something I hadn't really considered years before. I wanted a partner to go through middle age and old age with—I was finally ready to admit that. And I was also ready to try something new.

The ties that might seem confining to us when we're young often become a comfort to us later. In her twenties and thirties, when the future seemed endless, Lilly had no need for a permanent relationship. As she approached middle age, however, envisioning herself alone for the rest of her life became somewhat frightening. Ironically, it was both her fear and her spirit of adventure that finally propelled Lilly into seeking a marriage partner.

The desire to "try" marriage after years of exploring many other options, and the sense of not wanting to miss out on an important life experience, were themes repeated by many over-forty first-time marriers with whom we spoke. They wanted to know firsthand how *they* would experience this universally sanctioned—if often maligned—union. However skeptical they had been previously, when they reached a point where they became open to commitment, "ready" for marriage, they approached the possibility with a characteristic 1960s sense of explorative curiosity. Life was about trying everything, and here was something they hadn't "tried" before.

Viewing marriage as a kind of journey one hasn't yet taken certainly differs from the way in which most of our parents looked upon the state of matrimony. For most of them, marriage was a given; it was considered the *only* appropriate way to have an intimate relationship. But in the twenty-odd years since she'd come of age, Lilly had tried numerous other approaches to love and intimacy. Although she appreciated the freedom she'd had to become romantically and sexually involved with a number of partners, she now saw marriage as the next step in her life.

Lilly was "ready," however, before she had someone to be ready *with*. Yet she wasn't about to marry just anyone. Her socially conscious values were still intact, and one of her priorities in choosing a mate was to find the right person with whom she could share those values. The other essential was passion.

I had almost given up. I was forty-one, and while I had occasional dates, the man horizon was looking pretty dim. Not only was it harder in general to meet men my age, but it seemed the ones I did meet were from another planet in terms of consciousness. I was willing to compromise on a lot of things, but I wanted someone who was interested in more than certificates of deposit and real-estate values. And I also wanted someone who cared about me!

The problem was that Lilly rarely met available men through her work anymore, so she was forced to do things she would never have considered earlier—like asking friends to fix her up. She'd never had a hard time meeting men before, but it *wasn't* earlier, it was later. And Lilly had decided she wanted more than the fleeting romances she'd been used to.

None of the blind dates panned out, but, as the fates would have it, I met my husband through one of those fix-ups. Actually, he's the fix-up's younger brother! A friend of mine had set me up with Kevin's older brother, thinking he was more my age and more available—he was forty-three and divorced with two kids. Kevin was thirty-five when I met him, and he was still involved with someone else.

We met on a double date. I was with Kevin's brother, and Kevin was with his girlfriend. It was kind of embarrassing, because the whole evening Kevin and I were hooked into each other. First of all, he told me he headed up a clinic which was attempting to upgrade health care for poor people. We cared about the same things! Plus, we got each other's jokes, loved the same books and movies, and even ordered the same thing! There were some very heavy sparks flying.

We joke about it now, but at the time I remember cursing

*to myself, thinking, "Why do I have to meet this absolutely
perfect, adorable guy who's not available?" But he became available very shortly.*

After all the years of being with people in the moment, Kevin
was someone Lilly knew she could be with forever. Of course, they
had their problems—and still do—but part of the reason their relationship survived was that Lilly was *ready.* She told us she was willing
to overlook whatever differences existed in order to make this relationship work.

*I wanted to marry this man! And I was willing to do whatever
it took to make that happen. I felt passionately about Kevin, and
he felt that way about me, and we've held on to that.*

In the several years before she met Kevin, Lilly had serious
doubts about meeting a man who not only shared her social concerns
but also turned her on. Was it asking too much? She'd had opportunities to become involved with several very nice men, but she wanted
more than just companionship or security. So she waited—and at
forty-one she met Kevin. "And, boy, am I glad I held out," she told
us, "rather than talking myself into compromise!"

WE ARE/WE AREN'T OUR PARENTS

Lilly's and Chris's stories both focus on their continued resistance to
their parents' version of adulthood. Yet, as they approached forty,
they both realized that certain aspects of the traditional values their
parents upheld were valuable after all: constancy, loyalty, even a
certain degree of structure. On the other hand, Chris's and Lilly's
reservations about marriage, as well as their decisions about whom
and when to marry after age forty, had to do with preserving their
sense of vitality and personal identity. These were things they
weren't willing to sacrifice in order to have another person by their
side.

Chris didn't want to give up his youthful enthusiasm for life, as
he believed his father had. He saw in his parents' marriage a model

of adulthood he didn't wish to replicate. He witnessed his father being beaten down by the system and taking it out on his mother—and his mother putting up with emotional mistreatment in order to preserve her marriage. While acknowledging his indebtedness to his parents for some of his most deeply held values, Chris took a radically different path from theirs. He chose a risky career rather than become trapped in a joyless one. Although he's paying the price now by enjoying far less financial security than his parents had, he's happy with his choice. And he's glad he waited to get married, since he never felt ready until recently. Kelly fulfills his dream of having someone with whom to have an exciting, joyful life. They're equals in terms of career, and they basically agree on what they want out of the years ahead. Since they've been married only a year, they can't be certain of that future, but none of us ever can.

As for Lilly, she smiles nostalgically when she recalls that she had honestly expected a revolution twenty years ago. She had assumed then that marriage and all its trappings would be irrelevant to the life that lay ahead for her. While it may not have been as all-out a revolution as the twenty-year-old Lilly envisioned, America's various cultural uprisings during the sixties and seventies affected not only Lilly and her peers, but Lilly's parents' generation and the post-boomer generation as well. It's difficult to imagine what our present lives would be like had it not been for the antiwar and civil rights movements, the sexual revolution, the women's movement, and New Age consciousness—each of which challenged the fundamental precepts of American life and engendered a new awareness of freedom and self-determination.

What all of that societal change meant for Lilly was that her need to explore who she was and what she wanted out of life was sanctioned by society to a much greater degree than ever before. While the choices she made in terms of love, commitment, and work may not reflect the values of the majority of adult Americans, they do represent a significant minority.

Lilly spent her twenties and thirties learning about herself in connection with others, experimenting with different forms of commitment, testing herself against trial partners. She didn't want to make the same mistakes she thought her parents and their friends had made; she vowed never to take love or life for granted. She wanted to live passionately, with concern for the world around her, and yet she reached a point near the age of forty when she yearned to share that with the right person. Luckily, she happened to be fixed up with that right person's brother.

Both Lilly and Chris embody a spirit that Ashley Montagu refers to in his book *Growing Young*—a spirit defined by curiosity, imaginativeness, openmindedness, energy, the willingness to experiment, and the need to love:

> *The truth about the human species is that we are intended to remain in many ways childlike; we were never intended to grow "up" into the kinds of adults most of us have become. We are designed—in body, spirit, feeling, and conduct—to grow and develop in ways that emphasize rather than minimize childlike traits. By learning to act more like a child, human beings can revolutionize their lives and become for the first time, perhaps, the kinds of creatures their heritage has prepared them to be— youthful all the days of their lives.*[8]

As they both begin marriage at midlife, Chris and Lilly seem energized by the adventure of permanently committing themselves to another person. Having been certain for so long about what they *didn't* want, they now feel confident that they'll be able to create marriages that reflect who they are and what they want to be.

3

LIVING TOGETHER INSTEAD

Marriage was something other people did. I wasn't rejecting marriage, but I wasn't seeking it either—I was just being. It was never a requirement for any of my intimate relationships, and I figured if marriage was supposed to happen I would feel it. Even after being with Jenny for years, I was perfectly comfortable with the idea of simply living together forever.

—VICTOR, age forty-four, married three years

Come live with me and be my love. . . .

—CHRISTOPHER MARLOWE

The concept of what marriage should be and its place in young people's lives changed drastically during the sixties and seventies. Like Victor, many of us began to question the traditional definitions of holy matrimony. We were looking for new forms of intimacy that stressed respect for personal freedom, growth, and openness. Good relationships were defined as those that preserved an equitable balance between love of self and other, not obligation, self-sacrifice, and blind loyalty.

To achieve these lofty goals, the "love generation" knew it had to find and invent, if necessary, more flexible arrangements for loving. When free love, or freer love, became practice, the major rationale for marriage seemed to evaporate altogether. Sexual intimacy could be had on a continuum of commitment—all the way from one-night stands to a lifelong monogamous relationship. Hundreds of thousands of young people began experimenting; marriage became optional and living together took its place. Nancy, a veteran of a ten-year alternative arrangement, recalls her thinking at the time and echoes the sentiments of so many in our generation.

> The sixties signified a definite break from what my parents had expected for me. I lived with someone for ten years instead of getting married because of the era in which I lived. My husband, who is ten years older than me, got married for the first time to have sex. I was not under that constraint, but if I had met the first man I lived with five years earlier, I probably would have married him.

What is significant is that, like Nancy, more and more young people exercised the option of living together during a period in their lives when they otherwise might have married for the first time. By the time some of these individuals arrived at midlife, they had spent their twenties and thirties investing in long-term relationships that were just as intimate and emotionally intense as marriage, but less legally binding.

Living together before marriage has become as common now as it was taboo before the sixties. In fact, the number of men and women who cohabit *before* marriage has quadrupled over the last twenty years, from 11 percent of marriages in 1965–74 to 44 percent of the marriages in 1980–84.[1] Demographers believe this specific life choice has been a major factor contributing to the current upsurge of delayed first marriages and later-life families, and this was, in part, supported by our conversations with post-forty marriers.

Twenty-four out of the forty late marriers we interviewed had lived with *at least* one other person before their first spouse. And they mostly fell into one of two categories: those who regarded living together as a *temporary* way station on the risky journey from going very steady to full-fledged commitment, and those who considered it a *permanent*, preferred alternative to formal marriage. We wondered how living together affected the timing of their first marriages and whether choosing this alternative affected midlife marriers' attitudes toward married life when they finally marry. It was one of the questions we asked our "experts."

TRIAL MARRIAGE: FINALLY GETTING IT RIGHT

Luke, a forty-six-year-old newspaper journalist, lived with two women prior to meeting, living with, and eventually marrying Sally a year and a half ago. Had he been born a generation earlier, each of his unions would have been a formal marriage rather than an opportunity to explore the possibility of a long-term commitment: in that case, Sally could very well have been Luke's third wife instead of his first! Although Luke's relationship history is unusual, his experience was in keeping with that of his contemporaries and increasing numbers of adults who now regard living together as a natural and necessary preamble to marriage.

"Trial marriage," as it is called, is a kind of "hands-on" training that screens respective spouses for future marital competence and compatibility. In theory, couples who live together are freed from the pressure to conform to the stereotypical roles associated with marriage. That's because the implicit ground rules for living together are often more slack: personal independence and freedom need not be sacrificed to intimacy and belonging. Under these conditions, a couple can explore the complicated process of adjustment without the complications of formal wedlock.

But the reality is that *all* couples, whether they are husband and wife or cohabitants, must define and redefine emotional and physical boundaries on a daily basis. If a couple is unable to balance and blend interpersonal styles, rhythms, and needs, the relationship will most likely fail. Individual needs must be negotiated with those of the couple, and it's not necessarily any easier just because you happen to be living together. Not surprisingly, it is far from the perfect solution that many envision. For most people, living together tends to be a very short-lived and transitional state: out of ten couples who live together, only one will still be cohabiting after five years without marrying.[2]

This is precisely what Luke discovered for himself ten years ago, when he met a woman who appeared to be his perfect match. He was quick to exercise the option of not having to marry to probe the possibility of marrying. Living together helped Luke see through his first misleading impressions of his prospective spouse and his idealistic expectations—perceptions that had more to do with romance than with reality. The trial marriage allowed him to understand he wasn't ready to tackle the challenge of making a real one work.

> *We were actually very different in ways that we wouldn't have known if we hadn't lived together. It wasn't just the cap-off-the-toothpaste kind of stuff, but more our inherent rhythm and lifestyle differences. My idea of a great day was to be up at seven and go run—hers was to sleep until noon. I'm a frustrated athlete and enjoy going to the gym; she didn't want to get near a tennis shoe!*
>
> *I started to realize what major relationships were about. If you live day to day annoying the crap out of each other, the deeper issues often go undiscussed 'cause you are too busy fighting about the mechanics of living. We spent two years trying to make it happen, but I just wasn't psychologically prepared to see our relationship through to a marriage.*

With this first taste of marriagelike intimacy behind him, Luke spent several years dating women with the specific goal of finding his future wife. But his efforts didn't meet with success. As he became more settled in his career, he became all the more compelled to "catch up," to complete his "perfect picture" with a family and a white picket fence. Luke began dating a woman with three children, whose first priority was hearth and home—just what Luke wanted. It was a flushed courtship, and before he knew it, his "instant family" had settled into his house. Luke was way ahead of himself, playing dad and planning the wedding; what he didn't plan on was the "divorce."

> *At first I was saying to myself . . . "Here I go, I've got it all." And then my own worst nightmares came true. I found she was*

a much different person than she appeared to be on the surface
. . . one of those people who had learned to live a life using other
people, and it was just the kind of relationship I feared most. The
strange thing is that I had such a great relationship with her kids
that when I moved out, they wanted to go with me.

> *Nevertheless, it was my fault. I'd jumped into a situation*
I shouldn't have been in, tried to make it happen because I
wanted it so much, and stayed far too long— all with disastrous
consequences.

Although they weren't married, the dissolution of this relationship was no less painful and enmeshed. Luke's attachment to and concern for her children had developed over the course of their two years together. When he moved out of his house, he was forbidden to visit them and lost all direct contact. Luke felt just like any divorced dad who had been banished from his family and displaced from his home. But the breakup got even uglier: the woman with whom he'd been involved decided to hold his house hostage. More complicating still, she unexpectedly announced she was pregnant and planning to have Luke's baby. Unwilling to be manipulated into an unhappy marriage, Luke refused to marry, but was determined to fight for custody of his child. What followed was a protracted court battle that became as bitter as any divorce proceedings.

It took a year before the dust settled. Luke was able to move back into his own house—alone but able to win only part-time custody of his son, whom he financially supports. It was a dark, muddled time for Luke: sadness mixed with depression and guilt. Self-protectively, he went undercover emotionally and threw himself into his news assignments. In the course of investigating the resettlement of Southeast Asian refugees in U.S. cities, he met Sally, a social worker. Right away he was taken with her intelligence, sparkle, and verve.

But, this time around, Luke deliberately paced the courtship. He started out by telling Sally that he had made too many mistakes before, and wanted to try taking things a little slower. "I've got to stop jumping head-first off the high-diving board," he told her over dinner about three months into their relationship. Sally knew that Luke's persistent worry was whether he was going to get emotionally burned again. She also knew that what he really needed was reassurance and acceptance before he'd feel safe enough to love her. Without pushing for a commitment, six months later they decided to live together. As Sally's honest reactions and acceptance of Luke's past overshadowed his lingering doubts and reservations, marriage became the next natural step. For Luke, the third try was finally the charm.

> I'd made some very heavy mistakes in my past and brought those to my relationship with Sally—problems that were going to affect us for the rest of our lives. But I got all my skeletons out of my closet and Sally wasn't scared off. She said, "Ninety percent of the package is great, and I'll take the ten-percent downside." Once we lived together, I knew we had the basic building blocks to be able to say, "We can handle the problems that will come up; we can work it out." We no longer had that mountain ahead of us to climb in order to achieve togetherness. I had done it so many other different ways without success that I was really willing to try marriage. I was ready for the difference.

Looking back over his relationship history, Luke used living together to hone his relationship skills and ready himself for commitment. Were it not for the socially acceptable option of living together, Luke probably would have married his first live-in partner, gotten divorced, been forced to marry his second, gotten divorced again, and then made Sally his third wife. But this wasn't the case. Luke had the opportunity to warm to marriage, tempered by his successive near misses. By the time he and Sally met, Luke knew the direction he was going; he knew what he wanted from a relationship, and was unafraid to say it. In Sally he had finally met his match.

Although it's not uncommon for most other people to mature emotionally through the process of marriage, divorce, and remarriage, Luke and a good number of our late marriers accomplished the same thing through serial cohabitations. But with all the practice, does living together before marriage affect marital success? Research in this area is inconclusive. Recently, *Psychology Today* magazine published the results of two contradictory studies. The first, conducted in Canada, found that couples who had lived together prior to marriage were 7.25 times more likely to stay married than those who hadn't.[3] The second, conducted in Sweden, reported that within ten years of marriage, nearly 20 percent of cohabitants got divorced, compared to only 10 percent of those who did not previously cohabit.[4] Confusing? Somewhat, but not for those like Luke and others we interviewed. If you asked them, they'd tell you they wouldn't have done it any other way.

LIVING TOGETHER FOREVER—ALMOST

There is another variation on the theme of living together instead of marrying: late first-time marriers who were firmly committed to the idea that "happily ever after" meant living together happily ever after—*without* ever getting married. These individuals spent years in intimate relationships, the important difference being that they never intended to marry. Although they are in the minority, those who *never* intend to marry but choose to live together permanently share certain broad personality characteristics. As a group, they often pay little mind to social pressure to marry, or to the disapproval of parents and friends. And they tend to be more self-protective and are far less idealistic about marriage than are those who marry.[5]

Eric fit this description to a T. Living together forever was his way of guaranteeing his social freedom and safeguarding his fragile self-image as an autonomous, independent being. In fact, he and Sheila were so blasé about formal marriage and so completely unconcerned with anyone else's opinions that the thought of marrying scarcely occurred to either of them. When it did, they had already lived together for nearly a decade. Eric made sense of their choice this way:

> *See, when you are living together, people don't take the relationship as seriously and they still consider you a single person—so you're "excused" from certain "restrictions," which is what I was after. But when you get married, that changes. It's as if people are saying, "You're like the rest of us now." So you're not supposed to have female friends anymore, you need to become*

more conservative, have kids, and not hang out with the boys.
Right away it's implied that I'm owned by somebody.

Clearly, Eric and Sheila's attachment was strong enough to sustain them through nine years of living together (and, now, seven years of marriage). If they are any indication, there is certainly no doubt that long-term live-ins are capable of maintaining as deep and enduring a commitment to their chosen mates as couples who are legally married. But the same open-endedness that allows individuals who live together the freedom to shape their relationships according to their own needs may also require that they work harder to preserve their union in the absence of a legal bond. For some, this is the essence of the challenge.

These days a relationship with any kind of staying power is a gift. And for people who are committed to living together instead of marriage, each additional year that the relationship thrives is especially sweet, because many regard their commitment as deeper and "purer" than the compulsory caring associated with married love. For the ten years that Nancy lived with Joey—a man she affectionately refers to as "my almost-first husband"—she was convinced this was so:

> *I always thought of living together forever as a higher form of "marriage" requiring even more personal integrity and loving commitment than the formal kind. Living together is the deepest form of spiritual bonding because there is no one but the two of you holding it together.*

But there are social repercussions and inherent difficulties that come with the choice to remain permanently unmarried. In spite of the widespread acceptability of cohabitation, the prevailing social expectation is that a man and woman who appear compatible and continue to live with one another will *eventually* marry. When a couple has been together for about a year, the subtle and not-so-subtle pressure often begins. Friends and family begin to ask such pointed questions as "When are you two going to get married?"

This question comes up because most people find it easier to deal with relationships when they are predictable. Whereas marriage enjoys a fixed definition, living together is vague, indeterminate, and fails to peg the relationship on the continuum of commitment. So, for example, if you are going to have a dinner party and want to invite Lydia and your latest information is that she was living with someone, you might have to ask, "Is Lydia still living with that fellow Steve? Should we invite the two of them or just her?" Note that Lydia's intimate cohabitant, Steve, doesn't even have a convenient formal designation (one that parallels husband and wife). That's because the English language hasn't quite caught up with current romantic living arrangements. There is no word that explicitly names the counterparts of a living-together relationship apart from clinical-sounding labels such as "significant other" or nondescript ones such as "partner" or less-meaningful ones like "boyfriend" or "girlfriend."

Couples who are mutually comfortable with the status of their relationship may pay little attention to these minor complications. Keep in mind Eric and Sheila; neither felt any urgency to marry, and both were perfectly content to live with one another for years. But not all couples are as balanced in their agreements. In the next two separate stories, Tess and Derek, late marriers who never intended to marry, found themselves loving and living with mates for whom marriage and all its connotations mattered very much. Tess and Derek both eventually shifted their positions and ended up wanting and choosing the marriages they had long resisted. What prompted Tess and Derek to change their minds? We'll let them tell you.

KICKING AND SCREAMING

Tess closed her eyes tightly and blushed. "The *only* time I ever had fantasies about marriage was when I was five or six. I had a very brief stint with drawing brides and that was the end of it," she told us in her gravelly voice, which had suddenly become softer and more vulnerable. Until she was forty-four, Tess was always dead set against marriage. And even after she agreed to marry Mel, she did it kicking and screaming.

We interviewed Tess on a scorching California summer day, sitting around a patio table in the palm-sheltered courtyard of her charming apartment, built in the 1930s. Tess is a woman bursting with interests and vitality. She is quick to share her opinions, and she peppers them with flamboyant gestures. She seems very much her own person and is determined to keep it that way. She firmly feels that traditional marriage is a thoroughly corrupting institution, and, deep down, part of her still believes in the value of living together forever instead.

In the early seventies, Tess was influenced by the feminist movement and began to rethink her sexual politics. She came to agree with two commonly held conclusions: that monogamy was as outdated as admonitions against premarital sex, and that an "establishment marriage" would do nothing but strip her of her opportunity for personal growth and independence. She asked herself the same chorus of questions we did: Don't I have the right to do what I want with my own body? With whomever I want? Whenever I want to? The day Tess answered yes to all three was the day she thought she had rejected monogamy and marriage for good:

> I thought marriage was a trap where I'd have to trade off personal freedom for security and great sex for mundane intercourse. A stable life has never been one of my goals—neither was monogamy. I thought it was an unnatural state and that people were basically polygamists. There were very few times in my life when I wasn't living with someone either full- or part-time, and I always had sexual relationships on the side. In fact, I have never been monogamous until my marriage with Mel.

When Tess was twenty-six she began a long-term relationship with a man named David with whom she lived for eleven years—a commitment that outlasted most marriages. But splicing her progressive consciousness with the comfort and safety of a live-in relationship wasn't without its difficulties. As in any old-fashioned marriage, she was still faced with finding a compromise between personal autonomy and attachment. And when it came to her ideas about open sexuality, she thought she could have it both ways. But infidelity, an issue Tess sought so hard to avoid by not marrying, became the unspoken threat between them.

I just wanted to know that if I was away for three or four months, I could attempt some intimacy without jeopardizing what I had with David. I never slept with anyone [else] when David and I were in the same city, so it wasn't an "open" relationship in that sense.

I remember the first time I told him I had been with someone else. I thought he would be all groovy and understanding, but when he heard the news he was totally wounded. It was awful, and it hurt me that I had hurt him so. From that point on we decided it was okay to do whatever we were doing in our private lives, but that we would only tell each other the truth if one of us asked. Mostly we didn't ask, and it went that way for the rest of the time we were together.

Once Tess and David decided that what neither knew wouldn't hurt them, they tacitly agreed to sacrifice honesty and open communication inside their relationship in exchange for Tess's sexual freedom outside of it. Although it is difficult to estimate what price this agreement exacted on their mutual trust, it was a price both were willing to pay to stay together. And they did stay together—until the decision whether to have children divided them once and for all.

At thirty-six, Tess was still as uninterested in marriage as ever, but the urge to have a child—David's child—suddenly overwhelmed her. Both had their separate and active careers. Tess traveled extensively as an architect for a major hotel chain. David was afraid that with all her involvements elsewhere, he would be left alone to raise the baby. He wasn't ready to become a house-husband if Tess wasn't willing to become a wife. Tess now admits he was probably more realistic than she was. "He was right, but I refused to get pregnant 'accidentally.' " When she told us this, Tess paused in midsentence, and her eyes moved away to a distant point. She lowered her voice and said, "I don't regret *not* marrying David, but I do regret that David and I never had a baby together."

Tess, with regrets, left the relationship shortly thereafter. She nursed her heartbreak for the next four years. Despite all her prejudices toward couples, she couldn't feel complete without being part of one. Tess tormented herself with the common self-recrimination, "I must have some deficiency if I'm not in a relationship." After a string of short-lived and unsatisfying affairs, she deliberately chose to be celibate for a while.

It took me years before I could give myself credit for having had a happy and very successful relationship living with David. What I had mostly felt afterwards was the failure of it. I spent a lot of time putting myself down by saying I was somehow deformed, or that there was something wrong with me because I wasn't in a relationship. Then, about eighteen months prior to meeting Mel, I finally arrived at a point in my life where I was quite okay about myself and being single.

In this state of mind, Tess met Mel, an apprentice architect whom she was hired to supervise during the construction of a ski lodge in the Grand Tetons. Her first impression of him was "Ho-hum—a good person, nice, scholarly looking, with a great sense of humor." But definitely no bells. The next two months on the building site was like boot camp—thirteen-hour days, six days a week, holed up in a workroom above a greasy-spoon restaurant in the middle of nowhere. With little time for anything else, Tess and Mel joked and teased their way through all the deadlines and catastrophes and got to be friends. Tess was intending to keep it that way—after all, Mel was married and had a seven-month-old baby. Tess, now with a little sparkle in her eyes, went on:

I find anyone who makes me laugh sexy, but I never believed that you should mix sex and work. Furthermore—and this came from the deepest recesses of my feminist soul—the one taboo you really don't break is to fuck around with someone else's man, and there was this tiny baby too! So, instead, I spent several weeks having hot fantasies about him—the female equivalent of wet dreams.

This lasted until we were almost finished with the project and had our first day off. We were on our way to see the movie Christine *and Mel blurted out, "I think we should have an affair." My first thought was, How are we going to manage all this sexual tension and get the job done? Then I was pissed that he hadn't kept his secret to himself, but meanwhile I was thrilled.*

Neither of us knew what to do, so we decided to go have a drink. We ended up in bed and we made love all night. So, in one fell swoop, I broke every one of my taboos! The next day we went back to work and never said a word to one another until ten days later, when we finally finished the assignment.

As far as Tess was concerned, when the project was finished, so was her affair with Mel, "like ships in the night," she insisted. But after she returned home, she realized that Mel wasn't so easily dismissed from her mind. She thought about him, dreamed about him, and talked about him with her closest friends. Three months later, Mel telephoned, saying he had left his wife so they could be together.

Tess was in heaven. But things didn't remain angelic for long. It soon became evident that Mel was far from solid about his decision to leave his marriage. Tess was torn and terrified. With the support of her Al-Anon group and the Twelve Step program she began to prepare herself for a long emotional haul. Al-Anon taught her two guidelines for having a healthier relationship with Mel no matter what was going on: maintain clear emotional boundaries and stick around to fight for them if need be. She had always retreated from relationships—she had fled, either literally or figuratively, whenever she was put in a position to stand up for what she wanted.

But this time Tess chose to stay and fight. And fight she did—for the next six months, while Mel tested her mettle. First, Mel went back to his wife, then he left a second time. But when he returned to the marriage once more, twice was two times too many. Now on her way to recovery, Tess drew the line because, for the first time in her life, she could. Deeply hurt but adamant, Tess refused to see Mel again until his decision to leave his marriage was firm.

It was about eleven o'clock on a July night and Mel came to my door to tell me that he'd left home and his wife for the last time—it was final. So we moved in together right then and there, and we've been together ever since. But it wasn't until a few months later that I realized how committed to me he was.

In September I got pregnant accidentally, and without any hesitation he told me that he wanted me to have his baby; he wanted us to be together; he loved me more than he had ever

loved anyone; it was going to work out. No one had ever said
that to me before—especially [when I was] pregnant. I fell in
love with him again, right then and there.

Tess lost the baby at four and a half months, but she never
forgot the feeling of being so loved and wanted. Mel's pledge of love
and constancy moved her to reconsider her uncompromising attitude
about sexual exclusivity. Monogamy was a commitment Mel needed
and wanted. Tess said she'd give it a try.

Just when Tess had gotten the hang of monogamy and found
herself liking it, Mel proposed. Tess stonewalled; she was damned if
she was going to ruin things by getting married. Wasn't loving him
enough? Why did they have to get married? But Mel kept pressing.
He liked being married and wanted the security. Half jokingly and half
seriously, Tess offered Mel an irreverent marriage deal—one she
thought he would never agree to. Then Mel called her bluff.

We started kidding around a lot. He'd say he just wanted to
marry me to get a green card, and I'd say I'd marry him only
if we could get divorced. It was much sexier for me to think of
myself living with my ex-husband and fucking him than being
his wife. The word wife *is so depersonalized. To me it means*
subservient, dominated, housework, patriarchy, bad sex. Finally
I said yes, if he agreed to marry me on April Fool's Day and
if we could have a prenuptial agreement stating that we would
divorce, if need be, in Las Vegas—and live together as divorcees
instead!

Tess was willing to do anything to avoid becoming a "wife," for
being a wife meant bending to the will of a demanding husband and
living with frustrated dreams! That was what had happened to Tess's
mother, who had forfeited her separate identity after abandoning her
career as a social worker and devoting herself full-time to her family.
"If I married," Tess reasoned unconsciously, "I'll be swallowed up
whole, too."

Exorcising these powerful images was no small matter for Tess,
who seemed to be starting her emotional life over from scratch. In the
past she would just have picked up and left whenever fearful feelings

overwhelmed her. But this time she was locked into the most important promise she had ever made. The only way she could marry Mel and *not* become his "wife" was to pretend the wedding wasn't happening. The solution was easy: all she had to do was nothing.

> *April first was fast approaching and I hadn't made one arrangement. The closer the wedding came, the more terrified I got—migraines, sweats, stomach problems. I was terrified that marriage was going to alter my image of myself totally, and that I was going to fall prey to all the fifties conditioning I'd spent years breaking out of. My identity was going to crumble and I'd turn into June Allyson, wearing pointy bras and using his-and-hers towels.*
>
> *So, by March thirty-first, friends were calling about the plans. "Where is it going to be?" "Should we buy presents?" I was tongue-tied. Everyone was getting irate. I remember soaking in the tub for hours that day, nursing a migraine. When Mel came home, I was stone cold with fear and anger. We had a huge fight that night, and I told him that I was the bride and I didn't have to make the arrangements; so whatever the wedding was going to be, he'd have to do it. The night before our wedding, we slept back to back.*

On the day the wedding was to be held, Tess woke up to Mel singing "The Bells Are Ringing for Me and My Gal" at the top of his lungs. Tess couldn't stop laughing. Mel got dressed and went off to a pawnshop on Hollywood Boulevard to buy wedding rings while Tess called everyone to let them know that they were getting married at 5:00 P.M. and that plans were to follow. With less than eight hours to go, Tess began to organize her trousseau. Her first stop, a Spanish bridal shop downtown, where she bought a veil to go with the rest of her bridal gown—a white jersey dress with cleavage, white leggings, and white go-go boots.

> *We arrived by limo at the Forever Yours Wedding Chapel and all eight guests had shown up! When I put on the veil I became euphoric. There was no music in the chapel, so we all sang "Here Comes the Bride." When the ceremony began, everyone became*

very solemn and teary. Until then Mel had been calm, calm, calm, and then he turned as white as a sheet. Suddenly I was happy, loving, thrilled, and completely into it. It was definitely a union and a formalizing of something very special.

Some people might view Tess's wedding as a caricature of a solemn rite. But the photos in her album show her looking like any other bride: encircled by friends and family, dressed in white, and carrying a bouquet of tea roses down the chapel isle. Her face is beaming. Gone is the terror formerly hidden in her heart—for once she reached Mel at the altar, all her fears had given way to elation.

After nearly an entire adult life committed to the idea that living together beat marriage hands-down, Tess put her objections aside and became Mel's wife. Considering the ferocity of her prejudice against marriage, insisting on her own unique terms for a wedding (which is unlike any we have ever heard of) was probably the only way she could get through it! We can happily report that Tess survived her own wedding, and is flourishing in her marriage. She has been rewarded for her courage a hundred times over. Not only did she reclaim her ability to trust someone she loved, but she also unexpectedly recovered an even greater part of herself.

It has taken me a while to look back at my fears about getting married. I always thought that if I lived with someone instead of getting married, I could be whoever I wanted, but that if I married, I would lose that opportunity forever.

My old ideas about what marriage should be have changed. What has replaced them is a commitment to develop flexibility and intimacy, breaking down barriers to trust, and having faith in another person. Ultimately, our marriage is a commitment to honest self-awareness on both of our parts. . . . That, in the deepest sense, is our truest vow.

LIVING TOGETHER IS MORE ROMANTIC

Romance, we are told, is like a hothouse orchid: ephemeral and delicate. We are constantly admonished that it will wither and die if we don't work diligently to keep it alive—especially within the confines of marriage. It was this elusive intensity that Derek cherished most about new, unmarried love. And he was willing to preserve it at all costs, short of marrying any of the women he loved. For he genuinely believed that living together forever was just more romantic, and his fervent wish was to preserve the bloom of love. Derek might have continued in this way for a lifetime, but then he met Jackie. She was the one who had to take the next step for both of them.

At forty-three, Derek is actively building his career as a political media consultant. He has the eyes of someone who pays close attention—keen and blue, set into an aquiline face. Although his hair is shorter now, he still dresses as he did when he led political rallies in the sixties and seventies; a work shirt with rolled-up sleeves, tucked into a pair of bleached-out jeans. Like Chris in Chapter 2, Derek resisted giving up the sense of unlimited potential. But as he got older, it occurred to him that never choosing might also mean ending up with nothing. "Until I was well into my thirties, it was a world of too many girls and too many 'pretend relationships,' " he said, rolling his eyes and shaking his head back and forth. "It wasn't necessarily time to marry, but it was time to stop wasting my life." Derek thought he might want to experiment with making more of a commitment. Though he was still tentative, with this new slant on his love life, synchronicity, the matchmaker, just happened to join his side.

Jackie and I actually met at a campaign fund-raiser. I had seen her earlier in the evening and was immediately attracted. But the place was so packed that when I started to walk over to her, she got lost in the crowd. I couldn't find her the whole evening, and finally decided to go home. I went upstairs to say good-bye to my friend, who was the organizer. By coincidence, Jackie knew him too. She was sitting with him, so I walked over. He introduced us, and she and I started talking. The next thing we knew, it was

*2:00 A.M. and the waiters were folding chairs and sweeping up
the confetti. I liked her and I thought she liked me. I took her
phone number, and called her a few days afterward. That's the
long and short of it—well, almost.*

"Almost," because Jackie was coming from a very different
direction and wanted very different things from a relationship. She,
too, had never been married before, but, unlike Derek, she had *always*
wanted to be. In the two years prior to meeting Derek, she had gone
through a period in which she was completely fed up. Her sunny
disposition had turned angry, dark, and hopeless after a string of too
many disappointing relationships with too many wrong guys. The
way Jackie described it, she was walking around preoccupied with her
failures and completely absorbed in her problems. Under her little
black cloud, she succeeded in accomplishing one thing: no eligible
man dared approach her. On those rare occasions when someone
would get within dating range, she'd have a hundred reasons ready
why they were mismatched. Months would pass and no one would
call. "I couldn't get a date if my life depended on it," she shuddered
as she recalled those times. "I was getting back what I was putting
out."

As a spiritual person, Jackie believes that once she started acting
hopeless and desperate, the future of her love life became a self-
fulfilling prophecy. "The universe gives us messages all the time," she
said, "it is our mirror that reflects our deeper internal state—the one
we might not be aware of—and we always attract our spiritual
equivalent." Jackie decided to pay closer attention to the signals that
were surrounding her. One day she overheard herself "talking a good
negative game," and from that moment on, her first order of business
was to become as happy as she could be *inside*. She made a conscious
decision to become clearer about what kind of man she wanted, to
visualize him, and to deliberately open up to the world of possibility
again. Most important, she was no longer at war with herself. It was
at that juncture that she met Derek.

*The night I met Derek I felt I had a light around me. You know
how people say it always happens when you least expect it? I was
on my way to being more clear about who I was and what I*

wanted than ever before. I really feel there are right things and right people to get involved with. But I had always gotten hung up on pushing it to happen and getting impatient when it didn't, rather than surrendering to what will be. I was no longer coming from a place of desperation that was screaming, "I have to get married." At the same time I wasn't pretending I didn't want to be.

From very early on, Derek sensed that he was with Jackie for good. Not only was he physically attracted to her, but he described her as a "peer," not just someone to take to bed and have a good time with, which is how Derek had primarily operated in the past. He was immediately taken with her intelligence, humor, and "big heart," all of which convinced him that the potential for a more complex relationship was there. Without being fully conscious of it at the time, Derek was in the midst of making the commitment he was looking for.

Jackie and Derek knew each other for a year before they officially started living together, but Jackie began spending most of her time at Derek's house shortly after they first met. For Derek, their living together was as ideal an arrangement as he could hope for. He didn't need anything to change, and hoped it wouldn't.

I immersed myself in the relationship with Jackie, but I don't recall ever feeling as though getting married was an urgent matter. I felt we would stay together for the rest of our lives, and that marriage wouldn't make it any more so. I had even thought of having children with her—all outside the formal confines of marriage.

It is not like the idea of marrying Jackie had never crossed my mind. It would—like a dark shadow—and I would think of the finality of marriage and the pain of divorce: two feelings I wasn't eager to experience. Then, since we were just living together, I'd be free of those fears.

For the next two years he kept those fears buried and never mentioned marriage. Every now and then he had inklings that marriage to Jackie was inevitable, but he never discussed it with her, or let on that he considered it. Nothing changed. Ironically, Jackie's and Derek's emotional intentions were the same; they were, and are, very much in love, and they had every hope of remaining together permanently. But what differed were the personal meanings they associated with the idea of marriage, and their feelings about how it would affect their lives. For Jackie, marriage represented a safe harbor in which she and her relationship with Derek could grow.

> *I always knew that marriage would center me, and it did—but not in that white-doves-and-violins way that you think it will when you're a kid. I knew I would feel stronger not only because I was loved but because I would have a place where I belonged. I have always believed that I should find my mate, be married, and then move on with my life.*

It was no secret that Jackie was looking for permanence and considered each day together an investment, a sentiment Derek had understood from the very beginning. Derek's silence concerned Jackie; even though he wasn't saying he *didn't* want marriage, he wasn't saying he wanted it, either. One day they were walking on the beach. Jackie was looking far into the gray horizon and simply said, "Let's talk marriage, because I can't live with you anymore if it isn't a commitment for life." When Derek responded, it was clear that he didn't feel any less committed to her, just less committed to the idea of marriage. That moment of reckoning is etched in Derek's memory.

> *I told her that I was committed to her, and wondered why we had to marry to prove that. After all, it was just a piece of paper, I said. When she heard that, she replied, "Well, if that's all it is, then why don't you sign it? It's not a commitment if you don't make a commitment. Make me happy!"*
>
> *That stopped me dead in my tracks. I just said, "I don't want to do that because I have always felt that the romantic thing is to live with someone and be with that person for your whole life. I just don't want to get married."*

From that point on, Jackie wasn't comfortable living with Derek any longer. As far as she was concerned, the experiment was over.

Without making threats or ultimatums, she asked Derek to make a decision one way or the other so that she could make hers. One Sunday, a month later, Derek was shopping for a new Jeep and invited Jackie along. They were standing in the middle of the dealer's showroom bargaining with the salesman, but the word *marriage* kept popping into Derek's mind. Just as the salesman quoted his rock-bottom price for the model in question, Derek turned to Jackie and found himself saying, somewhat unromantically,

> *"Let me get this straight. If I don't marry you, you are going to leave me, right?" And she said, "Yes, absolutely!" I think we got it settled within the hour. First of all, I didn't want to give her up. Second, what we had was akin to a marriage anyway. And, third, we wanted to have kids. So I said, "Okay, you're right."*
>
> *Now, I know that this was not the wedding proposal that Jackie had imagined she might get someday. I think she felt monumentally ripped off. So, about a week later, we went out to dinner, and as we were on our way to a movie, I put my arm around her, nuzzled her, and said, "I want you to know that I've been doing a lot of thinking in the past week, and I am getting really excited about the idea. I don't want you to feel that it's something you talked me into; getting married is what I really want to do."*

The impetus to marry came from the unlikely combination of Jackie's certainty of purpose and Derek's fear that he would lose her if he didn't act decisively. As with Tess, Derek's ambivalence and lingering preference for living together expressed itself in the wedding arrangements. He was against a big wedding from the start, fearing that what they were doing would get lost in the sweep of events. Instead, he lobbied for "just flying away and marrying before some local clergyman." An elopement would have eliminated the need for a wedding—the most obvious symbolic act in the transition from living together to marriage. Jackie vetoed the suggestion and, as an unspoken compromise, scaled back the number of guests to thirty-five—no small task, given the number of friends and family both had accumulated over the last forty-plus years. It was a low-key affair—quiet, but with the definite feeling of unbounded joy. The clergyman's blessings even included a few jokes Derek had written for the occasion.

To this day, however, Derek stands by his conviction that his commitment to Jackie runs far deeper than the ceremony that pronounced them married. Some two years after the wedding, Derek feels that although marriage has redefined their status in the eyes of their friends and family, he insists that their growing love is a consequence of *them*, not of their marital status. He firmly believes the wedding was simply a formalizing of the existing bond between them; theirs is a seven-year commitment that started when they met, not a two-year marriage. By Derek's account, their anniversary isn't May 31, the date of their wedding, but August 1, the day they really came into each other's lives.

Our marriage intensifies the commitment to each other that we had already made, as opposed to some kind of exalted condition. But I am not sure that there has been any one moment in which being married seemed different from living together. You see, I felt connected to Jackie very early on, before we got married. That's what counted first—irrespective of marriage—Jackie is the woman I am going to spend the rest of my life with, barring some unforeseen catastrophe. And that is the feeling I grow more and more aware of every day.

SO WHY GET MARRIED?

Living together is so much a part of contemporary courtship that it has become nearly as common and socially acceptable as marriage itself. When couples begin living together, most who do end up marrying tend to make that decision within the first few years. But the longer a couple lives together without marrying, the smaller is the chance that they finally will. When this happens a couple of times in succession, the time invested may have been lost, but not necessarily wasted. This is precisely how some late marriers reach midlife without ever having been married.

After experimenting with living together to learn about intimacy or to avoid marriage altogether, some late marriers like Luke,

Tess, and Derek use it to ease into marriage. Because living together so closely resembles married life, it's a good steppingstone for negotiating the uncertain psychological territory between a temporary and a permanent commitment once they finally do meet someone they feel serious about. And because it isn't as "real" or final as marriage, it's a safe context in which to desensitize fears and soothe resistances. That was what Luke, Tess, and Derek did. Once their positive experiences outweighed their negative ones, the strength of the relationship drove them forward and each finally felt "ready" to marry.

In the complex and subtle vocabulary of courtship, "ready" can mean anything from "I didn't want to miss out on an important life experience," to "Getting married just felt like the right thing to do," to "I had tried everything else, so why not?" What these shorthand responses are really saying is, "I am prepared to move forward with this person and I feel competent to take the next unknown emotional risk." It's a process that each person approaches in his or her own way, on his or her own timetable. Time is what it took for Luke to trust Sally as his choice; for Tess to liberate herself from her own ideas about marriage; and for Derek to admit that commitment was sexier and more romantic than he ever dreamed.

Since living-together "togetherness" and married "togetherness" share countless surface similarities—meals have to be cooked, beds made, bills paid, and so on—we were curious to know how these late marriers themselves defined the difference. And like other researchers who have asked the same question, we found they could more easily explain why they married *when* they did, than *why* they married at all. Victor, who opened this chapter with his resolve to live with Jenny forever, came closest to expressing the intangible difference. He pondered our query and then said, "I can't say exactly how being married contributes to our relationship, but it does. It's a loop that passes through Jenny to me and symbolizes 'chosen companion,' commitment, and constancy."

A loop symbolizes security. If living together falls short of marriage, it does so because it fails to *symbolize* what marriage does. Marriage, as a rite of passage, is present in nearly all human communities worldwide. Few life transitions are given as much ritual attention; only birth and death are marked with equal seriousness.[6] In our culture, marriage embodies the highest expression of emotional commitment between adults, and it is against this standard that most other intimate arrangements are compared and judged. Ideally this commitment lasts a lifetime; no other arrangement except parenthood makes this explicit claim.

The symbolic power of marriage transforms our personal status and redefines our identity in society. The union has personal and public meaning. Marriage not only contains us as two separate individuals, but creates a third, ever-changing entity, namely "the relationship." The nuptial vows express the sincerity of the couple's involvement, and also publicly create a wider set of overlapping obligations. The moment they are spoken, unrelated people instantly become family to one another, and in this way communities are created. In the words of one woman:

> To live together seems to me to imply that the central relationship of one's life is nobody's business but one's own. To live together is a decision . . . put into motion alone. There is no community blessing or celebration of the decision.
>
> To marry is to acknowledge one's part in the human family, to recognize that one's life is more than one's own, that one's actions affect more than oneself . . . that [the relationship] is more than a private affair between one woman and one man.[7]

Marrying someone *is* a different kind of personal statement than simply choosing to live with them. This is particularly true when you marry for the first time after forty. By midlife we know who we are and what we want better than ever before. In seeking a life partner at this stage, we're less likely to entertain the possibility of divorce somewhere down the line. The stakes seem higher; there is less time to waste because there is less time to recover from a mistake. When we marry, we are essentially declaring, "I'm not disappointed with this person; this isn't a second-class fit; we belong together." As a self-affirming act, our marriage announces to us and to everyone we love and care about that we are finally willing and able to surrender our heart to another.

4

PSYCHIC BAGGAGE

Although I didn't realize it at the time, I needed women to be dependent so I could feel safe. But then their dependence meant I couldn't respect them, which gave me the perfect excuse to keep my distance and stay uncommitted. It was like having my unconscious cake and eating it too.
—ANDY, age forty-two, married two years

I was ambivalent about marriage and afraid of it. Part of me wanted it and the other part didn't. I spent too much time on doomed relationships—way past the point of knowing it really wasn't right, and yet still trying to make it right.
—HELEN, age forty-seven, married one year

HAUNTED BY THE PAST

For some midlife marriers, delaying marriage was more the result of unresolved psychological issues than sixties rebellion or conscious choice. Internal conflicts impeded the ability either to make a commitment or to choose a suitable partner with whom to make that commitment. Some found themselves forever choosing inappropriate, temporary partners to whom they were attracted but with whom a permanent union would have been impossible. In other instances, emotional wounds stemming from their families of origin left these women and men afraid of commitment—even with appropriate partners.

In every case, the dynamic between them and one or both parents was the root of each late marrier's subsequent problems with the opposite sex. We heard about fathers and mothers who were overly critical or harsh, and how that led to the adult child's inability to trust. One woman talked about how her father had depended on her to the extent that she avoided getting close to anyone for fear they too might depend on her too much. A forty-six-year-old man told us his mother had so failed to nurture him that, until recently, he had been unable to love or be loved by the women in his life. And a first-time bride of forty-seven revealed that her overly controlling parents set the stage for her anxiety about being trapped in an intimate relationship.

It was only after a period of self-examination—and often therapy—that this group of first-time spouses over forty discovered their troubled love relationships weren't accidental, but rather were connected to patterns they had learned in childhood. They had been unable to risk love on a permanent basis for fear that the consequences would in some way resemble the abuses of love they had experienced growing up.

Before they could rid themselves of the "psychic baggage" they continually lugged into each new relationship, most people found they had to go through the often lengthy process of confronting their particular psychological issues. Painful as that process often was, many emphasized that had they not gone through it, they would have been doomed to repeat and become imprisoned by the unconscious behavior that kept them from connecting successfully with an appropriate partner.

Often, when we're unable to "find the right person," what's actually inhibiting us is our unconsciousness about our past. When our unacknowledged fears tell us that being intimate means we'll have to relive uncomfortable or painful childhood experiences, we do everything we can to prevent intimacy. And since marriage, at least ideally, signifies the most intimate relationship we can have, we make sure to stay clear of it. We say to ourselves, "Even though I'm lonely and I want a partner, I never want to be in the position my family was in. So I'll look for love, get involved, but then I'll set up a conflict that will give me the excuse to breach the relationship or force the other person to breach it." In other words, we tell ourselves that we're trying, but we just haven't found the right person. In fact, we've set up our lives so that we'll *never* find the right person. A number of late marriers told us this had been the case for them.

It is important to recognize, however, that psychological problems related to intimacy and relationships are in no way exclusive to late marriers or never-marrieds. Unhappy marriages and divorce rates certainly attest to that fact. So while some never-marrieds indeed fear commitment or make the wrong choices, and some late marriers "waste time" fearing commitment and making wrong choices, some who marry at the normal age also set themselves up to fail at love. The only difference is that those who marry say "I do," and those who don't marry say good-bye.

"DAD WAS UNAVAILABLE"

Rita, forty-seven years old and married about seven years, had been habitually attracted to inappropriate or unmarriageable partners, and linked those attractions to problems she'd had with her father. Rita's dad was an alcoholic and a charmer, but he couldn't be counted on, either as a husband or a father. Like many adult children of alcoholics, Rita found herself choosing partners who were fascinating, sexually exciting, and fun to be with, but ultimately undependable. She was unconsciously trying to resolve with each of these men the very issue she had been unable to resolve with her father—his emotional unpredictability. Her father's alcoholism rendered him unable to ultimately come through for his daughter. So, when Rita grew up, the pattern with which she felt most comfortable was "having fun" with men she couldn't count on. The more irresponsible the man, the greater the challenge, and that challenge provided her with a sexual high.

*The whole first part of my love life fits into one chapter. All the
guys I dated before my husband were in some way like my
father—charismatic and fun, but thoroughly irresponsible. And
all my relationships were based on physical attraction. I couldn't
possibly have married any of them, but I felt passionately
toward them.*

Rita was unconsciously drawn to men with whom she could
reenact—and hopefully overcome—the struggle to win her father's
love. She could only play out that scenario with partners who were
as emotionally unavailable as her father had been. Since becoming
involved with such types rarely leads to marriage, Rita found herself
still single in her late thirties. When she met Rick, her husband-to-be,
a camaraderie and a deep friendship developed. Also, Rita wanted to
have a baby. So they married. But since Rick lacked the unpredictability that Rita unconsciously needed, she unfortunately didn't feel as
passionate toward him as she had toward her string of casual affairs.

*Rick's healthy and well rounded. Sadly, I'm not wildly attracted
to him physically. Part of what I'm trying to sort out now is why
I can't feel as sexual with Rick as I did with the guys I didn't
really love or respect.*

Rita appreciates her marriage to Rick, and they're both grateful
for their delightful seven-year-old daughter. But Rick is also the child
of an alcoholic, and Rita admits they both have problems with denial.
She wants to get into therapy with Rick, but since he isn't too keen
on the idea yet, she may begin the process alone. Although Rita told
us she's happy with her life most of the time—and doesn't regret
trading off exciting sexual affairs for a loving husband and child—she
misses the passion she felt with those less appropriate partners and
looks forward to resolving this core problem in a therapeutic context.

"DAD NEEDED ME"

Cheryl traces her resistance to marriage to her father's overdepend-
ency. She says that he needed her too much and that, in an uncon-

scious way, her decision to remain single was based in part on not wanting to betray him. An unhealthy bond was created that lasted for decades, with Cheryl's attentions being focused on taking care of her father. She consistently chose to date married men to whom she never had to commit herself, thereby remaining emotionally connected to her dad while at the same time avoiding the possibility of taking on another dependent male. In her mind, love threatened her personal freedom because it was all-consuming.

I always told myself it was just bad luck that I consistently fell in love with guys who were married. I went with one married guy for seven years, and he was intimately connected with my family—even came to my dad's sixtieth birthday party. I finally got a glimpse of what I was doing to myself when I pushed this guy into seeing a lawyer about getting a divorce, and he did just that. I couldn't get out of bed for a week—I was so terrified that he'd go through with it! I asked myself, "What is wrong? You should be jumping up and down, delirious with happiness!" But I wasn't. It wasn't until many years later that I figured out why I was avoiding commitment and marriage. It had to do with my feeling that if I made a real attachment with a man, I would be letting my dad down.

In her typical fashion, Cheryl met her husband, Michael, while he was still married to someone else. Shortly thereafter he divorced his wife, and Cheryl and he moved in together. She knew him for six years before they got married, during which time she worked on issues of separation from her father. She needed to know and experience that she didn't have to take care of a man for him to love her. In the course of their premarital relationship, Michael proved that to her, and Cheryl learned to trust him enough to become vulnerable. Eventually she and Michael were willing to risk marriage—he for the third time, she for the first.

CONTROLLING PARENTS

The issue of control was one that several late marriers raised when explaining their earlier avoidance of marriage. The fear of being controlled as they had been by their parents was one factor that kept both Kate and Maxine from finding mates before forty.

Kate's unhappy memories of a mother who was harsh and disapproving forced her to keep her distance from men who she suspected might be in any way critical or overpowering. Her involvement with younger men may have been one way to prevent being overwhelmed by a more powerful partner:

> My fear of commitment had to do with not wanting to be controlled—because my mother had been so controlling and so emotionally abusive toward me. It was preferable for me to keep my distance rather than opening myself up to that kind of maltreatment. I always had somebody in my life, but I was never really comfortable with permanence—and that took years to overcome. I would always find people I knew I wouldn't end up marrying and with whom there was little chance I'd be controlled. For one thing, they were often much younger than me. When I was twenty-eight I dated someone who was eighteen; then, later, when I was in my thirties, I dated someone in his early twenties. Maybe their age made me feel safe—I was in control, and there was no pressure to marry.

Maxine's worry was that marriage and the closeness it engendered might come too close to the kind of suffocating relationship she had experienced as a child. She clung to her independence, in part, as a way to prohibit such a reoccurrence. When she finally did marry, at forty-seven, she chose someone with whom there was no possibility that she would be emotionally smothered.

> I was an only child, and my parents loved me almost too much—that kind of "smother love." My not marrying was a kind of rebellion. I was afraid that a man would control me through love. That's one of the nice things about my husband— he's not at all that way. But my parents were, and I'm sure that I was afraid a man would try to do the same thing.

Both Maxine and Kate waited to marry until after they were able to identify the origins of their fear of control. Through counseling, they began to see how their relationship to their parents had created that very real fear. Eventually, risking love became possible for each of them, and the partners they chose had a lot to do with that risk-taking. Both women emphasized that their husbands had never pressured them or made any attempt to control them in any way. Rather, they created a caring, comfortable atmosphere in which love and mutual respect could flourish.

THE NEED FOR NURTURING

If too much parental control had its negative consequences, too little parental love resulted in a different set of difficulties for other mature marriers.

Ray told us that his mother lacked the nurturing qualities he so desperately sought. Her unsupportive treatment of him led not only to his need for mothering from other women but to his insecurity, his inability to trust women, and his subsequent need to control them. Having never received the proper kind of love from his mother, Ray was both needy and angry when it came to women. Inexperienced as he was at giving and receiving love, his need to control his partners was an attempt to protect himself from being betrayed. Ray had a long series of stormy relationships before he married two and a half years ago, at the age of forty-four:

> My mother was dominating and very critical. I was constantly told things like "Big boys don't cry," and "Children should be seen and not heard." I was never permitted to show my feelings or be myself. So I had a tremendous need to be recognized and nurtured, yet I couldn't allow myself to depend on anyone for fear they ultimately wouldn't be there for me.

Ray longed for a nurturing woman—the mother he never had. But he also needed to control that person. Several of the women he had lived with over the years told him they thought he hated women because his need to control them was so strong. Most of his relationships eventually ended in conflict.

All the years of battling with women finally caught up with Ray. He grew weary and began to question why he was repeatedly drawn to adversarial relationships. Upon reflection, he realized how he had vented his anger toward his mother on all the women with whom he connected. Two changes occurred in his early forties: Ray was no longer satisfied with volatile relationships; and he began to feel the urge to have children.

He took a break from his career in the music business and did some traveling and soul-searching. After months of assessing his past and thinking about what he wanted from the rest of his life, he came to the sobering conclusion that he needed to treat women differently. He was ready to try to make some profound changes.

When he met his wife-to-be, he had an opportunity to become the nurturing person he had so intensely and angrily sought all his life. Brenda was strong and confident, someone who was invulnerable to the kind of abuse and control he had inflicted on his previous girlfriends. Although they had their problems initially, Ray now takes enormous pleasure in his family and in caring for his two young sons. In fact, he's almost become a house-husband. But the scars of his youth haven't vanished. Ray is still in the process of building the self-esteem that will enable him to fully trust the woman he loves. Meanwhile, he and Brenda are in therapy together to deal with how his early experiences continue to affect their marriage.

WOUNDED IN LOVE

Parents weren't the only ones cited as the culprits who had deterred midlife marriers from marrying earlier. Several people pointed to previous lovers having so wounded them that starting up another love affair, with someone else, became virtually impossible. Their response to having been hurt early in their lives was simply to withdraw. They preferred to retreat from love rather than open themselves to the possibility of further rejection and pain.

Robert and Ivan, both attractive men, accomplished in their professions, disclosed shattering experiences that they say prevented them from considering marriage for close to twenty years. Robert married for the first time at forty-seven, Ivan at fifty-eight. First, Robert's story:

> *I shied away from women for a long time. Before I was twenty-five, I dated only a couple of times. After that, I only went out with women maybe once a year or once every three years. I used to get burned a lot—get my feelings hurt. It all started with a girl who betrayed me when I was in high school. I moped around for weeks after I saw her drive away in a '57 Chevy with another guy. I was depressed for years after that, and decided to focus on sports and my career rather than on women. I built this funny little wall around myself. It wasn't until my forties that I convinced myself to take a chance with women again.*

Robert was still gun-shy, but he finally decided not to be threatened by all those internal messages that told him, "That girl won't go out with you, so don't even ask her. She'll only refuse you." He told himself he couldn't be any worse off than he was—single and lonely—and adopted a what do-I-have-to-lose attitude. It was this new approach to life that gave him the nerve to approach his wife-to-be.

Ivan had a similar experience of getting "burned" by a woman and then retreating for a period of many years. When he was about forty-five, he lived with someone for the first time. She was adventurous, and they shared a lot of the same athletic interests. In fact, they met on a backpacking trip. The relationship went along fine for a while, until the woman ended the affair abruptly. It turned out she was seeing another man who lived in the same apartment building as Ivan. Ivan had never suspected she was seeing someone else, and he was completely devastated:

> *It was one of the roughest times I had ever had. I said to myself, "Never again!" and became a hermit. I had a good job, made good money, traveled—and I thought, "Who needs a woman?" From then on, I didn't look very hard anymore. I dated and went to bed with women occasionally, but I wasn't set on marriage.*

Ivan and Robert's sensitivity to rejection was rooted in their past relationships with their parents. People don't usually shatter to the point of avoiding intimacy unless they have a very fragile sense of self, emanating from childhood distress.

Without the unconditional supportive love of a parent, we find it difficult to trust that our opportunity for love will transcend any single rejection or disappointment. We tend to generalize on the basis of one or two negative experiences, thereby predicting for ourselves future failure in love. Since we were unable to trust that Mom or Dad would love us no matter what, when someone we love disappoints us, we can't believe we'll ever be able to find love again.

Robert's alcoholic father had never really been there for him, and Ivan's father's domineering personality created tremendous conflict within the family. Perhaps part of the reason both men were so easily disillusioned in love was that they had already suffered deeply prior to attempting any relationship with women. And once their first loves hurt them, it was one hurt too many.

"IF I LOVE YOU, WILL YOU LEAVE ME?"

The preceding short case histories touch on some of the psychological problems that inhibit late marriers from marrying sooner. We now turn to two core stories for a more in-depth look at how inner conflicts became barriers to commitment and marriage.

In Andy's case, the underlying issue of trust, or lack of it, colored all his dealings with women. Andy's adoptive mother died when he was thirteen. He experienced both her death and his biological mother's initial rejection of him as devastating personal betrayals. At the center of his inability to trust women was his fear that they would inevitably abandon him as his two mothers had.

Now forty-two and married for about two years, Andy is a successful educator, trim and athletic, who lives in a small house on a hillside overlooking a bay. When we walked in to begin our interview, his cocker spaniel bounded up to greet us, and Andy jokingly referred to her as his and his wife's "surrogate child." "We figured if we could handle a cocker spaniel, we may be ready for a baby in about ten years." Andy's answers to our opening questions were somewhat clipped and guarded. But once we began talking with him, he became extremely open about his relationship difficulties prior to marriage. He emphasized his struggle with painful personal issues and his ultimate triumph over an emotionally crippling pattern in his relations with women:

> *I lived with two women and dated a lot in between before I met my wife. I never gave marriage a thought. I didn't know who I was, and the women I was involved with didn't know who they were. I was just acting out this kind of "death wish" that seemed to be compelling me to get involved with women who were not the healthiest for me—or let's say my relationships with them were not healthy combinations. One clue was that I could never tell any of them, "I love you." Sometimes I had great affection for them, or liked them a lot, but I had serious problems using the word because I didn't understand what self-love was about.*

We were curious about how Andy's experience of losing his adoptive mother related to his lack of self-love as well as to his attitudes and feelings toward women. Since the loss of his mother was one of the first things he mentioned but hadn't elaborated on, we asked him to go into it more deeply.

What Andy told us was that being an adopted child, and then having his adoptive mother die when he was thirteen, left him with serious abandonment fears and a lot of unresolved issues about women. While no age is a good one for losing a parent, puberty is a particularly bad time to undergo such a loss, and that experience colored his future interaction with lovers:

> *Of course, I didn't consciously realize the pattern I was setting up until later in therapy, but I would pick women who I felt had potential, who I could mold and create in the image that I wished them to be. That would accomplish two things: I would have great women because they were hand-picked and hand-trained by yours truly, plus they would be so beholden to me that they would never abandon me. They would be hooked in.*

Andy went on to explain that his need to have control over women related to his unacknowledged lack of self-love. He only felt secure when the woman he was involved with was "hooked in." Since he had no experience of loving himself, he didn't trust that any woman would love him on his own merits. And since the women he chose were similarly lacking in self-esteem, his and their combined unresolved issues created a powder keg of emotions. Andy described the kinds of "scenes" that would ensue between himself and the various women he had emotionally ensnared:

> *My feeling is that when it comes to love, you pull in pretty much what you put out, and I was putting out very mixed messages about self-image and self-love. So I was getting a lot of troubled relationships in return. For example, one girlfriend was very fragile, suicidal sometimes, very dependent, very volatile. We would have like three days of absolute fabulous sex and relating, and then three days of basically trying to kill each other. Then we would take a day off to rest. So it was a very explosive relationship based on more drama and acting out unresolved issues than on reality.*

Again, owing to his family history, Andy lacked experience of trusting women and yet craved their love and attention. So he had unconsciously worked out a scheme whereby he chose women who also suffered from insecurity and allowed themselves to be victimized by his controlling behavior. Andy's need to control, combined with his girlfriends' need to be controlled, made for a perfect psychological "fit." Their unconscious needs created a compelling attraction, yet resulted in inevitable clashes. His contempt for controllable women was part of Andy's "mixed message," and it didn't take long for his girlfriends to receive his hostile signals. Ultimately the relationships would end. At one point Andy made a conscious attempt to "cool out" from a passionate yet troubled love affair by choosing someone who was more stable:

> *I found someone who was clearly at the opposite end of the sanity curve, very loving, always dependable. Whereas with my previous girlfriend I never knew if I was coming home to a lady or a tiger, with this one I always knew it would be the lady. She provided a very restful plateau—nice, but passionless. I was only*

with her because I needed a rest from two years of that up-and-down stuff.

The "restful plateau" didn't last long. Andy was unconsciously seeking to discover a solution to his anger and fear by alternating volatile women with calm ones. But his need for the troubled ones—with whom he could unconsciously act out his unresolved problems—persisted. He could only feel passionately about women who clung to him desperately and then dramatically threatened to leave him when he kept his distance. His next involvement, with yet another dependent, insecure, yet "exciting" woman, finally led him to do something about his roller-coaster romances:

My next girlfriend had all the old spark and flash I always seemed to go for. And she was dependent, fragmented, and basically had a bad self-image. I was beginning to be conscious enough to say to myself, "You're flirting with it again!"—like an alcoholic who's tempted to go on the wagon.

Then one or two serious incidents happened. When I told her I didn't want to see her again, she became almost like that woman in Fatal Attraction—*she would follow me, create scenes. Finally I said to myself, "Okay, out." I had had enough. This relationship was a final warning. I had become like an addict, trying to convince myself that if I didn't shoot it in the vein, I could still sniff a little bit. But you can't; you're either in or out. So I made a choice, and I was out.*

Ending that last disastrous relationship marked the beginning of a long, painful process of self-discovery and psychological "work," as Andy referred to it. He entered therapy, began a search for his birth mother, and openly grieved the death of his adoptive mother—something he hadn't been able to do properly in the twenty-five years since her passing. Andy recognized that unless he confronted the fear and pain associated with his past, he would remain stuck in unsatisfying, addictive partnerships that played out his internal conflicts surrounding trust and abandonment. He came to understand what it was he had previously been seeking in his relationships with women, and how that differed from what he actually wanted and needed:

I needed women to be dependent so I could feel safe. But then their dependence meant I couldn't respect them, which gave me the perfect excuse to keep my distance and stay uncommitted. It was like having my unconscious cake and eating it too.

It dawned on me that I was never devastated by a relationship breaking up, because I knew ahead of time that we would break up. I never felt a real loss in a relationship, because I just assumed it was going to end. That way I prevented the pain by remaining separate, but I also prevented the possibility of a sustained relationship.

When we consistently choose partners with whom we have unhappy, unhealthy relationships, we need to question those choices seriously and seek to determine what lies beneath those decisions. Andy was grappling with two very profound experiences of abandonment. He had been separated from his birth mother when she put him up for adoption, and had lost his adoptive mother when she died prematurely.

Unconsciously he had created a strategy to prevent any future losses. He chose women whom he could control and by whom he didn't mind being abandoned—since they weren't really the type of women he wanted to "end up with." Andy's need to act out abandonment/control issues was so strong that he felt a compelling attraction to those women with whom he sensed he could fulfill that need.

In her book *Women Who Love Too Much*, which applies equally to men, therapist Robin Norwood explains the powerful attraction to unhealthy partners and how it relates to childhood traumas. She states that when we choose such partners, we're often reenacting and reexperiencing unhappy family relationships in an attempt to make them manageable. If a particular partner offers us "an opportunity to grapple with and try to prevail over childhood feelings of pain and helplessness, of being unloved and unwanted, then the attraction becomes . . . virtually irresistible."[1] This behavior, Norwood explains, is similar to that of a young child who, having experienced a trauma of some sort, incorporates it into his or her play until he or she can overcome the negative experience.

As for Andy, he was attracted to women with whom he could

play out his fears of being left. He picked women he didn't ultimately want as a way to distance himself from any possible pain, and yet their dependence on him fed his need for security—a quality he deeply lacked, given his history of loss. Andy seemed to choose women onto whom he could project all his past fears. That way, *she* could act out the vulnerable, needy, dependent child he once was, and Andy could paradoxically experience his childhood from a safe distance. The "fit" between him and the women he chose was a perfect one—and accounted for Andy's compulsion to be with this type of woman over and over again.

The unhealthy cycle was broken when Andy embarked upon a period of self-examination and therapy. One of the essential things he learned was that he needed to love himself in the way he had yearned for his mother's love. He finally acknowledged the pain of losing her, accepted himself as a son in mourning, and began to love and nurture that grieving person within himself:

A lot of work and a lot of therapy helped me discover what self-love was about. I did a lot of grieving for my mother, and I did a search for my birth mother. Facing those two realities had to do with self-acceptance, with figuring out who I was, as opposed to who I thought I was or who I was supposed to be.

Andy admits that even when he became conscious of the unhealthy patterns he had set up with women, he still found himself slipping on occasion. Although the process of healing involved more than simply *determining* not to get hooked again, in time he found it easier to extricate himself from a potentially dangerous liaison:

I got to a period I call "conscious dating"—which didn't mean I was a genius, it just meant I knew what attracted me to women who weren't right for me, and I made an effort to stay away from them. My antenna would still go up. I would be at a party and inevitably be drawn to the woman who was the craziest in the room. I would zoom over there and do my stuff, and she would do her stuff, and in about ten seconds I would say to myself, "Aha. Okay. How do you do? Nice to see you. See you

*around," because I finally understood that that type of woman
was toxic to me, and that I wasn't good for her either. I got to
know the warning signs, and started wasting less of my time.*

Once Andy began to free himself from "toxic" relationships, he
started to think about beginning a healthy one—or at least wondering if such a relationship was possible. Could he be attracted to
someone with a good self-image? Someone with whom trust and
vulnerability were possible?

Andy met his wife, Carol, through a friend. He was impressed
not only with her looks, but with her intelligence and the altruistic
work she was involved in. He liked her energy and her humor, and
was attracted—but also put off—by a certain innocent quality. Perhaps he was afraid her naïveté was a sign of the kind of dependence
he had been so unhealthily drawn to in the past. But as he got to
know her, he found her to be quite independent, yet, at the same time,
vulnerable to his interest in her. They carried on a long-distance
relationship for two years before they decided to live together. Andy
admits that there was some significance to his choosing someone who
lived five hundred miles away. He had done this before as a way to
remain emotionally distant; but apparently, with Carol, the distance
provided him with the perspective to ultimately conclude that she
was the woman with whom he wanted to spend his life.

Andy was resistant to the idea of marriage when Carol first
brought it up. Some of his old fears of abandonment returned to haunt
him as he began contemplating the possibility. Before allowing himself to trust Carol with his whole life, he wanted to make certain their
relationship was on solid ground:

*When I first asked her to move in, about a year into the
relationship, Carol intimated that she'd be interested if—and I
said, "Forget about the if, 'cause there is no if. Either you choose
to move in, and we'll live together, or you won't choose to. I'm
not going to promise that we'll get engaged or ultimately get
married. I am interested in knowing who you are and having a
relationship. How can I make any promises if I don't know
who you are and don't know what's going to happen in the
future?"*

Carol was not happy about his position, and put off making any decisions. But a year later she finally earned Andy's trust. A catharsis involving his feelings for his deceased mother cleared the way for Andy's marriage to Carol. Carol not only proved that she could accept Andy for who he really was, she also had the wisdom to recognize that he needed to work through certain painful issues on his own. Andy described the turning point in his relationship with Carol:

I decided to go back to the mausoleum where my adoptive mother is buried, where I hadn't been since we put her in there when I was thirteen. I grieved, I wailed, I howled on the concrete floor of the mausoleum. Carol waited outside, listening to me, wanting to come in and rescue me, but realizing I had to go through this process on my own. It was tough for her, it was tough for me. But it was her ability to know when to be there and when to step out, when to allow stuff to happen, and when to give support that deeply impressed me. She saw the abandoned, hurt boy behind the image, but, unlike other women in my past, she didn't feel compelled to heal me or baby me or adopt me or come to my rescue. She was just willing to allow things to take place. Allow the little boy to do his thing, and then say, "Hey, that's fine. You can do that. It's not going to kill me. I am not going to run away."

This transformative experience served to build the trust Andy needed before he could feel comfortable committing his life to another person. By allowing Andy the room to feel his feelings and live out painful aspects of his life without interference, Carol demonstrated a deep maturity. Her ability to contain her own anxiety in order simply to *be there* for Andy was not an easy thing to do, and yet it was crucial. She provided Andy with the emotional space he required for healing.

Andy now feels that not only is Carol the right person for him, but the timing was right for their coming together. Had it been "one millisecond" sooner, says Andy, they might not have managed to clear away enough psychic baggage to make a healthy relationship or marriage possible:

*In my mind I knew this was the woman I could spend my life
with. Although we had our fights, most of the time we got along
tremendously well. We had both worked hard on ourselves to get
to the point where we felt ready to have this relationship. I'm not
saying it was perfect; I still did a lot of the old stuff that I had
done with previous relationships, and she did too. The thing was
that we were committed enough to each other to work hard at
ridding ourselves of those old patterns. We wanted to be with
each other more than we wanted to act out our old dramas.*

When we experience psychological barriers so deep that they
prevent us from getting close to people, simply wishing or willing
them away doesn't usually work. We must devote a good deal of time
and energy to working through these barriers, either with a therapist
or a support group or through intense self-examination. Andy recognized that he had a lot of work to do before he would be able to
overcome the anger, sadness, and fear associated with his childhood
losses. Meeting Carol when he did coincided with his having begun
that process. Carol was also a person who was actively getting to the
bottom of her own psychological issues regarding her father, so she
could empathize with Andy's struggle. The two of them were on
equal emotional footing, and they still feel that resolving their respective familial conflicts is essential to their own success as a couple.

For Andy, getting married at forty just happened to coincide
with becoming honest with himself, confronting his problems directly, knowing and accepting himself for who he really is. He doesn't
believe that one need reach any particular age before facing those
truths; yet he is aware of the benefits of having maturity on his side:

*As far as waiting until forty to get married, I don't think age
is really significant. It's how well you know yourself. If you're
a rare bird and you know yourself in your twenties, great. But
unless you have a pretty good idea what percentage of you is
bullshit and what percentage of you isn't, and have gone some
distance in resolving that—you end up working out your problems with, against, and through your spouse and then with your
kids. It makes for a lot of misery, because you just continue to*

dump all that horror that you didn't resolve on those you
supposedly love.

IF I TRUST YOU, WILL YOU DISAPPOINT ME?

When we spoke with Helen on the phone before our interview, she cheerfully told us she had married for the first time a year ago, at the age of forty-seven. After giving us directions to her house about an hour outside the city, she said she'd fill us in on her story when we arrived. Welcoming us warmly, Helen's vibrant dark eyes revealed an adventurous spirit that belied her outwardly conservative appearance. She beamed as she showed us through her quiet, comfortable home filled with Early American furniture. We settled in around Helen's patio table, and she smiled easily as she began answering even our most probing questions.

Marriage had always been Helen's "goal," although she soon revealed having had a tremendous amount of ambivalence about it throughout her life. After her parents' divorce, her mother remarried and divorced again and was left with very bitter feelings toward men—which she passed on to Helen. Yet she counseled Helen to prepare herself for a woman's only proper role in life: wife and mother. Although Helen attributed her mixed feelings about marriage primarily to her mother's influence, it became clear that her poor relationship with her father was also at the root of many of her fears. Like many children of divorce, she mistrusted marriage, and, like many daughters of uncaring or absent fathers, she mistrusted men.

As a little kid and early teenager, I received very conflicting
views about marriage. My mother told me I should marry and
have children, that that was a woman's reason for living. Yet
her's was a very bad example of marriage. So the spoken
message was, "Yes, marriage is what you should want and
have." But the silent message was, "It's not possible, it's not
good, it's not worthwhile, it can't be done." So I was ambivalent
about marriage and afraid of it. Part of me wanted it and the
other part didn't. Culture and society and my mother told me it

*was what I should want. Plus I craved the close companionship
that I thought marriage should be, but then I'd think about my
mother's divorces and both my grandparents' divorces, and I'd
say to myself, "Am I dreaming? Do I have a fantasy that's not
realistic? Am I wanting something that doesn't exist?"*

As it turned out, Helen spent much of her life trying to reconcile
fantasy with reality—choosing partners who she hoped would give
her the love and companionship she desired, yet who realistically
could never deliver. Ironically, her doubts concerning marriage,
deeply rooted in her family history, fed her fantasies about men and
love. As troubled as her parents' marriage was, and as unloving as her
father had been, Helen continually believed that each new man she
encountered held the promise of being "perfect," "idyllic," or "just
wonderful." She found herself falling "wildly" or "madly" in love at
first, only to become disappointed later on.

The Jungian therapist Linda Leonard addresses such disappointments and fantasies in her book *On the Way to the Wedding*. She
describes various obstacles women and men face in forming a meaningful union, and speaks of those who, like Helen, have difficulty
finding the right mate, yet dream about a perfect, romantic partner.
Leonard concludes that when we lack appropriate parental love and
role-modeling, our fantasies about love proliferate:

> *Sometimes the way to the wedding is blocked by an inability to
> get into a relationship, or even to meet a suitable partner. Over
> and over I hear the complaint, "There are no mature men" or
> "Where are the women who really want a relationship?" This
> complaint often covers up an inner image of the lover so idealized
> that no human could compare. [Those who tend to romanticize
> in this way may have formed] an inner idealized parental im-
> age to compensate for the parent's absence or rejection. Some
> of the men and women caught up in this syndrome find them-
> selves in love with married partners, wonderful but inevitably
> unavailable.*[2]

Helen's rejecting, absentee father was a reality she most likely
needed to mask with fantasy. And, as we'll later learn, her long-term

involvement with a married man protected her from risking further rejection. After her father's departure when she was eleven, Helen was estranged from him for most of her life. She talked about him only briefly during our interview, and when she did, her voice lowered and she looked away as she told us that her father had never been caring toward her, and that he had become even more distant after he divorced her mother. According to Helen, he's a very stoic man who can't express warmth or love.

As her father's daughter, Helen was disregarded and ignored. This experience probably led her to mistrust men, while at the same time she tried all that much harder to win over incompatible or unavailable partners. It was a struggle very familiar to her, given the difficulty both she and her mother had winning her father's love. Such a compulsion to replay the key psychological struggles of our childhood within the context of our adult relationships is common for most of us whose families were dysfunctional in some way, and Helen played out her ambivalence about wanting to connect with a man by choosing those who always seemed to be reticent or unaccessible or even more ambivalent than she was.

One of her most serious disappointments came when Helen was thirty-two and thought she had finally met the man she was going to marry. She met Matt just after he had gotten divorced and had only been on his own for a few weeks. Helen was "wildly attracted" to him from the start. Although they lived five hundred miles apart and only saw each other on weekends, she thought that would present no problem. They dated for about a year and were very happy when Helen finally gave Matt an ultimatum: marriage or nothing. Matt agreed to get married. And then . . . it didn't happen. When it came time to make plans, Matt wouldn't make plans. When it was time to buy the ring, he wouldn't buy the ring. Helen finally understood that the wedding was not going to be:

I can remember saying to some friends, "If I don't get married this time, then I'm going to give up." Because I really felt like Matt was the perfect guy for me. So when it didn't work out, I was devastated, and a part of me did give up.

Although I thought my relationship with Matt was idyllic, I think when it came down to it, he wasn't really there for

*me—even before he changed his mind about getting married.
I should have known when I had some health problems toward
the end of the relationship, and he didn't come to see me. He said
he would have been there if he could have been, but he had all
sorts of impressive excuses. That was when I realized I didn't
want a part-time relationship; I wanted marriage. I wanted
somebody who would be there.*

Unfortunately, wanting marriage didn't prevent Helen from continuing to choose men whose involvement with her stopped just short of commitment. Her next partner was Gabe, who, again, seemed to be the "ideal" partner, "happy, caring, loving, fun, attractive—and just all the really good things I wanted." Although Gabe lacked the basic intellectual qualities she valued, once again Helen's infatuation blinded her, and she became deeply embroiled. And once again she was determined that love would make it all work out between Gabe and herself, even though she sensed the very real differences between them.

But love did not conquer all; it couldn't erase the many disparities between them, and the relationship ended. After Gabe, there was another man who appeared to be a more realistic candidate for marriage, yet, after about a year, he told Helen he didn't think he was going to love her enough to marry her. Again, Helen was forced to step back from her illusions and face unforgiving reality. This time the disappointment was too much to bear. She sought the help of a psychotherapist, whom she saw for three years, and finally began to prepare herself for the possibility that she might be on her own forever:

*My relationship with Jonathan fell through about the same time
that a big earthquake hit, and the combination of my life falling
apart and the world falling apart traumatized me. I went
through a terrible depression. Once I started seeing a therapist,
it was like a rebirth. Before the therapy, I had so little self-
confidence; I didn't value much about myself. Now I started to
think I should just build my life as a single person—get into my
work, maybe start saving for a house. I felt stronger. I was
prepared to be on my own and live life by myself if I had to.*

*But again, I wanted marriage. I just didn't think I could
accomplish it. So I told myself that since marriage was probably
out of the question for me, I would just throw myself into my
career.*

Helen's striking ambivalence runs contrary to the widespread belief that unmarried women with powerful careers don't have the time or energy for marriage. Although not necessarily representative of all professional women, Helen thought of her career as a kind of booby prize for not having achieved her real goal: marriage. She was driven, in part, by the unlikely combination of her new-found confidence and her disappointments in love. Since work was an area over which she could have some control, she rechanneled nearly all her attention into her professional life. But little changed emotionally, and she continued her lifelong pattern of ending up with unavailable men.

Frustrated by her inability to make a relationship last, still unresolved in her ambivalence toward commitment, Helen took the safe route to companionship by getting involved with a married man—for nearly ten years. Since there was never any possibility that he would actually leave his wife, she was saved from having to make a real commitment and could play out her mixed feelings toward wanting a permanent mate:

*Jeremy was real handy. He didn't make any demands on me, and
I didn't make demands on him. We were together when we could
be, and when we weren't, that was okay too. In a way, it suited
my purposes. I was tired of all the problems inherent in dating,
and disillusioned that I hadn't found anyone to marry. So at
least I had Jeremy in my life to supply some of my needs, and
that was a positive thing.*

Helen's affair with Jeremy took her out of the dating pool for many years, and in a way this hiatus was a relief from the persistent sense of failure. When she was about forty-three, she went out dancing with a girlfriend and met Garth, yet another "one of those types who just couldn't be tied down." Once again she had her heart broken. She wondered if she was fated to be the woman men love to date but never want to marry. From her current perspective as a happily married woman, Helen had this to say about Garth, the last man to break her heart:

He was delightful, energetic, fun, and he got me out there into the world of single people again. He turned me on to all these great places to go dancing and meet people. But he's the one they must have in mind when they write books about men who can't love. After a while I knew he wasn't going to pan out as a serious relationship, so I stopped sleeping with him.

In a way, Garth primed Helen for her next change, but it was Kim, a woman friend nearly fifteen years younger than Helen, who became instrumental in turning Helen's life around. Kim took Helen under her wing and became Helen's "mentor." Every time Helen would talk about how men couldn't be trusted or say that they were no good, Kim would point out how those attitudes were counterproductive and had been the basis of Helen's self-fulfilling prophecy. Though Helen was also in therapy at the time, she attributes her ultimate success in meeting her husband to this young woman's positive approach to dating and relationships:

Kim said, "For your birthday, I'm not giving you a present, I'm giving you a man!" Well, she didn't exactly do that, but she did get me a book which opened my eyes to a lot of things I hadn't recognized earlier about realistically finding a man. It was called Beyond Cinderella, *and it really did cut through the fairy-tale stuff and get down to practical ways to meet people.*

So Kim became my "nag," and she stayed on me until I got rid of Garth and Jeremy. You see, all the time I was seeing Garth, Jeremy—the married guy—was always in the background. I would always go back to him. Of course, he was never going to leave his wife, but that didn't really matter to me; I still liked having him in my life.

When Kim told me I had to cut off completely from both Jeremy and Garth, I would argue with her, saying, "They're just my friends. I'm not even sleeping with them now." She said, "You have to have a clean slate. Unless there's a vacuum, a new

*man won't be able to fill it." We fought about that until I finally
realized she was right. I had to do it.*

Gathering up the strength to cut off these two "safe" yet limited
relationships was a crucial step in Helen's life. It meant opening herself
up to the possibility of a real relationship—one that would test her
ability to be truly intimate and committed. Given her childhood
experiences surrounding trust, her inherited fears that men would
only end up hurting her—as her father had hurt both her and her
mother—becoming vulnerable wasn't as easy for Helen as Kim may
have made it sound. But she struggled with it and finally decided she
was ready to face the daunting world of dating. Even seemingly
superficial changes made her feel as if her life was taking a whole new
direction:

> *I became a little more friendly and outgoing. When I went up
> in an elevator with a group of men, I'd smile at all of them. I
> began going places I never would have gone before on my
> own—dancing, for instance—and doing things differently just
> for the sake of making changes in my life. I even started dressing
> differently, 'cause I had always been like the little brown sparrow
> office worker. I started being more flamboyant, wearing more
> vivid colors. I even let my hair grow. A lot of these little changes
> made it seem as if I was a whole new person beginning a whole
> new life.*

Since her friend Kim was happily married herself, Helen was
exposed, for the first time in her life, to a marriage that worked. With
this positive role model, as well as her new ability to confront the
negative attitudes she'd had toward men and marriage, Helen was
now strong enough to return to the frustrating—yet potentially
rewarding—world of dating. She took more chances, got out more,
felt better about herself and her appearance than she ever had before,
and within a fairly short time met her husband-to-be, Dan:

> *I had on my new persona; I was going to be open to meeting
> people and doing new things. So I decided to join a ballroom
> dancing club. I had always loved ballroom dancing, and I figured*

it would be a great way to meet people without its being purely for that purpose.

There was a couple at the club who were both very outgoing and they introduced me to Dan. Quite honestly, my first impression of him wasn't great. He has a weight problem, and that put me off. But I liked him. He loved to dance, as I do, and talking with him I realized he was friendly and warm, and he seemed very sincere and sweet. I could also tell he was intelligent, part of the world.

The usual introductory questions came up. Bob, the friend who'd introduced us, couldn't believe I wasn't married or hadn't been married. He teased me, saying, "Okay, you can tell us about those seven husbands that you've murdered," and that lighthearted atmosphere made me feel more comfortable. Also, I felt more relaxed getting to know Dan with other people around. It took the pressure off.

After three or four weeks, Helen was beginning to see Dan as a person with whom she could at least be good friends. At first she wondered whether she could be physically attracted to him, because of his weight, but she grew to like him so much that it became less of a factor. She valued the fact that they laughed at the same things, had fun together, and had so many things in common.

The relationship was under way, but both Helen and Dan still had some serious doubts to overcome. A divorcé, Dan subscribed to a common bias that a woman who has reached Helen's age without ever marrying would *never* be able to be committed. He was worried she might lead him on and then leave him flat. As for Helen, when things began to get more serious, she began to have "commitment attacks." Although she had come a long way in her struggles with ambivalence toward marriage, negative role models, fears of becoming too vulnerable, and attractions to unavailable partners, she had never been put to the test in such a concrete way. When, about six months into the relationship, Dan asked her to marry him, she was riddled with doubts concerning commitment:

I was real worried about myself. Just the fact I had never done it before scared me. That old side of me that had been negative and had been sabotaging relationships all those years came out, saying, "No, you can't do this—who do you think you are?" I would get moody and withdraw, and that would scare Dan into thinking I didn't love him anymore. Boy, did I have struggles to go through!

Shortly before Dan proposed to me, I went with some friends to Hawaii. I had planned to go even before I met Dan, and had already paid for it, so I figured I'd go ahead. Dan was real upset, and I told him, "What's the big deal? I'm not going with any man—or to meet men." It turned out there was a fellow there who I had a flirtation with—just a fun vacation kind of thing, but it made me stop and remind myself, "This is what you'll give up if you marry."

With that uncertainty hanging over her, Helen returned home and did some hard thinking. It didn't take her long to decide that she wanted to commit herself to Dan. She'd had years of romantic experiences and figured the "fun" of single life was really more like a "second prize." She considered marriage to be the first prize.

Still, Helen wasn't certain she was *ready* for the first prize yet. Even when she got engaged, she underwent an internal process of questioning whether or not she could ultimately go through with it:

When Dan proposed to me, he had the ring and he handed it to me and I put it on —but it wasn't like I ever said, "Okay, yes, I will." I just started wearing the ring, and I told myself that if I really didn't want to get married, I would come to know that. I used the engagement period to know for sure if I could make a commitment. I couldn't know for certain until the reality was right before me.

I had been involved with men before. I had had them say they were going to marry me, and then they didn't. So part of me was saying, "Just wait and see." As I started going through all the mechanics of planning the wedding, I realized I wanted to go through with it, otherwise I wouldn't be allowing myself to go through the motions.

During the ceremony, I kept asking myself over and over, "Is this happening, is it happening? Am I really doing this?" And my answer was, "Yes, I really want to do this."

Helen's marriage is not without its difficulties. Owing, perhaps, to his own past disappointments, Dan still has insecurities about Helen's past, and questions her ability to remain loyal. Helen wonders if she'll ever be able to prove herself to the extent that he seems to need reassurance. Dan wants her to be more dependent on him financially and to conform to a more traditional homemaker role than Helen had anticipated. Although at first she thought giving up work would be a perk, Helen's not so sure she would want to give up her identity to that extent. And, to date, she's still unwilling to sell the house she bought when she was single, or to completely merge her finances with Dan's.

On the plus side, though, Helen seems very appreciative of having found someone to love and with whom to share her life. She has overcome a lot of psychological hurdles to get to where she is now, and her sense of accomplishment and satisfaction is apparent even without the words she used to describe it:

I've discovered I like being married, and I've adapted very well to it. I wasn't so sure I would be able to. I like having somebody in my life who is really in my life with me—not just someone on the perimeter. We are partners and best friends and more committed to our relationship than to anything. That's what I had always hoped marriage would be, but was afraid it wouldn't be. Having been single all those years, [I found] there was some chipping away at the ideal marriage in my mind. Finding that that ideal is still possible makes me value this marriage more than if it were my first marriage at twenty-five. I know there are a lot of men out there and a lot of different kinds of relationships. But I've been there, and I like this better.

Helen, Andy, and other late marriers who struggled with psychological barriers to commitment appreciate the distance they've come. Like so many of us whose families were in some way unable to meet our emotional needs, these first-time-marrieds over forty had been children lacking in the proper kind of nurturance. As adults they had to learn how to love themselves, how to be loved, and, finally, how to love and commit themselves to another without fearing the abuses of love to which they'd grown accustomed. In most instances they had help in this process of discovery and growth—from therapists, spiritual counselors, friends, or spouses. Still, the psychic journey that process required was one they ultimately had to make alone.

5

WHY GET MARRIED
UNLESS YOU WANT KIDS?

It was Jessica, my goddaughter, who helped me realize that I had to make a decision about having a baby. Whenever I would see her, she had a habit of nuzzling into my lap and asking me endless questions, most of which I could never answer.

One day Jessica was introducing me to her newest baby doll. She looked up from the miniature carriage and, pointing to my stomach, asked, "Is your baby here?" "No," I told her, "not yet." Then she pressed her tiny finger to my heart and persisted, "Is your baby here?" "Yes," I smiled, "a baby is always there." She wrinkled up her little face, looked up to mine, and, with the kind of innocent directness that only a child can have, declared, "Only grandmas have gray hair, not mommies!" She was right; I knew I had to get busy, find a husband, and have the baby who was always in my heart.

—TOBY, age forty-five, married three years,
mother of two-year-old Jason

AND BABY MAKES THREE . . .

Many believe that creating a family is part of our biological imperative and that parenting connects us to the life force in a way that no other experience can. If we have reached midlife without completing this connection, we may feel a particular urgency to bear our own children before it is too late. If we have spent all these years caring only for ourselves, we may long to nourish and care for little ones. Even though there are a number of options available to unmarried men and women who want to be parents—adoption, surrogate birth, or *in vitro* fertilization, just to name a few—most of us still equate parenting with biological children, and biological children with marriage.

What makes the late marriers in this chapter different from those portrayed in the previous ones is that these men and women postponed marriage up until the time when they could no longer postpone having children. None of them were willing to bear children outside of wedlock or forfeit biological parenthood forever, so they opted for a more strategic choice: they found a mate and married for the expressed purpose of having children. This explanation for why some people came to their first marriages later than others initially came to our attention when we interviewed Glen, a software designer in his late forties. When we asked him the question, "Why did you decide to marry?" he leaned forward, pushed his glasses back onto the bridge of his nose, and told us earnestly, "I always knew I wanted kids—there was never a doubt in my mind—but I spent years not knowing whether I wanted marriage. Once Julia and I lived together and were real sure that we were committed to being not only husband and wife, but also a mother and a father, we married—and it was for the sake of having kids. After all, for me, the primary goal of marriage isn't romance—it's family." The thoughts and feelings expressed in his response reverberate through many of the stories we'll hear in this chapter.

COUNTING THE MINUTES

Having to hurry up childbearing is directly related to having delayed it. And some of us did—in record numbers—until it was almost too late. From 1975 to 1985, first-birth rates increased 96 percent among women aged thirty-five to thirty-nine who had completed college![1] Our generation froze the fertility frenzy of the 1950s and early 1960s partly because we *could*. When birth-control pills and legal abortions first became available in the 1960s, young women finally had the means to decide if and when they would become pregnant.

Our decisions to stall childbearing were further supported by advances in genetic screening and prenatal monitoring. These medical breakthroughs promised us reduced risks if we delayed babymaking into our thirties and early forties. With our apprehensions in check, many of us chose to sidestep parenthood *temporarily* in order to become adults before having the children we knew we wanted. In exchange, we got the time we needed to realize our personal aspirations and build our careers and lives. But that same time, biological and otherwise, ticked onward. The next thing we knew, parenthood threatened to be out of our reach.

As we all know, procreative timetables differ between women and men. A woman's fertility is intermittent and finite—cyclically regulated month by month, and bounded in time between puberty and menopause. Until new reproductive medical technologies succeed in extending fertility, biology will continue to dictate the cessation of a woman's procreative powers, the timing of childbearing, and her ultimate choices.

By contrast, a man's fertility is relatively constant throughout his lifetime. Although his viable sperm diminish and become less motile with age, it is entirely possible that a ninety-three-year-old man, with a lot of luck on his side, can impregnate a woman. Without the deadline of infertility, a man's sense of urgency derives from the traditional notion that while a woman *produces* children, he *provides* for and *protects* them. While this oversimplification no longer reflects how most modern families actually survive, men still calculate their timetables according to the number of economically productive years they have left, as well as to how physically fit they'll be as older fathers. In addition, certain physiological midlife changes, such as a modest decline in overall stamina and sexual powers, serve to remind men that they, too, have their limitations. Men can't help feeling pressured by their shorter life expectancy relative to that of women, and the fact that as late-life fathers they are less likely than late-life mothers to see their children reach adulthood. Intangible as these considerations may be, they are no less real than the deadline imposed by a woman's impending menopause, and they loom just as large when a man assesses his future.

The female and male sides of this special dilemma are distinct. But the emotional and practical responses that men and women make to it have more in common than we might assume. Vicki and Ray, for example, were both in high gear to have families, and they married their respective spouses for that very reason. Their comments express the motivations familiar to many of us who are still unmarried and childless.

Vicki was thirty-one when she met Oliver—a self-proclaimed confirmed bachelor who never wanted children. They dated sporadically over the next eight years. It was a convenient arrangement that suited them both. Whenever Vicki would tire of looking for the man who would father her family, she always returned to Oliver's constancy and affection. After one wilted romance too many, it dawned on her that it was time to benefit from a known quantity—Oliver— rather than miss the opportunity to have babies altogether. Not only had he always been loving and supportive, but she knew he had the makings of a great father—even if he didn't. Vicki mounted a campaign and ultimately "eroded Oliver's will." They've been married for five years.

> At forty, I was going to marry whoever was there, and Oliver was there. But the qualities that first attracted me weren't the qualities that convinced me to marry him. Originally I had dated him because he was fun and never made demands on me. But I married him because he is honest and honorable and I sensed he would make a good father.
>
> Some of my other boyfriends would have been just as suitable for marriage as Oliver, but it doesn't mean I think I

*made a lesser choice. I'm happy we married. What I gained was
a family and someone who knows and cares for me—two things
I might not have had otherwise.*

Vicki and Oliver had both of their children during the first two
years of their marriage. So did Ray, who is now forty-six, with his
wife, thirteen years his junior. Prior to his delayed flurry of babymaking, Ray was having "too much fun to ever get married." However,
his life as a roué changed abruptly around his forty-second birthday,
when Ray's calculations began to sound vaguely similar to Vicki's.
After taking painstaking stock of his life accomplishments and his
failings and unrealized dreams, Ray asked himself what it was he *really*
wanted. When the answer was "family," he decided to stop treating
life as if he had a spare one in his back pocket.

*When I counted up the years it would take to date around, find
the right person, and get her pregnant, my deadline went something like this: I'd be at least forty-five before I could be a father
and fifty-five-plus when the kid would be old enough to play
baseball with me. I kept thinking, "Will I still be able to throw
a ball?" When I heard myself answering "No!" the next question
was, "How much longer can I put this off?"*
*So I didn't. My wife, Brenda, would like to believe that I
fell romantically in love with her and that she's the only woman
I ever loved enough to marry. But, in truth, I've had the same
deep connection with one or two other women—I just decided to
draw the line with her.*

In terms of having children, the biggest difference between Vicki
and Ray is the pressure of time. Men *do* enjoy the luxury of a few
extra years to search for and find a mate. Driven by his sense of
mortality rather than concerns about his ability to bear children, Ray's
moment to find a marriageable woman and start a family had arrived.
When childless men and women who *want* children reach midlife, some will respond to the push of their respective limitations and
the pull of certain compromises. If the number of strollers is any
indication, more and more men and women of this age are having

children; we are in the midst of a baby boomlet as increasing numbers of baby boomers make midlife babies.

Moreover, first-time parents over forty are a noticeable part of this trend. In the race against time, more women over forty are having their first children than ever before. Nationwide, 5,797 first children were born to women forty and older in 1987—nearly triple the number reported seven years earlier.[2]

Rita, Nancy, Andreas, and Ned are some of the real-life people behind these statistics. As late baby-bloomers, they were anxious to begin parenthood just when other people were sending their children off to college or becoming grandparents. Undaunted by the steep odds against finding not just someone to marry, but someone who also wanted a baby right away, they first began with a clear definition of what they wanted. Then they narrowed their priorities and shuffled their preferences. Finally they acted on their plans and decisions—decisively! And, best of all, they all bore the babies they wanted—just under the wire. How did they ever do it? Let's find out.

THE MOTHERHOOD RUSH

Has this, or anything like it, ever happened to you? You're standing in the checkout line at the market. The woman in front of you is busy unloading a shopping cart brimming over with what looks like enough Pampers for months. A six-month-old is plunked into the baby seat facing you. She's dressed in lime green OshKosh overalls and the smallest moccasins you've ever seen in your life. *Adorable* doesn't begin to describe her. She looks up at you with the biggest brown eyes and a toothless grin that you wish would last forever. Suddenly, you find yourself riveted to this little sugar lump, making strange cooing noises. And the more she smiles, the more you babble. You're hooked. You're in love. You want one . . . *this instant!*

Naturally! You've just had what we call a "motherhood rush." A fleeting reminder that even though motherhood may no longer be your primary destiny, you're still wired for it. Of course, this doesn't mean that all women experience the same drive or desire to have children. But, for a woman who wants children and has waited, one thing is certain: as her biological deadline fast approaches, these feelings *will* intensify. When they do, she may ask herself, "Can I give up some of the things I thought I required from a man and just find a good one who wants to marry and have children?" Rita and Nancy answered, "Yes." For them, finding husbands and fathers fast meant compromises, some easy, and concessions, some painful, in order to have the children they always wanted.

Rita's bouts with "motherhood rushes" rushed her into motherhood. On the day of her thirty-ninth birthday she made herself a promise: by forty she would be childless no more. With a string of unhappy relationships behind her, Rita thought she could do without marriage and decided to have a child on her own. Even though there was something about the security and stability of a family life that had always appealed to her, she didn't have high hopes of finding a man she'd feel good about marrying—especially on such short notice.

Rita met Rick at a sales seminar sponsored by her advertising firm, where she was the creative director. They eyed each other over the Cornish game hens at the buffet table. Rick cracked a chicken joke and Rita couldn't stop laughing. Over the lunch that followed, they discovered something else they had in common: Scrabble. Rick challenged her to a game and dinner. During their first month together they hunkered over the Scrabble board night after night, arguing playfully over the derivation of words and competing for triple letter scores. Apart from his virtuosity as a player, two of Rick's qualities impressed Rita. First, he was easy to be with, and, second, he was one of those men who, if you mentioned you wanted something, would produce it as soon as he possibly could.

Dozens of rematches later, Rick fell in love with Rita and Rita fell in love with the idea that Rick might simply father her child. Rick met her opening gambit on the subject with a reaction that quickly got Rita thinking in terms of the eight-letter word *marriage:*

We talked about a lot of things sitting there hour after hour with nothing but a Scrabble board and our wits between us. I found out that Rick wanted to have a child too; I had never met a man who expressed that to me. We'd been dating for about two months, and even though I wasn't wildly, passionately in love,

I asked him point-blank if he'd be willing to father my child. I made it very clear that he could take whatever responsibility he wanted, depending on his own feelings, but that I could handle it on my own. He was insulted. He wanted to have a kid, but, more than that, he wanted to get married to me.

I didn't necessarily feel the same way. I was mildly attracted to him—but not wildly. But I knew that if we got involved, it would stay on an even keel. I wasn't going to hurt him and he wasn't going to hurt me. As we approached the wedding, I was feeling a bit dishonest, but not enough to stop me.

Rita did marry Rick, and their daughter was conceived on their honeymoon. For the first two years of their marriage they felt like the luckiest couple in the world; their careers flourished and they had a beautiful little girl. Even so, the "mild attraction" she felt for Rick rapidly faded to no attraction at all. For the last several years, comforting affection has taken the place of sex in their marriage. "We are like compatible roommates now," Rita regrets with an uncomfortable sigh. It turns out that Rita has half-willingly sacrificed passion for parenthood.

While the decision is one she doesn't completely regret, the underlying tension between them has taken a silent toll on their seven years of married life. "The anger, frustration, and guilt are buried so deep," Rita says, "that at this point we talk about it once a year if we're lucky." Paradoxically, there is no one Rita would rather be with than Rick. She admires him for his loving nature as a person and a father. At the same time she sees no solution to their fallow sex life short of changing her sexual chemistry. But what bridges the gap between them is their sincere commitment to family. Honoring this principle holds them together and justifies the sacrifice both seem to be willing to make for now.

If I had married someone with whom I really wanted sex, it might have been different than it is now. But even then, everyone gets past that initial stage of being totally turned on. When I look at the whole spectrum of my life with Rick, we're like a

well-oiled machine in terms of daily life—ninety percent of the
time I am really happy. Ten percent of the time I'm tempted to
say, "Okay, let's call it quits."

That is not to say that either of us would trade it all for
a passionate relationship, even though we both would be happy
to have an affair. But I wouldn't cheat on him—not because of
him, but more because of our daughter. Rick feels the same way.
There is too much at stake; the family unit becomes sacred.

Not everyone who marries to have children has to experience these kinds of concessions. But based on the nature of Rita and Rick's initial compromise, the problems they are experiencing in their marriage shouldn't be entirely unexpected. Remember, both were seeking to satisfy their short-term goals as best they could, and perhaps this is a critical clue: Rita's first objective was to have a baby and to marry Rick *if* she had to, whereas Rick's first priority was to marry Rita, and if that meant having a baby, so much the better.

Even though Rita feels fulfilled as a mother, her marriage falls short of what she envisioned for herself as a wife. As much as she seems resigned to her relationship as it exists, she also genuinely believes that the trade-off has been worth it. For the present, Rita has chosen to protect her family life at the expense of resolving her sexual stalemate with Rick. We can only speculate that these unresolved issues are undoubtedly painful and can't be swept under the rug forever. And while Rita and Rick's arrangement is not one that most of us would like to have for ourselves, it is preserving, however imperfectly, the family that has become more important than anything else.

"I LOOKED FOR A FATHER FOR MY CHILDREN—NOT A HUSBAND FOR ROMANCE"

When Nancy casually mentioned, "It's not as if we're ultimate soul mates—having a child was what brought us together—with this *mutual* goal we felt we could work out our differences," we thought we were going to hear another story like Rita's. Although the two women were motivated to marry in order to start a family, there is one very significant difference between the two decisions. From the beginning, Nancy and her husband, Dennis, shared the same desire—*both* wanted to have children and *both* wanted to marry each other to have them.

If marital happiness can be tallied against the scoreboard of compromises, Nancy seems to have come out ahead of Rita, at least for the moment. Nancy and Dennis enjoy a satisfying sexual life and a well-rounded marriage. But that is not to say Nancy hasn't made her own set of unexpected trade-offs—ones we'll explore as her story unfolds.

At the time of our interview, Nancy had been married a year and a half. She was also on the eve of having her first baby—a little girl already named Janie, who might be lucky enough to inherit her mother's persimmon-colored hair. Nancy and Dennis live on a quiet, shaded street in the rolling foothills of an affluent suburb of San Francisco. It is a neighborhood that is a far cry from the Milwaukee working-class Catholic neighborhood where Nancy grew up. Their home is surrounded by a profusion of flowers, thanks to Nancy's love of gardening when she isn't hard at work as a certified public accountant. We believe it took someone with the patience of a green thumb and the talent to balance credits against debits to get where she is now.

As you may recall from chapter 3, Nancy's first long-term committed relationship was with a man named Joey. They lived together for ten years—from the time she was twenty until she turned thirty. For the better part of their decade together, both were finding themselves, and Nancy, knowing that ultimately she wanted a family, was refining her thoughts concerning the qualities she wanted from a husband and a father.

Joey was a wonderful companion, and they loved being a twosome. Compatible as they were, however, the progress of their relationship was hobbled by Joey's choice to pursue a career that took years to fall into place. Money was always a problem, and so was the central focus of their commitment to one another. Whenever the topic of marriage and children came up, Joey would ask if they could table the issue until . . .

"Until" never came, and Nancy almost missed motherhood altogether. Though their closeness as a couple compensated somewhat for the wait, Nancy came to wonder if Joey was really a family man. Would his professional ambitions always take priority over hearth and home? Sadly, Nancy came to the realization that until Joey achieved the success he aimed for, he wouldn't be ready to divert his energy to a family. They broke up. By the time they did, Nancy was well on her way to thinking about marriage and family in the same breath:

> When I got back into the dating world after ten years, I was surprised to find fewer available men than when I was twenty. The ones I did stumble across were either married and wanted to have an affair, or single with "commit-a-phobia."
>
> None of that bothered me until I got to be thirty-five. Then the urge to have a baby and settle down was like a tidal wave. Forty was my cutoff point for starting a family; if I had one baby by then, at least I could have a second before I got too tired out, around age forty-four or so. I had five years to meet someone, have an intimate relationship, and get pregnant. My possibilities were closing down much faster than I'd ever anticipated.

Coming from a huge family herself—she is one of thirty-five first cousins—Nancy pictured her golden years surrounded by loving children and grandchildren. True to her Catholic upbringing, she believes that marriage is the foundation for children—the more the better. Although Nancy respects and admires the courage of single mothers, she never considered becoming one. On the other hand, marriage alone, without the possibility of creating a new family, didn't appeal to her either.

Nancy dreaded having to accept the sadness of remaining child-less. She knew it would haunt her for a lifetime. After spending years on her own, she was far more prepared to deal with lifelong single-ness if she had to. If she had had to choose, never marrying would have been preferable to never having children.

It was a loss she was beginning to reckon with by the time she was thirty-six. In lieu of a family, Nancy began to contemplate a career move in order to find a profession that was more deeply satisfying. And while she didn't stop looking for what she hoped for—a man who wanted a child and had the time, money, and interest to devote to fathering—she stopped *expecting* that dating would necessarily lead her to him. "The key," Nancy advises, "is to stop trying so hard." Almost magically, shortly after she started listening to her own advice, she met Dennis. At this point their timing was off, but Nancy's intuition was on—full blast.

The first time I met Dennis, we had done some heavy flirting at a party, but he seemed unavailable. I can't tell you why, but when I went home that night, I said to myself, "I'm going to marry that man." I just knew that he was going to show up again in my life.

And he did, a year and a half later. With his second divorce decree filed but not final, this time around Dennis was in hot pursuit. Nancy couldn't help but be optimistic: Dennis more than filled her "shopping list." As a successful entrepreneur, he was financially secure and had complete discretion over his time. To top it off, Dennis told Nancy he not only wanted to father children, but he wanted to help raise his children as well. "Good timing, good draw!" Nancy said to herself, thinking her luck had finally changed.

But another part of Nancy was cautious. And with good reason. Dennis's first marriage had ended after seven years, when his only daughter was just six months old, and now his second marriage, of seventeen years, was on the rocks because his wife refused to get pregnant. Even with his divorce filed, Nancy sensed that Dennis wasn't entirely free to start his new life. Her instincts were right again. Dennis was living alone in his house, but his almost-second ex-wife promptly purchased a home for herself right across the street. When this happened, Nancy reined in her hopes.

The crowning blow came six months later, when Dennis's second wife suddenly had a change of heart and decided she wanted children after all—this at the same time Nancy and Dennis were seriously considering their marriage and discussing children. Dennis waffled: Should he start a family with someone new, or with someone he had been married to for seventeen years? Nancy's faith in the fledgling relationship was torn asunder by Dennis's indecision and ambivalence.

At that critical juncture, Dennis's business required him to go abroad for an extended period, and he asked Nancy to join him. Nancy weighed the risks and decided to go. But she kept her small apartment as a safe haven, just in case. She was banking on two eventualities: first, that the intensive time together abroad would solidify her relationship with Dennis, and, second, that the physical and emotional distance from his second wife would finalize their breakup. Nancy was right on both counts. They grew attached as a couple, and upon returning to San Francisco, Dennis sold his house and rented another one faraway from his former wife's neighborhood.

From that decision on, Nancy felt reassured, and even more so when Dennis's divorce became final. Still, Nancy had thought through the situation in her typical rational fashion and was careful *not* to push for marriage. She felt it was critical for Dennis to *choose* her and matrimony rather than the other way around.

And he did, but in his own good time. When Dennis finally proposed, they had known each other for four years.

Nancy and Dennis married near Santa Fe, on a windswept mesa overlooking the Rio Grande valley, on the first day of spring. For years Nancy had visualized just the kind of wedding ceremony she wanted—a spiritual blend of New Age, American Indian, and Judeo-Christian symbols and rituals—a celebration that couldn't have been farther removed from her doctrinaire Catholic upbringing. Her wedding, like so many other later first marriages, reflected her aesthetic preferences, not those of their respective parents. Also typically, the event itself was choreographed against the backdrop of Nancy and Dennis's separate and formidable pasts:

> *There was no way I was going to have the church wedding my parents always wanted for me. Dennis had already had two huge weddings and was a bit embarrassed to be taking public vows yet once again. So we decided to keep the ceremony small—twelve of us in all, one relative from each family. I didn't invite my mom or dad because I knew they wouldn't enjoy the kind of celebration I had in mind. Dennis's parents are ninety-one and eighty-five and don't travel well, so they declined.*
>
> *We both wanted Dennis's daughter there, but she didn't come. Between her father's three marriages and her mother's four, she's been to seven weddings. I have a feeling she just didn't*

want to invest herself in yet another one—and another step-
mother.

With the wedding behind her, Nancy thought the hard part was over. But the newlyweds barely had time to buy a house and settle in before a falling-out almost landed them in divorce court. Initially, Dennis wanted Nancy to get pregnant right away, but Nancy lobbied for spending more time together as a couple before jumping into family life. Dennis thought that sounded reasonable, and agreed. Three months passed and then the tables turned; Nancy was ready and Dennis started hemming and hawing:

> *Because we hadn't really lived together before we were married, we were discovering that our marriage was different from the other relationships we had been in, and that there were things to work out. Dennis started backpedaling on the baby issue and told me he wanted to wait until things were running smoothly. I could understand his hesitancy, but I also felt that you never have everything worked out in a marriage. We were at an impasse and, meanwhile, time was ticking away. But the baby got us over that hurdle. Dennis was in charge of birth control, and he slipped up. Now that I'm pregnant, that's behind us.*

Marrying a man who already has children can present as many challenges as opportunities. Although Dennis is utterly delighted with the pregnancy, he is less involved than Nancy expected. Nancy reminds herself that while having a baby is thoroughly exciting for *her,* Dennis has already been through pregnancy and birth with his first wife. Moreover, as she wisely observes, it's possible that on a deeper psychological level the impending birth of their daughter may have triggered Dennis's memories of leaving his first child when she was little more than six months old. But at that time Dennis was on the verge of leaving his marriage; now he's happily just beginning one. And it is this difference that gives Nancy comfort:

> *I always imagined that when I was pregnant, my husband would treat me like a China doll, like, "Oh, honey, let me get that pillow for you." Forget it! At eight months pregnant, I'm*

sweating out in the garden, hoeing weeds! The books say, "Have your husband rub cocoa butter on your stomach so you won't get stretch marks." And I am saying, "Have Dennis do what?" He is in his own world. But I think that, like most men, he will be more excited when the baby actually gets here.

Dennis *is* in his own world, to a much greater extent than Nancy realized before their marriage. "Our togetherness quotient doesn't sync!" as she puts it. For example, if they haven't seen each other all day, Nancy would like to spend the evening together—watching TV or just being in the same room exchanging small talk—while Dennis is quite content to go into his study for a couple of hours. If she doesn't remind him, she usually ends up reading by herself in the living room—not exactly her idea of intimacy. Even though Dennis is very loving and caring in his own ways, Nancy would like him to cuddle up with her on the sofa for a couple of hours without being asked to. There are times when she can't help wishing he were more like Joey, whose need for homey companionship matched hers more closely. But when she does a bottom-line comparison between Joey and Dennis, she knows she chose the right man at the right time for what she had come to value most:

I looked for a father for my children, not a husband for romance. In all honesty, if I had been beyond childbearing age when I met Dennis, I wonder if we would have gotten married—we're very different on so many accounts. The truth of the matter is that the first partner I had, Joey, was a real companion who loved being part of a couple. But my husband will make a much better father. So much of what he and I talked about initially and connected over had to do with family. There's no one better out there than Dennis to be the father of my children.

The enduring attraction that led to Nancy and Dennis's eventual marriage was based on their shared desire to create a new family. Nancy made her choice on the basis of a blend of pragmatism and passion: an uncompromising desire to have children combined with an honest, but loving, appraisal of Dennis's potential as a father. The added bonus is that Nancy and Dennis are also in love. They reveled in a full-blown courtship complete with streams of flowers, exotic trips, and a great deal of sex and romance. And although Nancy's prompt pregnancy has put a damper on their newly wedded bliss, she doesn't feel shortchanged. "I had romance my whole life plus a couple of years of it with Dennis before we got married," she told us resolutely. "Now it's time to get on with why we are together."

Marriage is teaching Nancy to step back from her expectations and to forgive the differences between herself and her spouse. On balance, she considers herself very lucky that Dennis is her husband, and she is grateful to be expecting a child. Above all, she cherishes her marriage principally as "an opportunity to grow, learn, and go through the changes of life together." With baby Janie about to make her debut into the world, Nancy and Dennis are well on their way.

"I DIDN'T WANT TO BE A DEAD BRANCH ON THE TREE OF LIFE"

While it is taken for granted that most women are equipped with a maternal instinct, many doubt that men experience a paternal urge that is just as compelling. Some argue that because men don't actually carry or give birth to babies, they don't experience internal pangs to procreate the way women do. It's a subject no one knows much about—first, because men don't often speak to women about these intense feelings (who knows if they even mention it to each other), and, second, because very little has been written about men's emotional and biological needs to procreate. In the course of our research we were struck by the number of men we interviewed who expressed a profound and urgent wish to have children. Their decision to marry, like the women we've just discussed, was based on their pressing desire to father.

Andreas gave us our first glimpse of what having children means to some men. As a graphic artist for an international film distribution company, Andreas has led a very full life. He lived and worked in Tokyo, Paris, and, for a short time, Bombay. His was an existence as adventurous as the lives of the heroes he depicted in the movie posters he designed. But long before settling down and having children was a conscious desire for him, Andreas remembers having a recurrent dream whose images clearly expressed his deep-seated wish to become a father. The dream would always involve a series of life-threatening predicaments: chaotic chases, inevitable capture, and torment. Andreas would free himself and then take flight to escape his enemies. He'd soar, faster and higher, homeward to a little boy. Cradling the toddler in his arms, Andreas would feel safe and strong again. The dream's persistent message finally broke through Andreas's awareness and he set out to make it come true:

> *This urge crept up on me after many years of sexual adventures and affairs, about five years ago, when I was in my mid-thirties. I found myself feeling envious whenever I looked at someone else's children. Whenever I'd spend time with my friends' children, I'd come away feeling like I was missing the point of life, which is to give something back—to pass the seed on.*

Two years later, still childless but more determined than ever, Andreas began living with a woman in her early forties. When she became pregnant, Andreas cried ecstatic tears. But elation turned to grief when she miscarried soon thereafter. Her subsequent decision to be sterilized sent Andreas reeling, and he pleaded with her to reconsider. She wouldn't. Three years later, at forty, he decided he had no choice but to leave the relationship in order to accomplish what he had set out to do nearly five years earlier—have a child.

Andreas, now forty-one, met his wife, Ellen, at a county-sponsored child-adoption fair, at a booth for single-parent petitioners. By coincidence, Ellen had recently broken up with a man who had no desire to have children, and she, too, was toying with the idea of single parenthood. They began to chat, shyly at first. Strolling together through the park, they each revealed that while they'd like to have their own children, adoption was the next best choice.

From that afternoon on, Andreas and Ellen were inseparable. It didn't take long for them to recognize their mutual good fortune in having found someone in exactly the same frame of mind at the same time. They dated, found they were wildly attracted to one another, and got married four months later. Now they're trying to have a child as soon as possible.

As a man, Andreas can't and doesn't feel the same biological link to pregnancy that a woman does. But that is not to say there isn't a physical side to his paternal urge. He claims he feels a procreative force in his body that is distinct from anything he's ever felt while making love before:

> I long to have someone small with my face! It is like a hunger—a quivering intensity. There are moments when I am making love to my wife, when, instinctively, "the animal" takes over my body and says, "Make a child with this woman," right now!"

Naturally, not every childless never-married man over forty feels the same compulsion toward fatherhood as Andreas does. But those midlife men who are considering first-time parenthood may have a slight psychological edge over their younger counterparts. Experts believe that as men age they are more psychologically available for the demanding job of parenting. Generally, as men mature, their attention shifts from an outer-directed focus on their careers to an inner-directed appreciation of their own emotional lives and the lives around them. In essence, they experience a kind of "wake-up call."

Daniel Levinson, author of a landmark study on men's life cycles, titled *Seasons of a Man's Life*, describes how these changes enhance a man's ability to feel and communicate the expressive, sensuous, and dependent sides of his personality. A man in midlife, Levinson tells us, "experiences more fully his own mortality and the actual or impending death of others. . . . At the same time, he has a strong desire to become more creative and loving: to create products that have value for himself and others . . . and to contribute more fully to the coming generations in society."[3] The flowering of these tendencies represents a male version of the "nesting instinct." Even if men use different vocabulary to express it, they *do* experience a paternalistic urge, and the signs are unmistakable. Listen to how Andreas communicates his need to create and caretake new life:

> I feel that once a child is born, my own wishes aren't that important anymore. My job will then be to give the child a chance to live a healthy life in a healthy environment with a

mother and a father. There is this urge inside of me, and I need to fill it.

As some men acknowledge these feelings, they may become acutely aware of the gaps in their interpersonal relations and seek to fill them with family if they don't have one. Andreas, Ray, and Ned, whose story follows, came to this stage at different points in their lives. But not until they became inwardly attuned were they primed to get on with marriage and babymaking before time ran out.

"HAVING A BABY IS A STEP IN THE RIGHT DIRECTION—A SIGN OF SUCCESS"

By midlife, some men have consolidated their careers and are savoring their professional success. But often there is an emptiness they yearn to fill. Achievement-oriented men may come to realize that the poverty of their emotional lives is the price of their careerism. So they begin to strive for another kind of "success," one that is defined not so much in terms of professional status and financial achievement as through a loving union that is mutual and supportive.

Ned is a good case in point. He is a prominent lawyer who agreed to meet with us for precisely one hour. A secretary ushered us into his wood-paneled office, and Ned, seated behind an imposing, well-ordered desk, stood up and greeted us warmly. He is a lanky, Lincolnesque man with thick black hair and close-set eyes. For the better part of his forty-five years he has committed himself to developing a substantial law practice. Until a year ago he was a bachelor.

Ned is the type of man that other people would say should have been married a long time ago: a solid provider, attractive and amiable, with nothing in his family history antagonistic to marriage. Quite the contrary. His parents were happy together for more than fifty years, and both of his two younger siblings began their marriages in their mid-twenties. But, unlike the rest of his family, Ned revolved through one long-term relationship into another, never quite finding "the one." None of these "quasi-marriages," as he calls them, were destined to last.

Most of the women Ned dated were as career-oriented as he was. "My relationships were pretty much operational," he reflected as he leaned back on his reclining black leather chair. "We had fun, heaps of intellectual rapport, and nonstop sociability—but none of those women—or I, for that matter—were ready to give of ourselves in a way that's necessary for marriage." In retrospect, Ned recognizes that the one quality all these liaisons lacked was what he now needs most and hopes to share with his mate—nurturing and the opportunity to nurture back.

We wondered if, over the span of all those years, Ned really *wanted* the committed bond he said he was looking for. Admittedly, a big part of him preferred staying "footloose and fancy-free" in Denver, a city brimming with diversions and a seemingly endless supply of eligible women. Not investing too heavily in any one relationship also made it easier for Ned to deal with rejection or disappointment if the romance didn't work out. But, like Derek in chapter 3, Ned had arrived at a point of diminishing returns and ultimately suffered the inevitable burnout of too many fizzled love affairs:

> *Because I craved female companionship and was morose when I wasn't involved with a woman, I enjoyed the highs and minimized the lows, whether the relationships worked out or not. But to tell you the truth, I was getting weary of raised expectations and disappointments. So a permanent relationship—without the ups and downs of single life—gradually became more appealing to me.*

But another factor was crawling into his consciousness: his desire to have children. At thirty-seven, Ned began to take emotional baby-steps, figuratively and literally, toward the safety and regularity of a stable relationship. One association, in particular, recalled his warmest family memories and gently nudged him toward fatherhood and marriage:

> *I've really enjoyed getting to know my nephew Timmy. He is five now, and one of my best friends! I got into the habit of*

visiting him and my sister and her husband every Sunday, so I got to see a marriage and children up close. And it seemed very worthwhile.

Being together reminded me of the positive experience I had bringing up my baby sister, who is twelve years younger than me. Like when I was sixteen. I remember taking care of her and getting a lot of enjoyment even though she was just a toddler. All those feelings encouraged me, and I got a lot less cynical about marriage.

Actually, Ned had always wanted to have children, and when he became more open to the idea of marriage, an opportunity presented itself. He met a woman and they fell in love. Ned would have married this woman except for one unnegotiable obstacle: she wasn't capable of becoming pregnant. The future possibility of finding someone who could ultimately bear him a child finally won out, and they parted company. Having come so close, Ned braced himself to continue his search.

Ned met Liza, his wife, seven years ago in a low-impact aerobics class at a health club. One night, after weeks of preclass chitchat about sore muscles and body fat, they played hooky and went for coffee instead. This led to their dating rather exclusively for about a year. Liza's personality was a good balance for Ned's low-key somber side. She was upbeat, an avid theatergoer, and loved to explore and travel. But the romance ran out of steam and ended. Ned isn't sure why, it just did. Still, Ned kept a warm spot in his heart for Liza, and every so often he would call her to say hello and to see if she was involved. Usually she was, and Ned's casual dating life would go on.

For four years the two lost track of each other completely. Then, by chance, one day they bumped into each other at a local restaurant. That meeting rekindled their involvement. In the meantime, Ned was being buffeted along by a combination of negative and positive forces: he wanted children in the worst way, was worried he wasn't getting any younger, and was concerned that his ailing father wouldn't live long enough to see another grandchild. The writing was on the wall. Ned took the leap with Liza, head first—he wanted a wedding and a child as soon as possible.

Having my own child, after having been so close to my nephew, was a big push. So this time, when I started dating my wife again, I was struck by her pleasant, healthy nature and I thought she would make a loving and lovable mother. She kept on saying that she didn't want just a casual relationship, so after about three or four weeks I said, "Well, we'll get married."

It wasn't a very romantic proposal, but I knew I needed to rush things along. My father was eighty years old, and even though I hoped he would have a couple of more years to go, I knew he wasn't going to live long. I wanted my dad to be at my wedding, and I succeeded in that.

Ned envisioned life with Liza as the source of renewal he so desperately needed in his life. For him, the marriage itself symbolized optimism and completion. Despite his considerable professional achievements, Ned was never able to shake the feeling that his unsettled life was a sign of failure. Through this long-overdue marriage he hoped to gain the personal sense of adulthood and fulfillment that had eluded him. Although he says he looked self-conscious and ill at ease during the wedding ceremony, inside he was bursting with expectancy and hope.

Getting married was a personal achievement—a kind of measure of my maturity. Still, I felt a little funny calling attention to a rite of passage that usually takes place at a much earlier age. The actual wedding was played down and very small, perhaps fifteen of us—just family and a few close friends.

Now, a year later, Ned and Liza are expecting the child Ned has wanted for years. But all is not well. While husband and wife have managed to create a new life, they've failed to forge strong ties to one another. Ned finds fault partially with himself. On the one hand, he takes pride in his self-sufficiency and doesn't want to let go of his "lifelong cherished privacy"; on the other, he yearns for a marriage in which he and Liza become an interdependent unit. Ned is in what seems to be an unresolvable dilemma. Troubled by the lack of connection to Liza, Ned is hoping that becoming parents will consolidate their parallel lives into one:

We're not separable, but we're not inseparable either. We are content to do our own things. The baby will force us to have a much more domestic household. The chores relating to the baby will be shared chores, so that may get us into the habit of doing things together. But if there were no baby involved, I'd be content to do my thing and let my wife do hers.

A marriage that runs on two separate tracks isn't what Ned pictured for himself. Nor has he been able to break through his own emotional isolation. The disengaged partnership with his wife isn't sufficiently intimate to bridge the void he feels. By Ned's own definition, his key to true happiness turns on being able to give and receive nurturing within a family. But can he really tolerate the closeness, trust his wife, and give of himself freely? One can only hope so.

So, while his relationship with his wife has not made him whole, Ned looks to the imminent birth of his child as something that will. The baby, he hopes, will transform his marriage into a family—the potential source of well-being and fulfillment. What a heavy burden to place on someone so small.

The baby's birth is a step in the right direction. My happiness will be more than what makes me happy—it will be what makes my family happy. I married for companionship and nurturing, and now I will have the opportunity to nurture someone even more when the baby comes. That will be a real sign of success.

The success and happiness that Ned wanted so badly at the time of our interview may ultimately prove to be out of his reach. Realistically, the baby may not be able to keep Ned and Liza's fragile alliance intact, let alone solder them into a family.

Just the opposite may occur. Withstanding the unforeseen stresses and strains brought to a marriage by any new baby is a challenge for even the most compatible spouses. In the absence of a strong bond between them, there may be too little for Ned and Liza to lean on when they need each other most. It is also possible that they have already asked themselves the question, "Why be with someone if you feel more alone when you are with them, than when you're by yourself?" Unless they can find a way to trust and give to each other more freely, it is doubtful that the marriage will flourish. Even with the new baby, if Ned's and Liza's lives remain in their distinct orbits, only a fragment of Ned's life's dream for success will have been realized.

A SINGULAR PURPOSE

Instinctively we know that we connect with life in a unique and precious way when we give life to a child. It is an experience that no other can approximate exactly, and one that the late marriers we discussed in this chapter weren't willing to pass up. For them, creating a *family*—not marriage alone—was integral to discovering life's deeper meaning. Through parenting they knew they would find an enduring purpose—one that is familiar to all of us who have or want children.

Children add breadth to our solitary lives by calling upon our unknown strengths and never-imagined talents. As parents we extend ourselves in completely unanticipated ways; we become several different people at once—disciplinarian, caretaker, friend, mentor —and in so doing we multiply our singular identity manyfold. Children also add depth to our awareness of time. Sharing the present with children intensifies the here and now, just as planning for their future accelerates and gives meaning to our own. Rita is continually discovering and rediscovering these connections, and brings these lofty notions down to concrete terms:

> I am happier married, more content than when I was alone and
> childless. I spent a lot of time as a single career person thinking,
> "Great, I just got this promotion or this raise, so what?" After
> a while it just didn't mean anything. That void, that feeling of
> not having a purpose, really did disappear when I had a child.

But we've seen, too, that with this void filled, other voids often open up. In their haste, some late marriers are propelled toward unions they might not have chosen had they been younger or forever fertile. If having children had not been a pressing consideration, it's reasonable to assume that Ray, Vicki, Rita, Ned, and Nancy could have continued either living on their own or looking for a mate. But getting married became their overriding priority once the deadline for having their own biological children was upon them. If these individuals hadn't strongly equated marriage with family, they might have considered becoming single parents. But when it came right down to making a concrete decision, even Vicki, Rita, and Andreas opted for marrying and having children rather than parenting on their own.

Setting out to find a mother or father for one's as-yet-unconceived child is no easy task. Most late marriers who choose this path are forced to compromise on qualities in a mate that they would have preferred. All with whom we spoke reordered their priorities: Ray simply drew the line with Brenda; Nancy chose Dennis on the basis of wanting a father for her children, not a husband for romance; Rita sacrificed passion for parenthood, and so on.

No decision is without its costs and consequences—and also its rewards. These late marriers created unions based on what they felt they could live *with* and what they couldn't live *without*. It is impossible, and unfair, to judge whether their compromises have been worth it. If you were to ask them, we have a hunch they'd all answer the way Rita answered us:

> Some people would say I "settled." But if that's what I did, I got a whole lot more in return than if I hadn't. I felt it was the right time in my life to give something up in order to get something else that was a hell of a lot more important in the long run—namely, my own child and my own family.

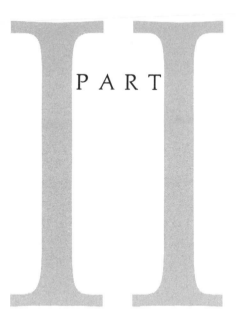

PART

II

WHAT ARE FIRST MARRIAGES AFTER 40 LIKE?

From Me to We

Sheila didn't want a big wedding, and I wanted something very casual. Since we're both sports fans, we arranged it in January so it wouldn't interrupt football season. I actually wanted to get married on a football field, but we compromised and had it in the condo rec room. Our closest friends were there, and it was a terrific party!

—ERIC, age fifty-three, married seven years

Rick and I would have preferred to get married at the courthouse, but my mother had been waiting forty years for my wedding. She started in with "You're not going to deprive me of my oldest daughter's wedding!" and completely took over. She picked out my wedding dress, bought Rick's clothes, got involved in all the planning. Since she had her heart set on it, we went ahead and let her. We knew we'd end up married either way.

—RITA, age forty-seven, married seven years

We had a huge outdoor wedding—invited everybody in sight. Joel's nine-year-old son played the guitar, and his two other boys served the champagne.

A lot of girls grow up glorifying the wedding day, but I didn't. I grew up glorifying day-to-day family life. Even though our wedding was a highlight of my life, I didn't feel as if "Christmas is over now." It was more like opening a beautiful door and this—our marriage—is the Christmas.
—KATE, age fifty-one, married nine years

WEDLOCKED

"She finally did it!" rejoiced one teary-eyed seventy-four-year-old father of the bride as he watched his forty-one-year-old daughter throw the bouquet into the crowd of her twenty-year-old nieces. "I never thought I'd live long enough to see this day!" joked the best man of a first-time married man, age forty-eight.

A wedding is a joyful occasion, no matter what the age of the bride or groom. For first-time-marrieds over forty, it is an occasion many thought they'd never celebrate, so, when they do, the day has a very special poignancy. Whether the ceremony takes place in an elegant hotel, on an idyllic hillside, or in a small living room, it is a cherished event. A few late marriers still have to contend with parents who want to "run the show," but most find their age gives them free rein to plan their weddings according to their own wishes. Their marriage celebrations are especially meaningful since they tend to reflect the social and spiritual values of the bride and groom rather than those of their parents.

From the time we're old enough to have fairy tales read to us, many of us create our own fantasies about what our weddings will be like. Although the fantasies may erode after forty-some years, what usually remains is the feeling that we're making a momentous transition in our lives. Some late marriers described to us fairy-tale weddings that lived up to their earliest projections, complete with flowing gowns, string quartets, and throngs of adoring guests. Others felt more comfortable scaling down their event to a few close friends and family gathered in a judge's chambers. Regardless, the wedding signified for each of them one of life's most important rites of passage, and in each case it was laden with emotional power.

Late marriers come to this significant juncture with years of life experience behind them and increased knowledge about who they are as individuals. Yet they still lack the experience of knowing them-selves as part of a fully committed couple. And when they take their marriage vows, the promise and uncertainty of what lies ahead are often as daunting as they are for much younger newlyweds. What is unique to older first-time-marrieds is the awareness that they're em-barking on a journey they almost missed.

Married for the first time at forty-two, Diana talked about what was going on in her mind during her marriage ceremony:

> *I had this feeling that it was all somewhat unbelievable. I loved this man so much that I had a funny, tingly feeling. Almost numb. I remember thinking I was glad I had waited, because I was getting just what I wanted. It hadn't been so long before that I had questioned if I would ever find someone I wanted to marry, so, standing there at the altar, I felt an overwhelming sense of happiness and closeness to my new husband.*

The wedding ceremony is a door to a new life. Those in our study anxiously and enthusiastically began married life at an age when most people have either long since adjusted to it, grown tired of it, or given it up altogether. In this chapter we'll explore the unique transition late marriers are called upon to make once they've said "I do."

LEARNING TO BE A COUPLE

Now what? Having waited or put off marriage for so long, how do first-marrieds over forty make the transition from single to spouse? How are their marriages unique as a result of their extended single lives? What sorts of practical adjustments must they make, and what kind of emotional changes do they go through when they marry for the first time in midlife? Over-forty first-marrieds have spent at least twenty years being single adults prior to connecting permanently with someone else. They've already established independent life-styles, friendships, careers, and leisure-time priorities. More impor-tant, they've created an identity on their own, a self that wasn't one half of a couple. Finding a way to create a oneness without compromising one's individuality or integrity is, for each of them, an ongoing challenge.

When we asked late marriers to talk about postmarital life changes and adjustments, a range of issues came up. The following are those most frequently mentioned:

♥ pride and power struggles
♥ balancing togetherness with independence
♥ compromise
♥ maintaining relationships with single friends
♥ resolving conflicts
♥ marriage as self-discovery
♥ confronting the "unexpected" in marriage

Although we're going to deal with each of these separately, many are interrelated. And while most of these issues tend to surface as "problems," they become opportunities as well—opportunities to learn about oneself and one's spouse and to deepen the bond that made marriage possible.

As we discovered in chapter 3, many interviewees who lived with each other before marrying reported a positive transformation in their postmarital relationships. They alluded to—but could rarely pinpoint—a sense that their commitment to each other had been enhanced by having publicly exchanged the vow to be together forever. But for a few post-forty marriers, living together first was no guarantee of a smooth transition into married life.

For Glen, the most trying period of accommodation began even before the honeymoon was officially over. The five years Glen lived with his wife prior to getting married hadn't adequately prepared him for the emotional turmoil he suffered in the earliest days of his marriage. Initially, at least, the marriage ceremony seemed to have jeopardized his ties to his new wife, Julia. The last day of their honeymoon signaled trouble ahead. Glen had enjoyed his vacation with Julia on the slopes of Aspen, but he ended up getting violently sick the last day. And for the next month and a half the couple went through some terrible times.

I had assumed that the day after the wedding would be just like the day before. But every little annoying thing that Julia did threw me into a depression, whether it was turning on the TV the second she got home from work or arguing with me over how to fix the stereo. I kept saying to myself, "Oh, my God, I'm going to have to put up with this forever." It was like buyer's remorse; I was in a real state of panic.

The thought of permanently accommodating himself to Julia's behavior left Glen anxious and angry. Although he had lived with her beforehand, he'd never learned to accept her fully. The impermanence of their premarital relationship allowed Glen, in moments of frustration with Julia, to fantasize about another woman "out there" who might more closely approximate his notion of compatibility. Marriage forced him to give up that fantasy and focus instead on a real, live woman with a few irritating habits, different opinions from his about how things should be done, and ideas at variance with his own. It also provided him with an opportunity to confront his long-standing stubbornness and pride. The need to have things go his way, to keep Julia's behavior in line with his own, was potentially destructive, and Glen realized he needed to change his expectations if his marriage was to succeed.

In our discussion with the noted Los Angeles psychologist Carl Faber about the unique difficulties middle-aged men and women have in becoming a couple, he mentioned the very issue with which Glen had to come to terms:

Pride is a big problem. When both people's identities are already strongly formed, the relationship tends to become a power struggle. And a liberated marriage has its best shot if people are about equally powerful. When the power balances are off, then things go wrong. And one of the faces of that—of two equally powerful individuals coming together—can be pride.

While Glen's "panic attack" lasted only a month or so, the lesson he learned was one he is still attempting to incorporate into his married life: the need to exchange a singular perspective for one that encompasses both his own *and* Julia's. Learning to see things from another's point of view may seem a simple enough task, but for those of us accustomed to being on our own, it can be a formidable one. Taking into account someone else's opinions on everyday matters isn't something we're used to doing. A significant step in the right direction was Glen's acknowledgment that pride and a struggle for control were at the core of his annoyance with Julia.

Distinguishing pride from individuality or integrity is difficult for most of us. We tend to lump them all together to mean "standing up for ourselves" or preserving our sense of who we are. But pride implies an *exaggerated* sense of self-worth and precludes compromise. Individuality and integrity, on the other hand, define who we are and can't be shattered by compromising with another person. We can relinquish pride, acknowledge that the other person's ideas have value, and still remain true to ourselves. And we can love others—respect them and care for them—without losing ourselves in the process.

In fact, the psychotherapist Eric Fromm bases his definition of love on the principle that each individual in a union of love must be a separate self. He declares that "mature love is union under the condition of preserving one's integrity, one's individuality. . . . In love the paradox occurs that two beings become one and yet remain two."[1]

Preserving one's individuality doesn't mean clinging stubbornly to the notion that one has a monopoly on the truth, nor does it denote that partners must keep their distance for fear of losing their sense of self. Paradoxically, only when we have a strong sense of self can we truly give of ourselves, because giving means expressing who we really are. Eric Fromm explains:

> *The most widespread misunderstanding is that which assumes that giving is "giving up" something, being deprived of, sacrificing. . . . Giving has an entirely different meaning. . . . What does one person give to another? He gives of himself . . . he gives of his joy, of his interest, of his understanding, of his knowledge, of his humor, of his sadness—of all expressions and manifestations of that which is alive in him.*[2]

As for Glen, he's in the process of learning to give Julia his understanding and tolerance. At forty-six, his maturity enables him to acknowledge his pride, his stubborn insistence on always being right. He recognizes that he and Julia are two distinct adults, with many exciting common interests as well as quite a few disparate opinions and habits. As Glen learns to honor Julia's differences rather than fight them, their love and their marriage grows stronger.

INDEPENDENCE VS. TOGETHERNESS

Getting married for the first time in midlife requires an openness to change. Prior to marrying, late marriers follow a well-worn path of independence and autonomous decision-making. Suddenly, just carrying on with their lives becomes a complex process in which someone else is involved. Their new role as husband or wife requires that they traverse an entirely new route in their day-to-day comings and goings.

One issue raised again and again among our interviewees was accountability to one's mate. Many late marriers resented relinquishing their freedom to do what they wanted, *when* they wanted. "Checking in" with another person on a daily basis became a jarring experience for them.

"I remember one time," said Diana, "I had gone grocery shopping at around ten in the morning and had run into a friend. One thing led to another, and I got back six hours later. Jim was furious. I couldn't believe he was so upset—after all, it wasn't the middle of the night, it was only four o'clock on a Saturday afternoon."

Diana's husband, Jim, expected her to call if she wasn't going to be coming home directly from the market. His expectation is just one example of the many unspoken rules that guide the conduct of every marriage. We internalize such rules by witnessing our parents' and friends' marriages, as well as those portrayed in the culture. But since our experiences differ, each of us acquires a different set of "rules," and unless they're articulated, they can easily be misunderstood.

Although spouses need to come to an agreement about which rules will apply to their particular marriage, newlyweds—even mature ones—are usually unaware of such protocol. Diana certainly was when Jim's seemingly minor "rule" infringed on her "normal" behavior. She wasn't used to being held accountable to another person, but her resentment eventually led to a discussion of the rules to which she and Jim could agree. Initially, Diana felt like a foreigner unfamiliar with the local customs, but now that she's begun to negotiate the rules with Jim, she's feeling more "at home" with marriage.

Learning to connect their life to another's, even when it comes to such details as telling their spouse when to expect them home, is a new experience for most first-marrieds over forty. Suddenly their private rituals and routines, how they spend their free time, how they go about the most mundane aspects of their lives, are all subject to discussion by this "other" person who is sharing their existence. Whether it's soaking in the tub for an hour upon arriving home from work, or religiously eating Chinese take-out on Tuesday nights, late marriers with years of singlehood behind them quite often have habits to which their mates have a difficult time adjusting, or that they have a tough time giving up. If the issue is a relatively minor one, simply bringing it out in the open usually goes a long way toward resolving it.

For example, Lilly's husband was initially offended when she would go to their bedroom in the evening, close the door, and spend hours with either a good book or her journal. Lilly was accustomed to having that time alone to read, write, and collect her thoughts. But Kevin felt shut out. It took weeks for him to approach her about it, but once he did, Lilly simply explained to him how important that routine was to her—and Kevin understood. Lilly also learned that living intimately with another person means that you are often called upon to explain your actions. What may at first feel like an invasion of your privacy or freedom can often bring you closer to your mate. Letting your mate in on your private rituals doesn't mean he or she must participate with you; it simply means they become aware of your behavior. And as your spouse comes to know more about you and you've learned to share new things about yourself, your marriage becomes more intimate.

Still, the desire to be close to a mate often seems to conflict with a late marrier's wish to preserve their independence. Forty-one and married just a year, Faith had a particularly hard time integrating her life with her husband's after so many years of cherishing her freedom. Her husband, Mark, had had a nine-year relationship living with a woman and a fourteen-year marriage prior to marrying Faith, so he wasn't used to independence. But Faith was, "to the nth degree." She told us that most of her life she'd done whatever she wanted, seven days a week. It drove her nuts to have to discuss her agenda with Mark. Even little things like getting up in the morning and making her breakfast became an issue. Mark thought it was rude of her not to make *his* breakfast for him. But the biggest bone of contention was Faith's schedule. She was so booked up with activities that there seemed to be little time left over for her to spend with Mark.

I had always had a lot going on in my life—classes, therapy, athletics, religious groups—and gradually I realized I'd better make some changes if I wanted to have a relationship with my husband. It wasn't easy, because it meant balancing what I felt I had a right to do against making him happy and us happy as a couple. Over time, I'm learning that some of my overscheduled lifestyle may have to do with my fear of losing myself in another person.

Faith had spent years becoming her own person. Although she wanted to have a close relationship with Mark, she was afraid of being "swallowed up" and losing her identity. She clung to her previous lifestyle until fate intervened. A serious knee injury forced her to stay home and be with her husband over a long period of time. The experience changed her life. She realized she enjoyed spending time with Mark, and felt neither suffocated nor put upon. Since then, Faith has been able to strike a balance between time spent with her husband and time reserved for herself. And she's discovered that she has nothing to fear from giving more time to her marriage.

Ned is also struggling to get closer to his new wife, Liza, and to become more of a unit rather than functioning as two separate entities. As we saw in chapter 5, he longed for a situation in which he and Liza would need each other more. He saw himself trapped by his own self-sufficiency and even felt nostalgic for the days—in his twenties—when he couldn't bear to be without his steady girlfriend for a moment. In those days, he says, he had a constant need to be

with his live-in girlfriend, and they did absolutely everything together. The situation with Liza is quite different, as Ned related:

> *[Having been] single for so many years, I became completely*
> *self-sufficient. I don't have the need to be with someone all the*
> *time, and the same goes for Liza. We've both been independent*
> *for so long, it feels natural for her to do her own thing and for*
> *me to do mine. She leaves without telling me where she's going*
> *or how long she's going to be gone, and there I am, with no wife*
> *around. And there's a duplication of chores—like I take my own*
> *clothes to the cleaners, she takes hers. Neither of us asks the other*
> *if we can do the errand for the both of us. It's almost as if neither*
> *of us quite realizes we're married.*

It sounds as if Ned *does* have a need to be more connected to
his wife, but hasn't quite acknowledged it and doesn't know how to
break the mold of self-sufficiency. An initial step would be to discuss
the issue with Liza; perhaps he's reluctant to do so for fear she'll react
defensively or critically. Ned's remarks indicate that he would welcome more togetherness with his wife, but he has yet to take the
initiative in changing the status quo. Instead, he's rationalized their
situation by declaring that he doesn't *need* to be with someone all the
time, as he did when he was younger. It's true that as we mature we
become more secure in who we are and less in need of someone else's
constant approval. But when we love someone and choose that
person for our mate, wanting to be close isn't a sign of immaturity or
weakness; it's simply an indication that we want to join our life to
theirs.

COMPROMISE

Although late marriers are more than happy to give up the loneliness
they have lived with for years, they have mixed feelings about
relinquishing certain other aspects of their single lives. They take
pride in having shaped their solo existence, and speak reverently
about their well-ordered lives prior to marriage. Learning to share
decision-making and control with their new mates thus becomes a

struggle for some and at least an effort for others. *Compromise* is a word that comes up frequently in discussing adjustment to marriage, but its meaning doesn't quite sink in until you've "been there."

For Derek, simply learning to give over physical space to Jackie presents a unique challenge. They both work at home, and as much as Derek wants to be gracious about letting Jackie do her thing in what used to be *his* house, he still finds himself on the brink of laying down house rules:

> *I told her, "You take the living room and let that be your work space, and you do whatever you want with it." But I guess I didn't really put my money where my mouth was, 'cause I'm continually sticking my nose into how she fixes up the living room for her office. I tend to be, if not compulsively clean, at least real ordered. Let's just say that Jackie has a looser relationship with upkeep. So that's become kind of an ongoing struggle.*

Although Derek would like to have both a meticulous environment in which to live and work *and* a compatible marriage to Jackie, Jackie is clearly more important to him. So he's given up on maintaining a showcase living room. He still squabbles with Jackie over her "looser relationship with upkeep," but he can't stay mad at her. Her passion and energy are worth the messy living room. And besides, a deal's a deal. Jackie originally agreed to let Derek keep the more secluded office in the back of the house if he'd allow her free rein in the living room. They both compromised, they're each getting something of what they want, and they agree that working together under the same roof is usually worth the sacrifices.

In Tess's case, compromise centered around a deeper issue than housekeeping. As we learned in chapter 3, her feminist ideology has always been a priority, and she's never allowed a man to jeopardize those values. A significant adjustment for her was learning to tolerate the traditional nomenclature of marriage:

> *I've always hated it when men refer to the women they're married to as "my wife." It's so depersonalized, and I didn't want to become another nameless woman. So I made Mel promise that he'd never call me his wife. The first couple of times he*

*slipped, I came down pretty hard on him. And then I realized I
was hurting him, and I didn't want to do that, because I love
him. So we arrived at a compromise. We decided it's okay for
him to call me his wife if he includes my name: "My wife, Tess."
As long as he doesn't say "the wife." The whole issue was
thrown back at me recently when Mel overheard me calling the
phone company. I referred to him as "my husband," and he ran
in from the other room shouting, "You see, you did it! You did
it!" We both had a good laugh.*

Tess's sense of fairness—as well as her sense of humor—helped
her through an ideological dilemma that pitted her sensitivities
against her husband's habits. Although her ideals had always come
first, compromising slightly resulted in neither hurt feelings nor abandoned values.

Robert learned about compromise in the context of balancing
work with his new marriage to Penny. For the preceding twenty-five
years he had always put his career first; he was overly conscientious
about his job, and made it a point to put in long work weeks. Since he
had no one else to worry about, and a lot of extra time on his hands, this
pattern was never a problem for him. Once he began sharing his life
with Penny, however, his extended workdays created a problem.
Robert had to find a happy medium between giving his marriage
enough time and maintaining his own high standards at work.

*I'm used to getting to work very early. I've done so all my life,
because I've always put my career as my number-one priority.
But Penny and I are newlyweds, and she wants that extra hour
in bed with me in the morning. I've come to agree with her that
we need the time together. After all, I waited until [I was]
forty-seven to marry, and I appreciate the importance of giving
my marriage the attention it deserves. Although it's been hard
for me to change my habits, our relationship comes first. And
besides, getting to work at nine instead of eight isn't going to kill
me.*

It's interesting to note that Robert is conscientious about his
marriage in the same way he's always been scrupulous about his work.

He is devoted to those things he truly values, and acknowledges the dedication a good marriage requires. He told us he'd always heard marriage was work and that he now understands what the word *work* actually means. It means "energy expended," and there's a lot of that when you're learning to become a couple for the first time.

Their previous single status affords late marriers the ability to determine for themselves how to define and manage their lives. Marriage requires their involvement in the somewhat unfamiliar process of compromise. As adults with considerable experience in the working world, as well as in dealing with friends and lovers prior to marriage, first-marrieds over forty are not strangers to compromise. Still, coming to terms with a spouse with whom you'll be living and sharing life's most intimate moments for the rest of your life is a distinct experience. In his book *Becoming Partners: Marriage and Its Alternatives*, Carl Rogers states that the true nature of commitment involves "a lasting quality to the relationship and the desire to continue to make the union mutually satisfying."[3] With that quality and that desire, it's easy to embrace compromise. When we know we've got a marriage that can last, and when we want our love to grow stronger, we look forward to doing what we can to settle our differences.

MARRIED COUPLES, SINGLE FRIENDS?

Until somewhat recently, it was assumed that upon reaching a certain age, one became part of a married couple, and the couple's social life would then inevitably revolve around other married couples. Most of our parents' lives looked like that. But when a person has delayed marriage beyond their thirties, they have usually maintained friendships with other single people for much of their adult life. When a forty-plus person gets married for the first time, what happens to his or her single friends? Must mature marriers make even greater adjustments in their social lives than newlyweds in their twenties or thirties since their single lifestyles and friendships have existed for a longer time?

In our interviews, both men and women who married late voiced their concern over losing touch with close friends they'd had before they married. As singles, first-time-marrieds over forty had placed a greater importance on their friendships since they frequently functioned as surrogate families. Before they had husbands, wives, or children of their own, late marriers often became part of a close-knit group of people who shared feelings, problems, and good times. These alternative families functioned as their primary sources of emotional support and provided the continuity and closeness that singles otherwise lack. They celebrated holidays together, came to each other's aid in times of illness or crisis, and were generally there for each other in the same way spouses or immediate family would be. Lilly described the deep connection she had to her friends before she got married:

> *My friends took the place of family. We took Christmas trips to Yosemite and celebrated countless birthdays together, not to mention New Year's Eves. If I had to have a root canal, one of my friends would be there to drive me home afterwards; if I had the flu, someone made sure there was a pot of soup on the stove. My two closest single women friends and I had a standing date every Sunday night to check out videos, call in for pizza, and swap our latest manhunting stories. My friends meant a lot to me. In fact, my desk used to be full of framed photos of our annual camping trips—the same way married people keep photos of their spouses and kids.*

Lilly has kept up with her closest friends, although she concedes that they aren't as integral to her life as they once were. Their time together is restricted to lunches or an occasional movie. The weekends and vacations she once enjoyed in their company are now reserved for her husband. Though this saddens her, Lilly sees no way to have a single lifestyle and a husband at the same time. She's working on including her friends in some of the weekend activities she currently enjoys exclusively with Kevin, but she admits that there's less need for the support of friends once you marry.

Even with the best of intentions, just finding time for friends becomes problematic. Oliver is swamped with family obligations now that he's married with two small children. He used to see his best friend on a regular basis. They'd go out to dinner or watch "Monday

Night Football" and chat about what was going on in each other's lives. They usually talked on the phone several times a week. But in the five years since Oliver's been married, he says he and his friend have gotten together only a half-dozen times—and then it was usually with their wives. And he still isn't used to the amount of scheduling that's now required in making social plans, since getting together with his friends used to happen so naturally.

Kids and schedules can't always be held responsible for the widening chasm between single and married friends. Sometimes it's the unmarried people who intentionally stay away—presuming that couples are in a self-contained world of their own. Nancy remarks that her friends just assume she's spending all her time either with her husband or "doing couple things" with other couples:

> I used to have a lot of single friends, and they just don't call me as much as they used to. The funny thing is, they all imagine that on Saturday night Dennis and I are out dancing or something, when in fact he's in the studio working and I'm sitting on the couch alone reading a book. If I call them and ask if they want to do something on a Saturday night or meet for brunch on Sunday, they're shocked. They assume we're joined at the hip and that we don't need anyone else anymore.

Nancy's friends made an erroneous assumption. It was probably based on their experiences with other married couples in which the domestic curtain had, in fact, been drawn. While most married people don't want to shut out their old friends, they often do desire a certain degree of seclusion—especially at first. When couples genuinely enjoy each other's company, being together alone is one of life's greatest pleasures. Such was the case with Victor and his wife, Jenny—although Victor confesses that setting up boundaries was initially Jenny's idea:

> One bugaboo in our relationship was that I had been used to friends constantly coming and going as they pleased before Jenny and I lived together. Jenny requested that they call first, so it's become much more formal. But I'm reaping the benefits as well, because Jenny and I do have more privacy now.

If it seems that there's little hope of bridging the gap between single friends and married folks, there *is* good news. There were several late marriers who seemed to be having little difficulty maintaining close ties with their unmarried pals. "I've found that most of my friends are still single," remarked Bonnie. "I still gravitate to single women—probably because most married couples have kids and that's all they talk about. But when I'm with one of my single girlfriends, I feel very much at home. I guess there's something about that mentality that I haven't given up."

Bonnie speaks for quite a few first-marrieds over forty who reveal that they still identify more strongly with singles than with married people. The struggles and joys of unmarried life were theirs for twenty-some years, and many say that those experiences fundamentally shaped who they are. Thus they continue to feel more *simpatico* with their single friends.

With Chris, the issue becomes almost a political cause. He's always been critical of married people who "ditch" their single friends and confine their social lives to other married couples. Such behavior smacks of the "old guard" to him, and therefore he and Kelly make it a point to maintain ties to their single friends. Chris's sentiments may reflect both his anti-marriage and pro-youth biases—the implication being that single friends are more youthful and therefore more interesting. Nonetheless, he shares with other late marriers a certain loyalty to premarital friendships. Difficult as it is to preserve those connections, Chris and others maintain that their single friends are worth the effort, because they were such an important part of their lives for so long.

CONFLICT RESOLUTION: "SET IN OUR WAYS" OR "MORE FLEXIBLE"?

Popular wisdom has it that with age come understanding, maturity, and the ability to deal with life's predicaments with grace and even temper. While our culture doesn't always seem to promote respect for our elders, most of us assume that the longer we live and the more we experience, the more tolerant we become.

But does age alone make us more reasonable or provide us with better judgment? And does being older enable us to resolve conflicts with our mates more equitably—even if we are married for the first time? Or does our *inexperience* in marriage result in incompetence? If we've waited until forty-plus to marry, must we begin at the beginning, just like any twenty-two-year-old newlywed? Or has our life experience—albeit experience as a single person—counted for something?

The late marriers we interviewed generally agreed that being older is a distinct advantage when attempting to resolve marital conflicts. Victor put it this way:

Age has made me less volatile, explosive, and pigheaded. Although it's an ongoing process, I've learned over time that it's okay to argue and fight, but that ultimately you need to explore solutions to problems rather than leaving things at loggerheads.

Roger Fisher and William Ury, the authors of the book *Getting to Yes*, agree with Victor. They claim that "negotiation is a process of communicating back and forth for the purpose of reaching a joint decision."[4] Learning to guide disagreements toward a solution can be as difficult for married couples as it is for warring nations. When we fight with someone, we often try to prove we're right, get revenge, hurt the other person's feelings or make him or her feel sorry for us. What we tend to forget is finding a solution to our conflict and resolving our differences. Mature marriers have an edge over younger couples when it comes to solution-seeking, for many reasons we'll explore in this section. The most obvious are the following:

♥ Older first-time-marrieds tend to be more secure about who they are. They don't need to be *right* in every argument in order to feel good about themselves.
♥ They've been around the block. They usually know from experience that name-calling, playing the victim, or emotionally punishing the other person doesn't lead to a good relationship.
♥ They're at the age when the expression "life is too short" has come to have real meaning.

Ray says his interpersonal skills have improved greatly over the last twenty years. But he concedes that he still has some way to go and that age doesn't necessarily make you "smart" about relationships. His determination to make his marriage succeed is what distinguishes his current behavior from the way he acted in prior dead-end relationships:

> *Now I find ways to stay in rather than get out. When you're married and you have a family and you're arguing with your spouse, you're arguing from a base of love and security. You want to work things out. You're not just trying to stick the other person in a corner so you'll have the excuse to walk away and end it all. That's what I used to do when I was single. As for my age being a factor, some smart twenty-two-year-olds might know what it's taking me all these years to learn. I think the key is self-esteem—and a real desire to stay together.*

Ray and his wife, Brenda, have certain issues over which they become deadlocked. He talked about their tendency to "detonate each other" in angry arguments, and said he feared their relationship couldn't withstand such battles. So they're currently seeing a marriage counselor to develop the communication skills to enable them to resolve their problems. Meanwhile, Ray avoids bringing up sensitive issues with Brenda since he knows neither of them is yet capable of dealing with the anger that inevitably surfaces. They both want their relationship to last. That desire, along with the wisdom they demonstrated in seeking help, will most likely ensure that.

What Ray is learning at forty-six—and what some very wise twenty-two-year-olds might already know—is that for two deeply connected individuals to get along on a daily basis requires positive traits almost too numerous to list here, but which include perspective, empathy, patience, open-mindedness, self-esteem, compassion, and a sense of humor. What we may come to understand as we get older is that truth is subjective and none of us ever knows the absolutely right way to solve a particular problem. The psychologist W. Robert Beavers claims that what distinguishes healthy couples from unhealthy ones *isn't* that they don't fight or that they fight more fairly. It's that, once the fight is over, they can negotiate solutions to their problems. The fight may be irrational, but once tempers have cooled, the process of resolution is a rational one.[5]

Successful couples are also intuitively capable of taking a more holistic approach to conflicts. They respond pragmatically to the *context* of an event as well as to the event itself. For instance, if one mate makes a harsh remark, the other stops to consider what might have caused it rather than becoming defensive. They can distinguish their mate's accusations and projections from what they know to be true about themselves. And they are capable of defining the boundaries between themselves—where each ends and the other begins.

Again, older, more mature individuals have usually had the time to build a stronger sense of self and to accept the lines of demarcation between themselves and their partners.

Ivan, sixty-one, attributes his success in resolving conflicts with his wife, Emily, to changes in his personality over the years. He claims that age has taught him to be more sensitive to another's point of view. Ivan also gives Emily much of the credit for his recent ability to be self-reflective after an argument.

In my previous relationships, I had difficulty seeing the other person's point of view. My attitude was, "This is my opinion, and if you don't like it, then that's tough." But Emily has helped me to sit back and reflect after we have a fight. Five minutes later I'll realize I did the dumbest thing in the world, and I won't resist talking about it. I wouldn't have been at all ready to talk in my twenties or thirties. I would have fought my battle!

The recognition that divergent opinions don't necessarily mean one person is wrong and the other is right comes with maturity. And while we don't automatically reach maturity at any given age, we can hope that our experiences with people over the years will yield some meaningful lessons. Maxine agrees that she's better equipped now to get along with another person than she was earlier on in her life. She's learned that not only is it okay for partners to have differences, but that it's also possible to express those differences without malevolence.

Hopefully, you've learned something by the time you get to be over forty. I think both of us are pretty good at expressing our feelings or saying what we want without hurting the other person. Hugh tends to hold a lot of stuff in, but he's working on that and getting better at it. Being older, we both know how to stand up for ourselves without knocking the other person down.

For some of us, patterns ingrained since childhood take longer to undo. Learning that he could simply get through a fight with his spouse without the fear of serious repercussions had an important impact on Derek's relationship. Like Ivan, he gives partial credit to his wife's peacemaking abilities in helping him find solutions to disagreements. But he also admits that they aren't always as mature as they could be. For both Derek and Jackie, being married motivates them to keep at it until problems are solved:

I'd like to think we're better at fighting than teenagers, but we can both be pretty childish at times. What's different, though, is that when we quarrel I don't have the sense that the relationship is about to be all over—which is something I had always felt before. As a child, I had terrible fights with my mother. Once, when I was ten or eleven, we were fighting and she ran to the window of our third-story apartment and said, "If this keeps up, I'm jumping." So I got it into my mind that fighting could lead to the point of obliterating one or both of us.

Now I remind myself that it's not about to be all over. And that, in itself, is reassuring. While it isn't like Jackie is some saint and I'm the sinner, she is more used to working things out, and I'm used to walking out. So I benefit from her experience.

Many of our interviewees came up with variations on the following pieces of advice: Don't go to battle over everything—let some things go. Enjoy the relationship that took so long to discover. Middle age teaches first-time-marrieds over forty to value the years they have left together; quarreling with the one they love isn't how they want to spend their time. Although it's unhealthy to ignore serious problems, it's also unnecessary to make a major issue out of every minor quarrel. No two people are going to agree on every detail of their life together, and it's counterproductive to analyze and discuss every hurt feeling. Sometimes the most mature thing to do is let it go.

After years of bad relationships, living alone, and fending for himself, Luke appreciates what he has with his wife, Sally. When the kind of little arguments come up that used to cause him to get his feelings hurt, he tells himself to forget it. "I don't have sixty years left to screw around and try to make things perfect," he says. "I have maybe thirty years or so. Wasting a single day tied up in knots is just not worth it."

Bonnie feels the same way. She and her husband used to squabble over things that were "simply not worth arguing about." When she caught herself in a confrontation with him over where to hang hooks in their new kitchen, something finally snapped. She burst out laughing at how ridiculous they'd both been. Now she credits her age with helping her remember the most important rule in conflict resolution: "Don't sweat the small stuff."

Middle age gives us the perspective to make light of potentially tense situations. Experience affords us the knowledge that most of what happens in life and relationships is survivable, and that keeping a sense of humor in the face of conflict is essential. Tess is a wonderful example of a late marrier whose trump card in the game of conflict resolution is humor:

> Around forty you're in the last half—you don't want to fuck around. You want to make it. It's just that it's not worth it to get so tooth-and-nail all the time, because there's more to life than that. For example, one of the things Mel and I fight about is sex. Sometimes we'll start to make love, and if I really don't want to, I'll go along with it anyway and then pull back. Then I'll explode, saying, "I don't want to do this!" But lately we've both noticed it hasn't gotten as nasty because I catch myself before I explode. I retreat for a second, think about what's going on inside me, and tell Mel how I feel. The other saving grace is that Mel has a great sense of humor. He can make me laugh very, very easily. So we'll admit that sex isn't working out, and then he'll say something very funny and we'll both end up laughing and loving each other again.

Conflicts are not only unavoidable, they're healthy. They allow partners to bring issues out into the open so that they can be resolved.

Our interviewees told us that, on the whole, their age allowed them more flexibility in dealing with marital problems. As many of the midlife marriers in this chapter attested, people actually tend to be more "set in their ways"—or "pigheaded," as Victor described it—in their twenties. Being more open about their feelings, seeking solutions rather than trying to win, letting minor issues go, and remembering their sense of humor were all things older first-time-marrieds had learned over the years in the context of other close relationships. And now that they were older, they felt secure enough in themselves to admit mistakes and make concessions. Their motivation to solve problems was much stronger than it had been earlier on; late marriers expressed a profound desire to make their marriages work. Waiting until after forty to begin a shared life made them especially appreciative of what they had, and they were committed to doing whatever it took to preserve that.

MARRIAGE AS SELF-DISCOVERY

For those who are open-minded, every experience in life, every new person encountered can provide an opportunity for understanding and growth. Even the hardships and tragedies that befall us can offer the possibility of deepened self-knowledge. By the time we're in midlife, we've formed firm ideas of who we think we are and how we'd like people to perceive us. When we marry, most of us come to view ourselves at least slightly differently from the way we did before. Living with someone who has promised to be with us for the rest of our life changes how we *feel* about ourselves and what we *see* in ourselves. The reflection of who we are in our mate's heart and mind tells us something new about our identity. What is it like to perceive ourselves from a different perspective at a point in our lives when we've supposedly already figured out who we are? What kinds of things do we learn about ourselves once we have a mate?

The mature marriers we spoke with were often quite surprised by what marriage unearthed, and their revelations ranged from mundane to deeply introspective. In some cases the self-discoveries centered around specific deficiencies and idiosyncrasies. Bonnie, for example, had the inner strength to face something about herself that wasn't particularly flattering:

It wasn't until I was married to Bill that I realized I wasn't as nurturing as a lot of women. I know women are supposed to have this quality as a matter of course, but it's just not something I particularly care to develop. When I have to do mothering kinds of things, I'm not into it. On the other hand, I don't have any doubts now that I can make a marriage work—and I had them before I got married.

Being unconditionally nurturing isn't necessarily a prerequisite for being a loving wife or husband. What's interesting is that Bonnie noticed her lack of motherliness only in the context of marriage—probably because women in general and wives in particular are expected to nurture. She isn't threatened by her discovery that she's less motherly than other women since she feels otherwise competent in her ability to create a loving marriage.

It's not only sexual stereotypes that are reinforced by popular culture; so are our oversimplified ideas about love. Ray's greatest learning experience derived from comparing the cultural images of love to the reality of his day-to-day marital experiences. It took being married for him to challenge his own definition of love.

I had an idea about love which I learned from the movies, comics, and books, and love is not like that at all. It's like saying we know about death because we watched Riff get stabbed in West Side Story, *right? Do we know about death? You never know about death until someone you're close to dies. And you don't really know about love until you consciously try to make a go of it. Real people don't just furrow their eyes into each other, have wild, passionate sex, melt into each other's bodies, and live happily ever after. The real living and real loving doesn't take place until you've gone through at least five years of fighting over each other's habits that you can't stand but have learned to live with somehow. Love has to do with loving yourself enough to accept and love others. I didn't have a clue about any of that before I got married.*

Other late marriers revealed that marriage provided a base of emotional security that enabled them to express feelings they'd previously kept buried. Knowing there was someone there to love them forever allowed them to expose certain unpleasant or threatening aspects of their personalities. In Cheryl's case, being married to Michael made it possible for her to finally show anger:

Not long ago I had a medical problem, and my husband came with me to the emergency room. They wouldn't treat me or give us referrals to doctors. I was furious because the nurse wasn't taking me seriously. Yet Michael was being so nice to her. How dare he be nice to this woman at my expense! We got back to the apartment and I was steamed!

I had never gotten angry at anybody in my life. I picked up the nearest thing, which was a coffee can with pencils, and threw it at him, shrieking, "How dare you! I am in danger!" I had never raised my voice at him or anybody else—much less thrown anything! But it was the beginning of my being able to be angry when I felt angry—to have access to that part of myself which had been completely submerged in my family. I always felt that if I got angry, the person I loved would abandon me. But this time I took the risk. And I came out of it trusting myself and Michael much more than ever before.

Why is it that we tend to need someone to push against in order to get to know ourselves? While some fear giving up too much of their identities by merging with another person, others, like Cheryl, find that they gain access to previously hidden parts of themselves. Newly discovered traits may not always be flattering or easy to face, yet we need to accept them in ourselves and in our loved ones if we are to continue growing toward wholeness. Cheryl had to face the darker side of her normally easygoing nature before she could fully integrate the disparate parts of herself. In turn, she found that the experience brought her closer to her husband. By becoming more whole herself, she became stronger; by showing more of herself to him, their union became stronger.

In her book *On the Way to the Wedding*, Linda Leonard explains that Rainer Maria Rilke's notion of love encompasses all aspects of existence—even those we sometimes wish would remain hidden:

Love requires giving up one's preconceptions and demands on the other and on the universe, accepting whatever comes, the whole. The way to . . . love is . . . enduring the tension of opposites within and without, seeking always to unite them.[6]

Discovering the "tension of opposites within and without" was also a significant aspect of Nancy's adjustment to marriage. She eloquently described how her attraction to her husband, Dennis, and her discovery of their basic differences were connected not only to her relationship with her mother but to undeveloped portions of her own personality. Dennis is a very flexible, unstructured person, and Nancy has just begun to see her own rigidity in contrast. She's always thought of herself as simply very efficient and organized, and she's chosen friends and lovers who were somewhat like her in that respect. Adjusting to Dennis's looseness has been difficult for her, but it has also been a signal to Nancy that she needs to be a bit more relaxed and spontaneous:

It's painful for me to confront things about myself that I'd rather not see. But that process is an inevitable next step in my life. I had never been forced to deal with certain aspects of my personality because I hadn't been with someone who contrasted with my traits so distinctly. Interestingly enough, someone pointed out to me that Dennis is quite a bit like my mother. Maybe that's why I knew when I met him that there was something about him—that unspoken part of myself—that was compelling me forward into a relationship with him. As if marrying him had to be the next step.

Revelations concerning how we are or aren't like our parents come forth in many different circumstances, but none are so powerful as the circumstance of marriage. We don't have the opportunity to unravel fully what our parents' effect on us was, until we play the role of husband or wife ourselves. Although you need not be married to be haunted by parental ghosts, if you *are* married, the experience most likely goes deeper. Newlyweds of all ages often find themselves baffled by the fact that their behavior so closely mirrors that of their parents. A woman may wonder, for instance, "Am I treating my husband this way because that's how Mom treated Dad—or because I'm actually choosing this behavior for myself?" First-time husbands or wives are called upon to separate their own roles as spouses and their own adult values from the roles their parents played and the values they embraced. Marriage offers the opportunity to consciously choose whether or not to live your life according to parental models or your own.

Our interviewees often spoke of confronting "parental ghosts" for the first time in the context of their own marriages. Frequently they found that they resembled their parents in the role of husband or wife; for some, that realization was horrifying or troubling. For others, it was gratifying. Faith spoke of her discomfort upon recognizing that she possessed some of her mother's worst flaws. This hidden side of her personality hadn't shown itself until her marriage, and Faith is grateful to her husband for helping her deal with the consequences:

I do to my husband what my mother does to my dad. I hear myself sounding like the critical, intolerant person she is. I never acted this way in my other relationships—my problem then was always that I kept things inside. When I got on overload, I simply left the relationship. But now, because there's a lot more openness and because I don't want to leave—I seem to cope with problems by being real hard on Mark. What's great about Mark is that he doesn't let me get away with it. He goes out of his way to stay with me until I can get past it. He'll either try to joke me out of it or show that he's hurt or just bicker with me about it until it blows over. But he doesn't abandon me.

Dealing with unwanted familial patterns inherited from her childhood is less of a burden for Faith because she is aware of what's going on and secure in the knowledge that she can change. She also has her husband's understanding and support. Robert was also surprised that he tended to take on his father's characteristics in certain situations. But rather than perceiving the similarity to his dad as something negative, Robert realized that his father had often been a role model.

My father was usually tender with mom. I realize now when I'm behaving in a certain way toward Penny, there's a lot of my father in my behavior. It's what Dad would do. There was always a gentleness in his expressions and words. He was a tough person, but he could also be gentle, and I call on that a lot. I think that's what has enabled me to get past certain arguments with my wife. I was never really willing to put up with women before. Even with my sisters, it was rough for me, because I didn't understand girls. If they didn't act like John Wayne, I couldn't relate. But I've changed. I remember how my dad was with my mom, and I try to learn more about Penny and be patient in that process.

Ideally, all of us would like to be able to select which parental traits to discard and which to inherit. Unfortunately, we aren't automatically given that choice; it's something we have to learn to change. Only when we understand how our behavior resembles what we experienced as children can we make an effort to prevent the past from controlling us. Some may be psychologically equipped to undo certain "psychic habits" on their own; others may benefit from peer-group support or therapy or spiritual guidance. In either case, successful couples must have the ability to live in the present without being plagued by childhood events. W. Robert Beavers wisely advises that we ought to learn about our past and use that information as a "guide, not a directive. Capable spouses can usually do this because they possess . . . an 'observing ego'—the ability to watch oneself interact—to critique, and to experiment with new ways of achieving goals."[7] By middle age, many of us have struggled diligently to develop our "observing egos"—our ability to be objective about ourselves. All the better for starting a relationship off on the best footing possible.

CONFRONTING THE UNEXPECTED

When women and men over the age of forty marry for the first time, they make adjustments in their lifestyles and redefine their identities. They learn about resolving conflicts within the context of a permanent relationship, some for the first time. Priorities shift; they discover pieces of themselves they hadn't acknowledged or noticed before. They come up against their pride and vulnerability. Newlyweds of any age experience dramatic changes in their lives. But for those in midlife, the transformation from being single to being a husband or wife is uniquely poignant, since they've spent at least twenty years of their adult lives on their own and generally look forward to twenty years' less time with their new spouse. They've also had a longer time to anticipate marriage or, in some cases, to hold on to both positive and negative myths about married life.

As we talked with our interviewees about their early years of matrimony, we wondered how their marital experiences differed from the way they'd always envisioned married life. Some said they had had no preconceptions; others said they couldn't picture what marriage would be like until they met the mate who would be in that picture with them. But there were those who admitted that the reality of marriage contrasted radically with what they had expected. Often they were surprised by the simple fact that marriage need not fit any preconceived mold—that, indeed, they were free to create their own parameters and ground rules and live happily ever after while living quite unlike any other married couple they knew of. They were pleased by this discovery, having previously feared that somehow the marriage police would arrest them if they didn't abide by certain unwritten laws. Even free-spirited Tess found herself comparing her relationship with "some kind of fifties stereotype" in the early months of her marriage:

> I thought you should have a house and the husband should come home from work and find dinner on the table. My comparison wasn't that explicit, but emotionally there was some connection to that. I translated the fifties image into my own terms and began to mentally measure our marriage by those standards. Of course, I quickly understood that that's not who Mel and I are,

that those expectations were false. But there was this kind of
residual cultural flotsam. Once I let that go, we both became a
hell of a lot happier.

What surprised Cheryl the most about marriage was how her life
changed in a much deeper way than she had ever anticipated. Remember, before she met her husband, Cheryl's love life was predominated
by affairs with married or otherwise unavailable men. There was no
risk of being overwhelmed by someone else's needs—as she had been
by her father's—but there was also little chance of her getting very
close to anyone. Cheryl began her relationship with her husband with
few expectations. Slowly but progressively, each of them was able to
open up to the other, and Cheryl was surprised every step of the way.
She had never quite anticipated giving and revealing more of herself
than she had in her premarital affairs. By doing so—learning to accept
herself and trust Michael's acceptance of her—love became a reality
rather than an intangible.

> *Throughout my life I had it in my head that no one was going*
> *to love me very much. I thought people would want me, and*
> *want to be with me, but no one would really love me.*
> *By the time I got married, I thought that I would have this*
> *playmate whom I could have a great time with, but that there*
> *wouldn't necessarily be this depth of love. It turned out to be just*
> *the opposite. I have a guy who isn't at all social like I am, but*
> *he loves me a lot. And that's a pretty good trade-off, because*
> *where it counts the most, he's there for me.*

Carl Rogers believes risking the communication of one's feelings
is one of the keys to a continuing successful partnership. He defines
communication in the following way:

> *I will risk myself by endeavoring to communicate any persisting*
> *feeling, positive or negative, to my partner—to the full depth*
> *that I understand it in myself—as a living, present part of me.*
> *Then I will risk further by trying to understand, with all the*
> *empathy I can bring to bear, his or her response, whether it is*
> *accusatory and critical or sharing and self-revealing.*[8]

For the first time in her life, Cheryl decided to communicate with someone in this manner. In doing so, she allowed Michael to experience not only her understanding and her joy, but her anger and sadness as well. She's now glad she took the chance.

Like Cheryl, many other late marriers are happily surprised by what married life has to offer. Having spent much of their lives intimidated by commitment, afraid of making the same mistakes their parents did, or simply not finding the right person, they find marriage—on balance—a comfort and a joy. Kate delights in the unanticipated joys of marriage:

> I spent so much of my life either enduring the loneliness of not having someone in my life or having relationships that didn't work out. When I finally had Joel, [with whom] I mesh so well . . . I simply loved it. And still do, after nine years. Just sitting on the couch listening to opera, or going outside and watching the sunset, or walking along with him with my hand in his hand—it's so wonderful. It's been much more gratifying than I would have dreamed. And yet, in the old days, when I would describe to my friends the kind of life I wanted, they would tell me I was too idealistic. "That's not the way real life is," they would say. But they're wrong.

7

MONOGAMY? AFTER ALL THESE YEARS?

*I appreciate having good sex now because I had a lot of bad sex when I was
single. I remember being horny for years. Joel is not only a good lover, he's
kind, I respect him, I look up to him. From a sex standpoint, I know I have
the best—'cause I've had everything else—the gamut. Holy cow! You
wouldn't want to know.*

—KATE, age fifty-one, married nine years

Sex—either having it or thinking about having it—occupies a good
portion of most people's attention. When we are single we wonder
what steady married sex will be like. When we are married we fondly
recall the unpredictability of single sex. What is particularly special
about older first-time-marrieds is that most have spent their entire
adulthood as sexually active *singles*. Until their first marriage, the
majority have felt free to act on their sexual proclivities—whenever
or with whomever they've wanted—restricted only by their own
discretion and appetites.

Out of the forty late marriers we interviewed, only one man and
one woman were virgins on their wedding night. As for the rest,

they'd sown their wild oats and enjoyed a variety of sexual arrangements over the lengthy course of their unmarried lives. Although there were exceptions, most late marriers had practiced cyclical monogamy during singlehood: they were faithful to their intimate partner when they had one (some had been in unmarried monogamous relationships longer than they'd been in their current marriages). When they didn't have someone steady, they indulged in casual sex or remained celibate for months or even years like any single person. Most late marriers have always *understood* the difference between unmarried and married monogamy; only now were they beginning to *experience* the difference. Derek's comments touch on this distinction:

> *Despite all of my excursions with women, I was never really one to cheat, even though technically I could have. Now that I am married, I no longer consider myself free to fool around. I still look at and appreciate other women. There are either the beginnings of impulses to move toward them, or what is left of archaic impulses. I don't think they will ever go away until I stop being interested in women. But now there are limits.*

The limits Derek refers to are created when we take marriage vows. We call upon our husband- or wife-to-be "to forsake all others" and promise "to have and to hold until death do us part." The moment we utter these words, or phrases like them, to our betrothed, we are declaring our resolve to choose *one* mate for life. What makes these prime-of-life brides and grooms unique is that with half of their adult lives behind them, they are *officially* signing up for sexual monogamy for the *first* time.

How has their adjustment been to the possibility that their husband or wife might be the *last* man or woman with whom they will ever have sex? How does married monogamy affect late marriers' attitudes about fidelity, sex, romance, and intimacy? Is monogamy a natural state, or does our form of marriage demand a kind of sexual exclusivity that is restrictive and unrealistic in this day and age? From the vantage point of some late marriers who have wistful recollections of their wilder pasts, this question has particular relevance. After two years of marriage, Ray, who has neither strayed nor is planning to, openly contemplated the ambivalence he felt initially when he first married:

I used to think about monogamy a lot. Most other animals don't mate for life, and, besides, humans are built to love in a lot of different ways. Have we made too much of a pressure out of fidelity? If I'm part of this animal kingdom, how much should social pressure dictate the way I respond? If I get curious about wanting to explore another human being, don't I have the right to act on it? If I do have the right, then is it simply a matter of the way I do it?

Even in the aftermath of the sexual revolution, our first impulse is to regard monogamy as intrinsically "good" and extramarital affairs as irredeemably "bad." Few of us would openly admit it if we did have an affair, for fear of the recriminations. Our society still places the greatest premium on a sexual relationship that is exclusive, and casts a questionable eye on those that are not. So do most of us. Nearly everyone enters into wedlock expecting that his or her spouse will be faithful; over 91 percent of all Americans disapprove of extramarital sex.[1] But, as we all know, what people say is one thing, and what they do is another. Just because they *believe* in sexual monogamy doesn't necessarily mean they *act* monogamously.

Conservative findings suggest that 37 percent of all married men and 29 percent of all married women have had at least one extramarital affair.[2] In most cases an affair is disruptive to a marriage. If kept secret, it is often at the price of deceit and deception. If discovered, it is usually considered the ultimate breach of trust. Prior to no-fault divorce, adultery was one of the few legal grounds for the dissolution of a marriage.

Some who think monogamy is a natural tendency argue that it is a legacy of survival deeply rooted in our evolutionary past. Anthropologists and sociobiologists speculate that originally our female ancestors needed the support of a mate to help feed and protect vulnerable offspring through the first four critical years of infancy.[3] Humans pair-bonded to maximize the survival rates of their highly dependent infants until they were weaned. This makes sense.

But an equally legitimate counterargument can be made for multiple mates. While there may have been a strong evolutionary bias for couples to remain together until infants were weaned, there doesn't seem to have been any necessary advantage in lifelong monogamy after the reproductive years were over. In fact, having many reproductive partners in a lifetime may have promoted survival. Rather than producing children from the restricted gene pool of one woman mating with one man exclusively, multiple partners might have contributed to offspring with a broader mix of inherited traits *more* adaptive to hostile environments.[4]

If we look at forms of marriage worldwide, what we discover is that monogamy is far from universal. Surprisingly, fewer than one-fifth of all human cultures ever documented have insisted on monogamous unions. It may be that our culture's predilection for monogamy is more a result of historical antecedents than of evolutionary ones.

Our contemporary attitudes concerning monogamy in marriage are largely based in the myths and traditions of European medieval "courtly love"—a morality that held almost sacred the exclusive sexual compact between two lovers. True love demanded virginity before marriage and absolute fidelity thereafter; sexual restraint forged an inviolate covenant of body and soul that sealed a couple's lifelong commitment. These high-minded ideals have colored our present-day attitudes toward contemporary sexuality and marriage. And it hasn't been a perfect fit.

Today premarital chastity is rare, opportunities for sexual expression seemingly limitless, and fidelity ever more fragile. We've come to live in a society in which sexual restraint alone no longer guarantees a lifelong commitment. Most of us believe that a satisfying sex life—not just an exclusive one—will sustain the connection to our spouse well after our marriage vows are spoken. Fidelity isn't enough; we expect sexual fulfillment too. Essentially, the majority of us still want the commitment of "courtly love," but not at the expense of individual growth or potential for exploring new experiences. Sex has become the means through which spouses can grow and learn about themselves as individuals and as a couple.[5] The new monogamy puts less emphasis on giving something up. It offers instead a pathway to discover self and other.

IS VARIETY THE SPICE OF LIFE?

Since more than two-thirds of the first-time marrieds in our sample have yet to celebrate their fifth wedding anniversaries, the difference between unwedded and wedded sex is still very distinct in their minds. A few recalled initially chafing at the restrictive implications of married monogamy not because they were aching to make love to someone other than their spouse, but because they felt as though a bit of their freedom was being yanked away. The great majority, however, couldn't wait to put dating behind them and were grateful to settle down with one person.

So far, none of our interviewees had broken their marriage vows—or at least they didn't confess to us that they had! But several were openly nostalgic for the spicy interludes and risky love affairs that predated their marriages. All the feelings associated with a sexually charged first encounter—the fantasy, anticipation, and discovery— were difficult to forget. After so many years as free agents, late marriers had accumulated a considerable store of amorous memories that were tucked away in a special corner of their libidos. Although they knew it was unfair to make comparisons, some couldn't help but make them anyway.

For example, Eric, after seven years of marriage, still plays at harmless pursuits. He claims it's hard to make the adjustment to marriage when you've spent years playing the let's-jump-in-bed game. "It becomes part of your being," he told us with a foxy grin on his face. "I'm faithful, but I still drive around the block when I see an attractive woman. That was part of me for years—and still is."

Exploring a new person is like taking a mysterious expedition: you make special preparations, you don't always know where you're going, it's a little bit uncomfortable when you get there, but that's part of the excitement. Married sex is just the opposite: you know the territory, there aren't as many surprises, but at least you can relax. We all have at least one tingling reminiscence in our past. Vicki's erotic tryst with one man in particular sends a little shiver down her spine to this day:

I had a relationship with a guy I saw once a week. We were devoted to it and got ready for sex. I'd take a shower, brush my

teeth, and get dressed to get undressed. I'd change the sheets on
my bed and everything was sparkling clean! He would bring a
bottle of champagne or we would get stoned and it was a
wonderful evening. We had great anticipation and great sex!

Single sex is often by arrangement only, so there is usually
plenty of "prep" time between meetings to make it special. Without
a steady partner, the opportunity to make love just isn't a part of
day-to-day life. This uncertainty plagues many singles. It is not
uncommon for unmarried women, in particular, to wonder, "When
will I ever make love again?"

Rarely does anyone choose to be celibate for long periods of
time. But the older and more discriminating one gets, the easier it
becomes to find oneself precisely in that predicament. Rather than
sleeping with someone simply to take the edge off the isolation, most
of us would prefer to share our beds with partners who will be there
in the long run. A lovely thought, but then again, it doesn't always
work that way.

Late-marrying women, especially, recalled their longings for
even fleeting physical contact in the absence of a regular sexual
partner. As single women, some slept with men expressly to fill this
void. Charged with pent-up emotional and physical need, these intermittent affairs shook with a heightened passion quite distinct from
married relations. Diana, drawing from her own experience, comments on the difference:

Dating sex is elusive. It always had a needy feeling to it that
married sex doesn't have. When you get a chance to fill the need,
it's very erotic. You never know when you'll have the chance
to make love again, so sex starts to represent a whole lot more
because it may not be there again.

Casual affairs are often spellbinding—for a reason. This lusty
sexual energy is enchanting *because* it is transient and leaves generous
room for romantic fantasy that temporarily lifts us out of our loneliness and sense of incompleteness. The abandon of needy passion is
sweet but also greedy, grasping, and all-consuming, at least momen-
tarily. Short-lived involvements are mostly about oneself and less

about the other person. They're often based primarily on our projections of how we would like things to be and how this person can make them happen.

Only with commitment and loyalty can we experience the bothersome disappointments and undiscovered joys that come with *accepting* another person for who he or she *really* is. Ideally, this happens in marriage. If it does, marriage transforms us and our sexual energy into something else. Diana continued:

> *When I first got married, Jim and I were "in lust." Then, after we'd been together a long time, we didn't make love as much. Also, the sex is less passionate, and that's frustrating. I started thinking Jim was bored with me or that our relationship was no good anymore, because that's how it used to be when I was dating. But I've learned that when you have commitment, sex is just pleasant sex. The commitment doesn't go away if you are not making love, as it does when you're just seeing someone every now and then.*

Diana's thoughts perfectly describe the adjustment involved in shifting the focus of love from hot sex with impermanent partners to constant and companionable sex with a permanent one. On balance, it was a task that most late marriers were ready and eager for. After two decades filled with the whims and woes of sexual wandering, they had accumulated a kind of carnal wisdom. Unlike men and women who married earlier and spent the greater portion of their marriages living vicariously through the sexual escapades of their single friends, late marriers have no hidden lust to fulfill. Having sex for the sake of sex is behind them; married monogamy looks better because they've experienced everything else but.

When we begin to know someone as an ordinary human being, as we do in marriage, our illusions about love, romance, and sex change. Inevitably, the *real* person we've chosen for a mate won't necessarily match our dreams and ultimate desires. If we are only interested in passion, once the real person intrudes into our fantasy, our passion may falter or fade. Then we're left with a shadow of a relationship and we may be tempted to move on. But if we are committed to commitment, then the discovery of who that person is, with all of his or her imperfections, holds the potential of enhancing the rich mixture of our love.[6] Such was the case when Glen chose Julia for a partner. By age forty-six, he'd come to value relating authentically and completely to a woman, not just the sum of his sexual fantasies:

> After years of sexual experience with a lot of people, the number of surprises isn't that great. It's no longer, "Gee, if I can get this woman in bed, it will be fantastic." Part of it is that you settle down personally and make a decision to make something out of the relationship with the person you've chosen.
>
> From the time I started going with Julia, I have been very pleasantly surprised that I don't find myself being attracted to other women. Julia isn't the only person I could have ever been married to—it's not like we are cosmic souls—but she is the person I chose. Not just a choice, but a good choice.

The challenge of monogamy isn't just in resisting the lure of a new lover. It's also in resisting the impulse to bail out of our relationships either emotionally and/or physically when things get boring, bumpy, or downright bad. Our near-mystical belief that once we are paired we will never suffer loneliness or unhappiness again doesn't make getting through the rough times any easier when the *last* person you want to be with is the person you've married.

What does help, however, is the memory of so many more *forgettable* love affairs than unforgettable ones. Late marriers know from experience that searching for sexual solace outside a relationship never solves any of the problems inside it. For example, Cheryl's resolve to remain monogamous in her marriage was stronger for all the times in her unmarried life when she hadn't been:

> Both Michael and I had a lot of sexual experience before we found each other. I think it is easier being monogamous since I wasn't for so long. When I moved in with him I told him, "I am not interested in being cheated on." We made this deal that since we both knew what could be gotten from sexual relationships for their own sake, we would be monogamous. And if either one had

any trouble with our relationship, we would talk it through. But
we wouldn't use other sexual relationships to solve it.

Committing ourselves to monogamy means we aren't willing to throw our married love away just because it isn't absolutely blissful every single moment. Consciously choosing to honor our marriage vows demonstrates devotion and allegiance to our chosen mate not only physically but spiritually. The two are inexorably intertwined.

Monogamy has the potential of anchoring us to our spouse's side, where we can experience the sense of belonging, not just for today or now. It establishes a fixed point of loyalty and trust, part and parcel of what true marriage is. Ray, the skeptic who questioned the concept of monogamy early on in his marriage, expressed what he has grown to understand about the privilege of his connection to his wife. It's a bond he has decided to protect and revere:

I haven't thought about another woman in four and a half years.
If you asked me to remember one beautiful lady in that time that
I wished I would have gone to bed with, I can't think of one. And
that was never the case before I got married. Before, just the
potential of being with a new woman was a turn-on. Now I
don't get the same buzz at all. I feel very comfortable, very at
ease, and actually quite satisfied—even though I don't get nearly
enough *sex.*

I recently saw a play that has a lot of personal meaning
for me. The central character's wife is dying at the age of
thirty-five. She asks her husband if he's been faithful in their ten
years of marriage. He thinks back to when they were making
love for the first time, and how their lovemaking was like
creating this beautiful bubble filled with light. He had always
felt that if he ever strayed, it would be like puncturing that
bubble and allowing all the light to leak out.

I feel very much like him. I want to try to keep the light
for my wife and my family—the light that belongs only to us.

MONOGAMY IS MORE ROMANTIC

Romance can and does bloom in the glow of "the light that belongs only to us." This comes as a surprise to many late marriers who have never experienced anything quite like it before, irrespective of all their past relationships and commitments. We usually think that romance evaporates after marriage, or, at best, struggles to survive. But many discovered that the longer they were together with their new spouses, the more romantic their marriage became. Why?

Communicating romantic sentiments or showing loving attention doesn't necessarily come naturally, improve with age, or have anything to do with when someone first marries. But universally, these tender moments touch the well-being of every couple's emotional life. A *truly* romantic relationship, in the opinion of most late marriers, is based on the genuine appreciation of a partner as a person.

"I feel cherished and known for the first time in my life," Lilly told us. "Nothing is more romantic than that." Every year on her birthday, Kevin revises a love letter he first sent Lilly two months after they met. It's entitled "Fourteen Ways You Know You've Met the Right Person." In it he prizes her qualities and celebrates her quirks—all that makes Lilly Lilly: the two tiny freckles that adorn the back of her left knee, the grouch she becomes if someone telephones too early in the morning, the mania she has for making love on trains. With each passing year, Kevin admires Lilly all the more for who she reveals herself to be. He tells her what he notices, what he's learned. To Lilly, this is utterly romantic.

These reminders of shared intimacy and sweet tokens of desire telegraph our respect and acceptance straight to the heart of our beloved. Incidental touching and physical closeness is another way we let others know we trust and value them. Of course, not all affection is sexual or romantic. But taking the liberty to touch and flirt physically with someone usually is. Emotionally expressive partners do tend to be more caring of their mate's feelings and are more likely to initiate sex.[7]

Late marriers, who spent so much of their lives without this special affinity, savor the privilege and romance of familiarity. The ease and comfort of freely expressing affection with an intimate partner is one of the great gifts of a relationship. Simple pleasures like the ones Kate describes next have kept her nine-year marriage filled with more romance than she ever dreamed possible:

We still kiss a lot, we hug a lot, we hold hands. One thing I do with Joel, that I never did with anyone else, is I'll see him standing there and I'll slip my hand into his. The basic feeling is trust—and the willingness to be vulnerable. I'm vulnerable with Joel because he's trustworthy. Not only do I trust his behavior and his feelings toward me—I trust my feelings toward him.

Kate's romance with Joel comes close to sounding like "two hearts beating as one." Theirs is our ideal notion of real romance— one that is as effortless and natural as breathing itself. But sometimes it takes a while for a pair to synchronize their rhythms. Couples with different ideas about the place of romance in their lives must work at adjusting their expectations and developing a common vocabulary for expressing their love. With gentle (or even not-so-gentle) intimations, a reticent partner can be encouraged to initiate romance— especially if he or she reaps pleasurable benefits afterwards.

For the entire time Tess has known Mel, she has wailed, pleaded, and "ragged like a shrew" to persuade him to "spontaneously" buy her flowers. Nothing worked and she had all but given up on the idea. Then, one day, for no special reason at all, there was a knock on her front door. When she opened it, at her feet was an enormous bouquet of scarlet long-stem roses. Tess lights up just talking about it. "It's such a small thing," she says, "but one flower equals days of good sex." From that moment on, Mel and Tess were busy for months!

A romantic gesture can be as lusty as hiding your lace bikini in the breast pocket of your husband's favorite business suit or as endearing as his drawing you a scented bath and sticking around to chitchat while you take it. There are endless ways to pluck a lover's heartstrings, but two elements enhance romance immeasurably: unpredictability and intimacy. True romance is knowing someone so well that you can predict what will stir their passions or delight them unexpectedly! Expressed caring that is sincere and spontaneous keeps love alive and marriages fresh.

What makes romance romantic also depends on the individual

ways that each lover expresses love. Many late marriers have such well-entrenched romantic tastes and amorous habits by the time they marry their spouses that attuning to the nuances of their mate's style takes time and practice. Jackie and Derek's marriage is a good example of how a couple learned and taught each other about romance. Derek is a self-proclaimed "unromantic" while Jackie is just the opposite: he's more reserved and she's more gushy. First, let's hear Derek's side:

> *Romance has never been my strong suit. I don't gravitate toward whispering sweet nothings; I am not practiced at it. Since I'm self-conscious about being romantic, I enjoy playing off how unromantic I really am. My way of being romantic is pretending to have forgotten some occasion or omitting a gesture and then having it right there. Just by that you can see that romance doesn't come easily for me. But I think I'm going to get better because Jackie likes it and now I finally have an opportunity to change.*

Jackie, who has always adored words of love, is learning to live with Derek's verbal disclaimers that he isn't romantic. Little by little she is paying more attention to what comes naturally for him and accepting that love can be expressed in many ways. Ever since she's been more attentive to what he *does* rather than what he *says*, she's better at reading his underlying intentions—his teasing omissions included! Even though Jackie still wishes Derek were more verbal about his feelings, she's come to appreciate that he's much more romantic than even he gives himself credit for:

> *Derek is not classical romantic, and sometimes I wish he could express how he feels in words. But he is not a big dud either. He's sentimental in a lot of ways that aren't conventional—like the way he'll cook me a gourmet dinner or pick out a special gift that is just right for me—something he knows I've been wanting. In the very beginning, I didn't always know how he felt about me if he didn't tell me. Now I can read his signals and feel them.*

Becoming fluent in one's lover's romance language is a part of the give-and-take of every good relationship. Most couples develop a cryptic code that becomes their own private vocabulary, one that only they can decipher. Each time we celebrate the gift of love, we are being romantic. Our first-time marriers pay special attention to these belated opportunities. With each romantic gesture—whether it be a cozy weekend camping together by a wilderness lake or a book of "Cupid's coupons" redeemable anywhere, anytime, for a hundred kisses—they're saying "I love you" in the devoted dialect of the heart.

MARRIED SEX IS SEXIER

Late marriers are newlyweds at the same time some of their contemporaries are on the verge of becoming "old married couples"! As almost perennial singles, they've endured erratic sex lives, thousands of lonely weekends, and hundreds of going-nowhere "dates from hell." By comparison, the sexual stability of marriage is nothing short of thrilling. Nancy still can't get over the abundance and availability of married sex: "What I love about marriage is the luxury of having sex when I want it. When there wasn't a man in my life, I'd always be wondering if I was ever going to have sex again. I remember thinking, 'What a waste.' Now all I have to do is ask for it when I am in the mood and it's there!" Tess, too, was struck by the plenitude of married sex. Actually, "overwhelmed" was closer to her initial reaction. But again, as with romance, couples must find a balance between too much and too little of a good thing. Not to worry, however. She quickly turned her embarrassment of riches into a more modest sexual advantage:

> In the beginning, whenever Mel wanted sex we would have sex. But it was just way too much for me—like having a chocolate mousse every single night of the week. It started to be a turnoff because I never had any room to be sexually assertive.
>
> My sexual drive is very erratic. It is either really strong for a while or it falls off completely. I can go for as long as two weeks without really having any desire for sex. I do need cuddling, intimacy, and sensuality, but I don't have to have an orgasm or actual penetration. And none of this necessarily has anything to do with my attraction to Mel.

*I've had to learn to "just say no." But then I had to learn
to take on the responsibility of being the aggressor, and that's not
so easy because it requires a certain amount of self-confidence.
The first time Mel told me he wasn't in the mood, it was
thrilling. His saying no made me want to have sex with him
even more!*

If a couple shares control of who takes the lead sexually, there
is an increased sense of mutuality between them, and it's likely that
they will be happier with their relationship in general. Paradoxically,
when both partners feel that they can refuse and initiate intimate
contact equally, they end up having more frequent sex.[8] Of course,
it's not always as simple as "just saying no." While quantity and
quality can be related, fighting for and finding mutual sexual gratification often requires more: two committed partners who are determined to stick it out until the sweeter end.

Hammering out the inequities of different sexual rhythms and
temperaments with a sexual partner can be uncomfortable and embarrassing. Sexual negotiations such as these rarely surface between
couples in shorter romantic involvements. If we know a relationship
isn't destined to last, it seems easier just to have sex than to go
through painstaking accommodation. In the long run, however, this
approach creates more problems than it solves. Inevitably, when the
passion fades, partners often terminate the relationship and move
on rather than face the problem. A real commitment to monogamy
forces us to do otherwise. After a lifetime of other options, what
did married monogamy teach our late marriers about the quality of
sex?

By the time Tess married Mel, she was ready to experiment with
the problems and payoffs of monogamy. After all, she had tried
everything else *but* monogamy, and "none of it seemed like the real
thing." Little of it had been. Besides always putting men's satisfaction
before her own, she had never had the courage to be sexually authen-
tic for herself. At the expense of her own pleasure, she faked orgasms
well into her late twenties and kept her sexual frustrations to herself.
Rather than risk honest self-disclosure with her bedmate, she'd simply
search for "perfect sex" with the next perfect partner:

I came into my marriage with the idea that if it is not perfect sex, it's bad sex. As a single person or even a person having an affair, if you have bad sex, you let the relationship die. Or you set up situations that would make sex close to perfect: a nice quiet room, the right music, the candles, the bath, the hotel—the works!

In marriage you can't afford to have that idea—especially if you promise to be faithful. I had to be able to say, "I have to live with the times when it is going to be 'ho-hum.'" I had to get off "perfect sex."

Mel once yelled at me, "If we only had sex when you wanted it, it would be only on Friday morning, when it's not too hot and we're both well rested and we've had our coffee, with milk, no sugar. . . ." He went through this whole list. It was hilarious. I realized I needed to let go of "perfect sex or nothing."

Letting go of our *singular* idea of "perfect sex" allows us to redefine perfect sex *mutually* with our partner. According to the noted psychologist Adolf Guggenbuhl-Craig, author of *Marriage: Dead or Alive,* "alive" marriages allow for and tolerate sexual experimentation and the playing out of fantasies of both partners. He believes that when we aren't holding back or hiding, we can learn "to know the other person in all of his or her heights and depths. Thus, one actively traverses the soul's primeval forest . . . the peculiarities of oneself and of one's partner must be bourne, accepted, and integrated into the interplay between the spouses."[9]

Marriage offers fertile ground for great sex. At its best, it combines loyalty, trust, and companionship with affection and love—an ideal context for achieving sexual gratification. Under these prime conditions, partners generally feel safe enough to take risks with each other sexually. When there is confidence between spouses, the marriage can breathe freely in all respects, and the sky, or our imagination, is the limit.

This has certainly been true for Ray, who, prior to monogamy with his wife, had different sexual styles depending on the person he was with. He found it difficult to let go sexually *and* connect emotionally with a woman at the same time. As a nonmonogamous single, he wasn't much concerned by this split. Ray sated his diverse sexual needs with many partners. But as a monogamous married man who was promising fidelity to his wife, he knew something would have to change. It did.

Ray and Brenda worked at giving each other freer and freer rein to explore the full range of their sexual styles *within* their marriage. Even though Brenda is still more inhibited than Ray would like, he finally feels free enough with her to reveal all the sides of his sexuality. The double pleasure of being able to satisfy his erotic drives and express his deep caring with one woman is one of the great rewards of his marriage:

> *Before I married, I remember going out to fuck a woman—like a mission. I get tense when I'm fucking, but I lose myself when I'm making love. What changed in monogamy is that I fuck my wife and I make love to her. I've had experiences with her that are totally different from anything I've ever had before.*
>
> *Sometimes when I am feeling vulnerable, tender, caring for my wife deeply, something completely holy happens when we are in bed together. Then there are times when it's been a long time since we've had sex, so I'm just horny. I start talking dirty on the phone with her—really gross—and I make a game out of trying to embarrass her. It builds a tension, and by the time I come home we'll usually end up fucking—she's into it as much as I am.*
>
> *But the best times have been when I've wanted to make love, and all I could think of doing was fucking. So I did the fucking to get the release and become relaxed, and then we'd really start to make love.*

Feeling safe to expose our vulnerabilities can potentialize all aspects of our sexuality. Without being tied to one sexual style or another, Ray's sex life is integrated in a way he's never experienced before. Jackie, too, has opened up to a new level of responsiveness when she makes love to Derek. "I'm much more uninhibited now," Jackie told us, "because I am making love to my husband, who is a part of me—there are no restrictions on anything. The more Derek and I are together, the more we nourish this marriage, the better sex is."

The sexual freedom that Jackie relishes feeds and is fed by the wholeness she experiences in her marriage. Like other fortunate late marriers, Jackie and Derek consider each other "found treasure": nearly out of reach, difficult to unearth, but more bountiful than they ever expected. It is a bounty that makes their marriage, and its physical expression, more precious and often more ardent than they've ever known before. For many, it isn't always the actual sex that changes with monogamy, but the *meaning* that takes on new dimensions. After six years of marriage, Duncan is still replenished and sustained by the physical and metaphysical relationship he has with his spouse:

> *God knows how many women I've slept with in my life, but I've only made love to one wife. Annie is the best! Married sex with her is sexier than anything I've ever known before—it's real union. This may sound very old-fashioned, but when we make love we join our bodies, our brains, and our beings. Lovemaking mirrors the joy we found when we joined our lives.*

Marriage creates a *we*—an ongoing entity that contains and connects two individuals before and after sex. Many of our late marriers mentioned the continuity that marriage provides. "Marriage means that I can get off the gypsy caravan of sex I don't have to keep an extra toothbrush in my purse anymore," Lilly remarked. "It finally belongs somewhere, and so do I." Married sex isn't just steadier or more stable than single sex; it can be a metaphor for the giving and receiving implicit in the entire love relationship. Making love is, for these late marriers, an extension of "making life" with their mates. And they are reveling in the privilege of both.

WHEN IT ISN'T ALL ROSES

Many factors influence sexual satisfaction in marriage. Unfortunately, the relative newness of late marriages is no guarantee that sexual bliss will last forever, or that it will even be there in the first place. A handful of men and women in our sample were grappling with problems that typically don't cluster for other newlyweds: declining overall energy, diminishing interest in sex, the draining demands of young families, and the peaking pressure of careers and financial responsibilities. Any one of these can undermine sexual relations. But in combination they are guaranteed to drain midlife libidos.

Changes in sex drive affect women and men differently. Women are most sexually responsive in their middle to late thirties, and remain at the same high plateau for decades.[10] Not only are women capable of having orgasms their entire lives, but some also experience increased sex drive after menopause, when they are no longer hampered by the possibility of pregnancy. By contrast, for some men, middle age brings a drop in stamina and a range of other physiosexual changes; fewer spontaneous erections, a decreased need to climax as often, and weaker ejaculations.[11] These gradual shifts don't necessarily mean less lovemaking—just minor adjustments in foreplay and pacing. For example, Eric's sex life with Sheila is still satisfying after sixteen years together. However, his age, combined with the debilitating stress of his workload, *have* affected his sexual energy— but not his enthusiasm:

> *The quality of our sex is the same, but the quantity isn't as crazed. We used to be naked for a whole weekend—start on Friday night and come out on Monday morning. Neither of us can afford to do that anymore—we're working too hard! Both Sheila and I wrestle with the lack of energy. The perfect remedy to our stamina problem is daytime sex—after a good night's sleep I've got energy for anything!*

Physical fatigue is also an issue between Vicki and Oliver. Their energy is further taxed by the all-consuming demands of two toddlers. Unlike couples who began families when they had the fortitude of youth and fewer career pressures, late first-time marriers are starting families just at the time when the demands of their jobs may be the greatest. These factors combine to put an untimely damper on the initial passionate years of late marriages.

Vicki's professional schedule involves extensive travel. When she's away, Oliver comes home from his office and takes full charge of their children. Their nonstop agendas leave little time or inclination for romancing; when they are together, by bedtime, Vicki and Oliver are dying for sleep, not sex. It's been that way from the first day of their marriage, when they went from being long-term lovers who had never lived together to being expectant parents, with no newlywed time in between. Vicki says:

I got pregnant right after we got married. First I was a big, huge person and then I was nursing. That happened twice in a row. My body went and so did sex, even though I have more energy than Oliver does for it. I have some disappointment about that. It's not like the same old wonderful passionate things we used to do, which were great. When you are with the same person it's not like that—particularly when you have kids. I don't even sleep next to him anymore, 'cause we have this baby curled up between us! There is some passion left between us, but I would like him to be more loving, to occasionally say, "I think you are terrific. . . ." But who knows? Maybe sex does become less important.

With time, the primary bonds of companionship, financial interdependence, and children become important in a couple's relationship. If a couple's sex life is less than great, these other attachments may even compensate and promote a commitment that is just as enduring and permanent. The role of sexuality can become less binding in keeping a couple together, and this is as true for some late marriers as for anyone else. Oliver's compelling connection to Vicki isn't sex, but rather the comfort and pride he takes in his family:

I am fifty-two, not thirty-two. Sex is a physical act which takes energy, and I have less each day. I am neither that thrilled with our sex life nor that interested, but I am being faithful. Being involved with one person every day, in every respect—meals, sexual relations, finances—is not easy. Although I don't find that particular aspect of marriage that appealing, I would never trade it for being single again. Sex aside, I would say that marriage with children is the most rewarding way I could have led my life. I can't imagine having led my life without it.

Vicki and Oliver didn't launch their marriage on a wave of sexual desire. Neither did Ned or Rita —whom we discussed at length in chapter 5. Remember, these late marriers had a primary goal: to begin a family and home life, which they did, successfully. Although these individuals complained about their married sex lives, not everyone felt the same degree of dissatisfaction. Only Ned and Rita's admissions left us with a sense of debilitating cynicism and resignation.

As you may recall, a great deal of the well-being of Ned's marriage is riding on the birth of their child. Caught in the squeeze between his expectations of how family life will change his life and his doubts that his marriage is viable, he's under enormous pressure. Poignantly, he is seeking the restorative benefits of intimacy while at the same time he believes less and less in the redemptive value of romance. It doesn't take much imagination to figure out that his sex life *and* his faith in love are faltering:

> When I was twenty or thirty, I fell in love more passionately and more often than now. Love was more important to me then. And I think the same applies to sex. Although I did the same things back then, I enjoyed it more. I used to look upon romance and sex as a salvation. And, at least in my own experience, it isn't.
>
> Life goes on. Reality sets in. Believe me, I've got a lot less expectation and energy for sex—all these things take their toll. In my life, romance has become less tangible, less realistic.

Romance seems to have evaporated from Rita's life as well, but for different reasons. Ironically, her marriage is good; it's her sex life that's bad, and she laments her sexless marriage with worn acceptance. For now she seems to be preparing herself to live asexually in order to preserve her family and her marriage:

> Inside of all of us is this seething animal in search of the right partner, and it's usually not your husband. I thought I would be sexually attracted to someone forever. "Settling," for me, was realizing that I wasn't going to marry one of those guys that turns me on. They're never good marriage material.
>
> I've been with Rick seven years now, and sex has never rekindled for me. That's hard to accept because I'm someone who

was incredibly sexually active. It's not enough to drive me to divorce, but it's been the only sorrow of my marriage.

Our assumption that late marriers might avoid the notorious sexual "midlife crisis" because they were in the midst of enjoying new-found love and lust clearly turned out to be true for some and untrue for others. As we discussed in the preceding section of this chapter, some midlife marriers felt more sexually attractive, vital, and hopeful than at any other time in their lives. They looked to the future with glowing anticipation—"like vintage wine that just gets better and better."

But, as we've just read, this clearly isn't the case for everyone. A segment of our late marriers were dealing with troubled sexual relations. And they ranged from making the best of their anemic sex lives to tolerating them with a debilitating aura of forbearance.

Our interviewees who had strong mutual sexual energy going into their marriages seemed to fare better than those who didn't. But the fact that a spouse was less than satisfied with his or her sex life didn't necessarily equate with a lack of satisfaction in the marriage. We all know from experience that it is possible to have good sex in a bad relationship and bad sex in a good one. The same is true for matrimony, in which every conceivable variation on this theme is possible, and later first marriages are no exception.

MAKING MONOGAMY WORK

How many times have we heard that single people fight loneliness and married people fight monotony? Does this hold true for late first marriages as well? After all, just about this entire chapter has been devoted to the idea that late marriers are tickled pink that they've found each other and that they're in love with love. Can they actually be contemplating having an affair already? Well, the shorthand answer to that question is no, for many reasons.

First, intrigue is time-consuming. The amount of juggling required to keep an affair under wraps eats into precious time. Unlike long-time-marrieds with empty nests and fewer demands, late marriers' schedules are stretched taut between new spouses, newer families, and full-time jobs. Even thinking about covering up clandestine liaisons sounds more like effort than it's worth. Nancy concurs: "There's a premium on life energy at this point in life—it's wasteful to give it over to keeping secrets."

Second, and more important, even if time was for the taking, most late marriers aren't bored with their spouses, sexually disgruntled, or even trolling for outside action. But life always has a sneaky way of testing our resolve, and the commitment to fidelity is no exception. Rita reminded us of this irony when she observed jokingly, "Once you've finally made a commitment, the whole universe gets together to gang up on you to see if you can keep it. It's like when you stop smoking and everyone starts offering you cigs." Some late marriers who aren't the least bit interested in having an affair have declined offers; some who might have been open to the possibility haven't had any opportunities; others may have had them but didn't tell us. But the topic does come up, since most late marriers are relatively new to married monogamy. They are human, too, and wonder, "What would happen if . . . ?"

There's an old-fashioned saying that "monogamy is like good crystal—beautiful, but all it takes is one chip and it's never the same again." As touchingly quaint as this simile is, it possesses a lot of truth. While it doesn't necessarily follow that one sexual transgression, or even a series of them, automatically leads to divorce, the possibility that one *could* is deterrent enough. And this is precisely the crux; late marriers are *very* concerned that their relatively new marriages will last, and they aren't about to place them in jeopardy.

In their hearts, sexual betrayal simply isn't worth the deception; unquestionably the emotional and health risks of having an affair far outweigh the fleeting benefits. Late marriers are consistently preoccupied with the repercussions of dishonesty on their primary relationship. Inasmuch as only one husband in our group had spoken hypothetically to his wife about an agreement that permitted nonmonogamy, those remaining would be required to deceive their spouses if they *acted* on their fantasies.

This is not to say, however, that some didn't cheat in their minds when passion flagged. With ample escapades to draw upon from their single years, Henry and Toby spiked their married sex with fond forbidden memories. First, Henry:

I have fantasies of having a lot of sex, 'cause I'm not having enough now. I stand in the shower and get off thinking about all the women I've had in the past. At times my wife has been the surrogate for whomever I've been thinking about. I don't talk to her about it because it would feel as though I'm cheating on her in some way.

And Toby:

Even though I love Frank to bits, our sex gets terribly predictable. I'd never think of actually cheating on him, but I do have a very naughty little secret. When I can't come with Frank, I make him my imaginary lover—the composite of all the great men I ever had. He's got Frank's face, but all the rest I owe to them. It isn't like I'm really being unfaithful to Frank, except in my mind.

We live in a sexualized society with every opportunity to live out our wildest erotic fantasies, not just imagine them. Temptations of the flesh abound in the course of our daily lives: old lovers, new flirtations, close friends, business associates. It's naïve to assume that we or our partners will stop feeling sexually attracted to others, no matter how much they love us or we love them. Yet, even in the face of a momentary weakness, most late marriers steadfastly honor their vows of fidelity. Cheryl is one of them:

About three years ago, out of the blue, an old boyfriend called and dropped by for lunch. He said that I hadn't changed and what he felt before was still there. By the end of the meal, I was feeling a little bit the same way. Something that had been sleeping inside me was starting to stir, and that made me nervous. I was saying to myself, "I am not available for this guy!" I looked at my watch and told him, "Listen, I've got dinner guests coming, you better leave." A baldfaced lie. Even though someone might be interesting to me, I can't do it, 'cause I promised Michael I wouldn't.

Other late marriers have come much closer to having an affair than Cheryl did. But the stakes seem high when marriages with children are involved, and especially high for late marriers, who have waited so long for both. For example, before Henry and Rita decided not to take their final leaps, they meticulously weighed the consequences of their actions.

Henry is discouraged by the possibility that he would lose his wife and child if he were discovered having an affair. The threat of these concrete losses is sufficient to keep him from acting on his desires: "If I were to cheat on my wife, it would damage the relationship—maybe irrevocably. I don't want to hassle around with that, even though I have fantasies and the rest. I'd be risking not only losing the relationship, but losing my child, too."

Rita's concerns have less to do with betraying her spouse, and are focused on the implications of betraying the innocent trust of her daughter. She has symbolically extended the monogamous principals of sexual accountability and exclusivity to her child. This earnest consideration has tempered her successive impulses to take a lover during the seven years of her sexually barren marriage. Once she went so far as to arrange the use of a friend's apartment for a rendezvous. But at the last minute the power of Rita's loyalty overruled even her longing for physical love:

> The reason I couldn't go ahead with it had nothing to do with my husband. I was feeling infidelity to my child. What I've done is turn off that part of my life now because of her. It is her innocent trust in family that I could never betray.

Although our generation has been long accused of disdaining monogamy, our late marriers appear to be taking fidelity to heart as well as to bed. No matter what the state of their married sexual relations, late marriers stay monogamous because they *want* to. They want their new marriages to last and their even newer families to remain intact. They want to live up to their vows of loyalty. They want to protect the mutual trust they share with their spouses. And they want to be able to live with their own consciences.

Living monogamously requires the joint effort of two minds, two hearts, and two bodies. But even with the loftiest ideals and the best of intentions, we can't necessarily *assume* our partners will be sexually monogamous unless we discuss the issue explicitly with them. Nor can we *insure* fidelity through emotional sabotage using intimidation or coercion. Monogamy works only if both partners have the willingness to stay faithful and the courage to confront themselves and their spouses when they don't.

Midlife marriers feel that all their single years may have inadvertently given them an advantage in monogamy. After all they've been through, and given who they have become, they're convinced they have more respect for the boundaries of the marriage it's taken them so long to find; more experience to know that sex without intimacy is vastly overrated; more maturity to keep their fantasies fantasies; and more wisdom to work on the problems their relationship may have. With all of this in their favor, men and women who marry for the first time after forty claim and treasure what D. H. Lawrence poetically christens "the sapphire of fidelity—the gem of mutual peace emerging from the wild chaos of love."

8

MONEY AND CAREERS:
YOURS, MINE, AND OURS

Until I got married I was somewhat of a perennial student—smart but broke! I told my husband, "The only thing I can bring to this marriage is ten thousand dollars in debts and my Karmann-Ghia." He said, "That's okay. I love Karmann-Ghias!"

—ALICE, age fifty-eight, married eighteen years

In some ways marriage is cleaner than living together because you can have financial issues put down in writing. I have been successful in my profession for a long time, so I have quite a bit of equity. I wanted to make sure that if the marriage didn't work out after just a year or so, I wouldn't lose all that.

—LUKE, age forty-six, married one and a half years

Along with sex, children, and in-laws, money is the subject over which married couples most frequently come to blows. How much is enough, who ought to earn it, and who ought to decide how to spend it only begin to enumerate the questions inherent in the interplay between marital partners and income. The recent economic squeeze

186

and women's evolving status in the workplace especially figure into any discussion of couples and money, since both have profoundly altered the financial foundation on which today's marriages are built.

For the majority of couples, whether or not a woman will work is no longer a choice; a wife *must* work if they are to make ends meet. And for most college-educated women, a professional career is considered a given. Still, the role women take in supporting their families has become the hottest topic of debate in the area of love and money. Books and articles abound on how to manage a "dual-career family," and there is great controversy over whether working mothers are an asset or a liability to their families and society.

Married couples of all ages continue to grapple with the pros and cons of having two breadwinners in the household, as well as numerous other money matters. But what about first-marrieds over forty? How do the classic marital money issues apply to them? Late marriers face a unique set of circumstances surrounding finances and work. Most of them are established in their careers and hitting their stride financially. With rare exceptions they have been supporting themselves and making their own monetary decisions for twenty-some years. They haven't been financially burdened by dependent spouses and/or children, but neither have they necessarily had the benefits of two-income households.

The financial concerns of mature marriers are unique as well. The problems most couples have with pooling or separating income, or with money management, were scarcely mentioned by those in our sample. And a prevalent crisis experienced by many middle-aged families—women either returning to work or entering the workforce for the first time after being full-time mothers and housewives—was, of course, irrelevant to our population. Of the twenty women in our study, sixteen worked full-time. (The other four relinquished full-time work outside the home to raise children.) Thus, nearly all of the forty people we interviewed—both men and women—were part of dual-career marriages. Dual-career relationships were not only accepted but were taken for granted by mature marriers, with one exception: Helen's husband wanted her to quit her job. Her account appears later in this chapter.

There were, however, unexpected consequences—positive and negative—in the financial dealings and working lives of those who married for the first time after forty. The issues that came up most frequently were these:

♥ prenuptial agreements
♥ finally getting serious about work and money
♥ (for women) emotional consequences of being supported vs. supporting oneself
♥ sharing the financial burden
♥ juggling financial needs: new families/aging parents/retirement

In exploring each of these topics with our interviewees, we found we agreed with the financial writer Grace Weinstein, author of *Men, Women and Money*, who contends that conflicts over money usually have to do with the deeper issues of control, security, self-esteem and love.[1] Our earning power can make us feel good about ourselves, but it can also be used as a means to control our partner. On the other hand, when our partner supports us financially, it may make us feel loved and secure or guilty and insecure, depending on our particular psychological issues surrounding money. Ultimately, it's one's sense of well-being that's at stake in assessing the relationship between oneself, one's livelihood, and one's mate.

IS WHAT'S MINE STILL MINE?

Unlike younger couples who begin their careers and marriages at roughly the same time, late marriers usually approach the peak of their working years just as they begin sharing their lives with someone else. They've spent at least half an adult lifetime creating a financial base. They may have bought a house on their own, or accrued significant investments. Regardless of the particulars, late marriers often worry that what they've spent years building up could be lost in the event that their marriage doesn't work out. With the odds of marital success being about fifty-fifty, fear of divorce and ugly battles over financial settlements are, unfortunately, well founded. Such apprehension leads some to consider prenuptial agreements.

A prenuptial or premarital agreement is a legal document written and signed before the couple marries and effective upon their marriage. It can stipulate whatever the couple wishes, but often its essential purpose is to declare which monies and properties were owned by each partner prior to the marriage, which assets are to be kept separate, and which are to be shared or divided in the event of divorce. Premarital agreements are usually drawn up by remarrying partners with children and amassed property. One or both partners want to make certain that their own children or other beneficiaries will receive designated property in the event of dissolution of the marriage or of death.[2]

The intention of prenuptial agreements is to override the law. Most states have community-property laws that stipulate that earnings prior to marriage and earnings after the end of the marriage are considered one's separate property, but whatever is earned during the course of the marriage is community property. But a prenuptial agreement can nullify the community-property stipulation. For instance, some couples agree that money they earn during the marriage will be treated as separate property.[3]

Since these agreements are usually drawn up to negotiate how property is to be treated in the event the marriage doesn't last, many look upon them as cynical declarations. "The sting of prenuptial agreements," says Los Angeles mediator Kenneth Cloke, "is that many people feel 'Here we are about to get married, and we're already planning our divorce.' "

Late marriers' primary worry stems from the uncertainty about what they stand to lose should the marriage fail. Those in our sample who considered premarital agreements were realistic about the possibility of divorce. Having been involved in failed relationships prior to marriage, they were particularly cautious.

As we learned in chapter 3, Luke had an especially difficult relationship history that greatly contributed to his financial insecurity. Specifically, he and his ex-girlfriend (the mother of his first child) were embroiled in a bitter dispute over their financial settlement. Although Luke is now very close to his four-year-old son, he still deeply resents the boy's mother—not only for deciding unilaterally to have a child, but also for taking advantage of the situation financially. In addition to child support, he pays her a monthly sum and complains that "for all practical purposes I'm paying alimony, even though I was never married to her." With all of this only recently behind him, Luke felt

the need to investigate prenuptial agreements before marrying Sally
a year and a half ago.

> *Sally and I spent a fair amount of time preparing for the
> prenuptial agreement, but ultimately decided it wasn't necessary.
> I learned that what's yours before the marriage is still yours—
> whether or not you sign an agreement. The law is very clear on
> that point. I had to be certain about it, though, because I'm
> forty-six years old and I came into this relationship with a lot
> of baggage, part of which is monetary. I've been successful in my
> profession for a long time, so I have quite a bit of equity. I
> wanted to make sure that if the marriage didn't work out after
> just a year or so, I wouldn't lose all that.*

Luke's concerns weren't solely financial. His prior relationship
undermined his trust in women to the point that even though he's
very much in love with his wife, Sally, he admits having had fears that
she might "change on him overnight" and take advantage of him
financially. Should that very unlikely possibility occur, resulting in
dissolution of their marriage, Luke sought reassurance that he was
financially protected. More important, he needed confirmation of the
loyalty between him and his wife. Sally's willingness to explore the
topic of a prenuptial agreement promoted the trust between them that
Luke previously lacked.

> *My whole feeling about marriage is: a woman has really "got
> you." They've got you at a definite financial disadvantage be-
> cause of the commitment you make. My fear was that once I got
> into the thick of it, Sally might become a different person and
> we'd both want out.*
>
> *Now that we've been married awhile, I've learned to trust
> her, and she has earned my trust. So even if it doesn't work out,
> I know what we have together will have been worth the time,
> effort, and finances.*

The property law in effect in Luke's state stipulates that what he
owned coming into the marriage remains in individual ownership
unless he chooses to mingle it with property belonging to his wife.[4]

So, in the end, with this legal clarification, he felt protected enough not to require a premarital agreement.

But Maxine did. A successful stockbroker who owned her own condo and maintained her own investments prior to marriage, she was strongly in favor of drawing up a premarital agreement. So was her husband, Hugh, who had been married and divorced twice before and, along with Maxine, faced the possibility of divorce pragmatically. Maxine explains:

> *Obviously, when you're in your forties, you have more property to protect than when you're twenty. Hugh had quite a struggle in his second divorce, and doesn't want to go through that again. This way it's all there in black and white, and there's nothing to fight over. It's also good if, God forbid, one person dies, because apparently a will doesn't divide up everything the way this would.*

A prenuptial agreement is tailored to the parties' specific needs and desires and, in that sense, can specify certain things that a will might not. But a personal will is still necessary. Unlike a standard prenuptial agreement, a will stipulates who will be the executor of the estate, whether he or she will serve without bond, what happens in the event the will is contested, and other important issues.

Additional financial concerns also led late marriers to consider premarital agreements. Responsibility for a spouse's debt was one. After working hard to establish their own financial security, some older first-time-marrieds were concerned about "marrying into" debt. And at their age they were more likely to marry someone with debts, since the older one gets, the more likely one is to accumulate them.

Helen is a case in point. She was worried that her husband's financial liabilities might jeopardize her own economic stability. She looked into drawing up an agreement that would protect what she owned independently, so that her hard-earned assets wouldn't be used to pay for her husband's premarital indebtedness:

> *Before we married, my husband told me that he had a lot of serious financial problems with the IRS. That upset me, so I immediately spoke with an attorney before the wedding. He told*

me that as long as I kept things in my own name, my property was safe. It had taken me years to acquire my own house and an IRA. I didn't want my husband's creditors to take my only security away from me. Once I knew that nothing of mine could be touched, I calmed down.

As a single woman, Helen had struggled for twenty-five years at modest-salaried nursing jobs to ensure her future well-being. It's understandable that she felt the need to consult a lawyer before possibly endangering what had taken her so long to establish.

Similar doubts concerning potential loss of assets led Rita's parents to counsel her to draw up a premarital agreement. Rita's trust fund was at stake, and her mom put pressure on her to get things in writing before the wedding. But, as Rita found out, legally divvying up "his" and "hers" can create adversaries out of loving spouses-to-be.

Rick and I share finances totally. All the money is mixed up—so now it's not really an issue. But it sure was before we got married! I came into the marriage with a considerable inheritance, so my parents convinced me I needed to draw up a prenuptial agreement. Their feeling was, "You never can tell." I went along with it, but it almost prevented our getting married.

Suddenly, Rick and I were between these two armed camps, each side declaring the assets of the other. Rick didn't have anything—except his collection of bootleg records and cassettes! I was an ignoramus about the whole thing. I should have turned to my parents and both lawyers and simply said, "Stop! This is ridiculous!" But I assumed they knew what they were doing, so we went along with them and got the agreement. Luckily, Rick and I trusted each other enough so that we didn't let the lawyers' hostility put a damper on our relationship.

Then there were those late marriers who had *very* negative feelings about premarital agreements. They believed firmly that unless they trusted their spouses to be fair and equitable in financial matters, their marriages wouldn't stand much of a chance. Since the existence of a prenuptial legal document signified, for them, a lack of mutual trust between husband and wife, they looked upon it with disdain, seeing it as undermining the economic unity implicit in the marriage vow that states "for richer, for poorer."

Both Vicki and Ray were vehemently opposed to premarital agreements. A physician with a flourishing practice, Vicki came into her marriage with a higher income and more inherited money than her husband Oliver, an insurance investigator. Yet she strongly condemned the notion of a prenuptial agreement as detrimental to marriage:

> We have never said, "This is my money," or "This is yours." I have more money than Oliver does, and I think he's more careful about it than I might be—out of some sense of honor, I guess. He's not out to get my money, and I'm not possessive about it, so we have no reason for one of those agreements. It would feel as if we were uncommitted.

Ray also emphasized that he and his wife based their economic relationship on a sense of honor. Even if they were to break up, Ray believed he and Brenda would act in good faith as far as dividing up assets.

> Brenda and I once talked about what would happen if we didn't stay together. She just flatly said, "I know what I came into this relationship with, and I'd take it with me. I'd expect you to do the same." I know it gets stickier than that, but neither of us can understand how people can get so entangled and ugly like the Trumps—when they came together so lovingly. I would just say, "This is yours, and this is mine." I think we'd both be fair with each other.

Those couples who opposed prenuptial agreements were usually either convinced they'd be able to work out any differences that might lead to divorce in the first place, or certain that their spouses would be fair, even if the marriage were to fail. A number of late marriers, however, felt that their unique life circumstances warranted legal assurances that a divorce wouldn't result in personal financial loss. Premarital agreements gave them the peace of mind to begin married life without feeling that they might be jeopardizing what they'd worked so long to earn.

FINALLY GETTING SERIOUS ABOUT WORK AND MONEY

For some first-marrieds over forty, delaying marriage meant forgoing the trappings of middle-class life—as well as some of the pressures. Without a spouse or children, some found no reason to "settle down" and took advantage of their single status to travel, experiment with a succession of career choices, and live more simply than others their same age. Rather than getting bogged down with house payments, IRAs, and life insurance, they rented their living space, got by on less income, and felt unencumbered. There was no need for them to consult with anyone else on how to spend their money. But marriage has a way of changing one's lifestyle and priorities. Chris discovered this when he and his wife decided to buy a house:

> *I'm absolutely freaked out about our new house. The mortgage payments will be six times what I pay in rent. Kelly doesn't seem to worry about where the money will come from, and maintains this wonderful belief that things will work out—while I'm scared to death I'll end up in debtor's prison! My fear is that the financial pressure could mess up our marriage by creating so much stress we won't be able to enjoy each other. What's scary is that I always had the freedom not to work if I didn't want to. That's the toughest thing—the idea of giving up that freedom.*

Chris's fears were threefold: that he might not be able to earn enough money, that the pressure to earn the money might place too much stress on his relationship with Kelly, and that he might lose his cherished sense of personal freedom. Some may feel Chris is simply not accepting his adult responsibilities in a mature way. But as for his purely economic concerns, the fact is that financial pressures *have* sharply increased for most lower- and middle-income families. Chris's transition to a more settled, upscale lifestyle is certain to require continued emotional and financial adjustment as buying into the American dream of home ownership becomes increasingly forbidding. In 1973 the average thirty-year-old man could meet the mortgage payments on a median-priced home with about a fifth of his income. By 1986 the same home took twice as much of his income.[5]

Granted, Chris's wife also earns a decent salary, but they both still feel the strain. The slow growth of our economy in recent years has meant that most of us, Chris and Kelly included, can't necessarily assume our income will steadily increase.

But Chris's concerns go beyond spiraling inflation and mortgage payments. Having built his life on the principles of spontaneity and experimentation, he's now reached a juncture where his personal freedom is on the line. For the moment his work is going well, and he and Kelly are meeting their payments. Chris is hoping that taking on considerable financial responsibilities, having a great relationship with his wife, and holding on to a freewheeling spirit won't necessarily prove to be mutually exclusive.

If Chris's fear of losing his freedom is simply one of the trade-offs of marriage, the positive side of relinquishing an unhampered lifestyle is that one begins focusing on a chosen career. Certain late marriers told us that they felt "at loose ends" until they married and settled down. The emotional security provided by marriage enabled them to "get their act together." And as a rite of passage into the "adult" world, marriage paved the way for these late-blooming spouses to finally flower. Glen is a case in point. He didn't begin training for his career as a software designer until his mid-thirties; before then he had no idea what he wanted to do with his life. "It took me a real long time to get a sense of who I was in the world," he said, and it's only recently that he's begun to come into his own in his profession. Glen and other late marriers attested to the fact that their careers benefited from the support they felt from their spouses; having a partner with whom to share work-related problems and triumphs was a boon to people accustomed to slugging it out on their own. Mates also served as motivation to surpass previous accomplishments. Being part of a couple, first-marrieds over forty were energized by the thought that they were now working for the good of another person as well as themselves.

Forty-two and married two years, Henry affirmed the positive influence of marriage and family on his career:

My career perspective has changed a lot in a couple of respects. For one, Shawna has looked after me being successful. She pushed me to finish my work for advanced training in my field.

*And when we found out she was pregnant, she was the one who
said, "You know, the finances are going to require that you get
additional work." So I did that, and I've never worked so hard
in my life, nor have I been as prosperous.*

First-time marrieds over forty who considered themselves "late
bloomers" told us that marriage served as a catalyst for career growth
and stability. With personal lives on a steadier course, vocational
pursuits became more focused. In Cheryl's case, the economic consequences were pronounced:

*My husband and I became financially self-supporting only in
the context of marriage. Before that, we were thirty-five-year-old
babies. Neither of us had ever owned a car or had enough money
to take a vacation. Before we got married, we lived in a one-
bedroom apartment which neither of us could pay for by ourselves with our unemployment checks!*

*It was marriage that made it possible for me to make
money. Having a permanent relationship is a developmental
stage, and I couldn't do anything else until I had that. Once I
finally had a partner, I moved on to other things—taking care
of myself, separating from my dad, switching to a money-
making career, being successful. All that stuff was linked
together.*

For Cheryl, marriage represented a rite of passage that enabled
her to go on to the next stage of her life. She got serious about
supporting herself, rather than continuing to bank on artistic pursuits
that were unlikely to yield any real income. After years of attempting
to eke out a living selling her photographs at art fairs and small
galleries, she set up shop as a children's portrait photographer
and started earning serious money. Ironically, she became more
self-sufficient once she had someone with whom to share financial
responsibility.

Several women in our study found that they clearly directed
their energies toward achieving professional goals *only after* marrying.
With worries about meeting the right guy behind them, their work-
related efforts became more concentrated. Jackie is a perfect example:

I would certainly still be doing my work if I wasn't married, but I expect my work to get better for not having to worry about relationships with men anymore. Being on the same course with my husband, I feel stronger, more centered—and my work improves as a result.

Late marriers who were less achievement-oriented prior to marriage gave two distinct reasons for their premarital lack of career focus: they either wanted to enjoy a freer lifestyle or they felt too "unsettled" or "uncentered" without a mate. Both men and women credited marriage with motivating them finally to get serious about their financial and professional goals.

TO SUPPORT MYSELF OR TO BE SUPPORTED— THAT IS THE QUESTION

Gone are the days when gender automatically determined whether we'd work outside the home and, if we did, how much money we'd make. In 1988, according to the Bureau of Labor Statistics, 64 percent of all married women worked, and 65 percent of all mothers with children under eighteen brought home a paycheck. This is in contrast to 1960, when only 30.4 percent of mothers had paying jobs.[6] Women who work do so out of necessity, desire for fulfillment, or both. Although, on the average, women still earn only sixty-five cents to every dollar a man earns,[7] 12 percent of *married* women earn more than their husbands.[8]

But the emotional reality behind all the statistics is that many women still harbor the desire to be taken care of financially. We often find ourselves straddling the line between traditional and feminist values because we were part of a generation that grew up with one set of expectations and matured with another. Most of our families were structured along the conventional roles of male breadwinner and female homemaker, and so, as young girls, we expected to follow our mothers' lead. But as we grew into young adults, career expectations changed, opportunities opened up, and women had choices to make. Then, when the economy slowed down in the late seventies, choices narrowed and most women couldn't afford *not* to work. Still, the radical cultural changes of the sixties and seventies left some women feeling one way and acting another. Late-marrying women who stayed single for the first twenty-some years of adulthood got used to fending for themselves. Yet several of them revealed that their long-standing independence clashed with old notions about wives being supported.

Tess, a self-declared feminist, was frank about her hidden wish to be taken care of. Although she makes about $15,000 more a year than her husband, Mel, a recent business venture left her broke. Suddenly the issue of being supported by a husband began to surface:

> *When we first got married, I used to joke with Mel and say, "Ha, ha, now that you're my husband I can retire and eat bonbons and watch daytime soaps!" Then I realized there was a part of me that really wanted Mel to support me.*
>
> *Unconsciously, I had bought into the "marriage myth" that your husband should provide for you. But Mel was having a hard time getting work himself, and I had to come right up against feeling that he was less of a husband because he had less earning power than I did.*
>
> *Ultimately, I concluded that providing for me is not Mel's job. I have to deal with my own financial security. I know that there've been times in my life when I've taken care of friends and lovers financially. And when they didn't give me back what I felt I had given, I felt used and unappreciated. So how could I expect Mel to do that for me? Supporting me isn't his obligation.*

Although the fantasy of being taken care of is sweet, women who value their accomplishments and independence prefer not to turn back the clock. For most of us, remembering the days when women had no choice but to be supported conjures up the restricting reality of living in a man's shadow.

Helen's scenario was the reverse of Tess's. All her life she thought she *wanted* a man to support her. Once the opportunity presented itself, however, she discovered she was actually a closet feminist. When her husband suggested she give up her job as a registered nurse once his business became more stable, Helen realized that to do so would mean giving up her sense of self-worth and identity:

I enjoy my work, and I'm good at it. I think it's important to me to have income of my own and a job of my own. Without it, Dan would tend to wrap me up like a fig leaf. He'd like me always to be available—to have lunch with him, talk to him about his business problems, go to meetings with him—and that would make me feel like a very important part of his life. I'd probably like it to a certain extent. But at some point I think I would get the feeling that I didn't have any identity of my own.

Balancing old conventions against new realities, women in their forties and fifties have had to profoundly alter their expectations concerning the role of "wife." In light of the divergent values they grew up with, the ambivalence voiced by Tess, Helen, and others is understandable. Their ultimate commitment to both shared financial responsibility and personal identity is no small testimony to how far we've all come in the last two decades.

There was another group of women in our sample who also came up against the dilemma of being supported versus supporting themselves. They were those who had given up full-time careers for full-time parenthood and, for the first time in their financially independent lives, were economically dependent upon a man. Interestingly, learning how to be financially *dependent* became just as much of a challenge for these women as struggling to be financially *independent* is for middle-aged married or divorced women who have never supported themselves.

Late-marrying women who chose to stay home and raise children planned to go back to work at some point. But by temporarily giving over the breadwinner role to their husbands, their status as full-fledged financial partners was called into question—not by their husbands, but by their own inner voices.

Nancy couldn't help hearing her voice loud and clear. Although it was her decision to take a break from her busy accounting firm to stay home with her baby, losing her own income was one of the most difficult transitions she ever had to make. Having her husband, Dennis, pay all the bills made her feel "strange and awkward," and she assumed she needed to be much more frugal since it was now Dennis's money she was spending. She talked to him about her reticence to spend money, and he simply replied that it was *her* problem. The money was there for her to use when she wanted to. But Nancy still couldn't help feeling guilty about buying anything but necessities—expensive shoes, for example.

Nancy's upbringing accounts for some of her attitudes. During the Depression, her father, who was the oldest son in a large Irish family, wound up supporting them all. He counseled his own children to get a profession—something to "fall back on"—and warned his daughters never to depend on a husband. He had seen too many examples of men "running out" on their wives to want that for his girls. So, for Nancy, issues of financial dependence are associated with vulnerability and trust:

> *I've wrestled with this question about being dependent on my husband for a long time. It finally occurred to me that it's an important emotional experiment for me. You need a certain level of trust to have someone support you. I was always taught not to trust anyone but myself.*

Nancy's feeling that somehow she wasn't entitled to spend her husband's money was initially shared by fellow late marrier Alice. Married eighteen years, Alice has two teenaged children. She completed her Ph.D. sixteen years ago, when her first child was an infant, but subsequently put her career on hold. At that time she felt she had many years of professional fulfillment behind her, and wanted to focus her attention on the children she had waited until she was over forty years old to have. Recently, Alice went back to work—out of financial necessity—but she recalls what it was like when she first traded in a paid career for an unpaid one:

> *When I first got married, and [became] pregnant soon thereafter, adjusting to financial dependence on my husband was very difficult. It was a traumatic experience for me to write a check on a joint checking account! And although we never spoke in*

*terms of "my own money" or "your own money," the bottom
line was* I was not paying my own bills.

It's common for some spouses to feel that whichever partner is
making more money has the right to control it. But enlightened
couples know that it's unfair for wage-earners to pull rank on child-
rearers. The contribution a full-time parent makes to his or her family
is hard to compute in hourly wages (although activist homemaker
groups have rightly attempted to do so in order to gain political and
economic rights). But however much we value full-time homemaking
and parenting, that value is usually undercut by the importance our
culture places on money: earning power is synonymous with self-
esteem and personal power.

Luckily, neither Nancy's husband nor Alice's bought into that
ideology. Both continued to treat their wives as equal financial partners even when they temporarily exchanged professional careers for
full-time parenting. And when both partners feel they have equal
control over how money is spent, they tend to have a more harmonious relationship. Although Nancy and Alice initially had difficulty
adjusting to the loss of their own separate incomes, they continue to
share equally with their husbands in managing their financial affairs.
The key to the success of their marriages is that the money is not used
as a wedge to undermine the spirit of marriage, which declares, "We
are working in a *joint* enterprise, a partnership that transcends dollars
and cents."

TWO CAN LIVE BETTER THAN ONE!

If Madison Avenue copywriters had their way, they'd have us believe
we live in a slick, yuppie world where our only care is which new
adult toy to buy next. Such cultural propaganda also accounts for the
popular belief that single people have fewer financial concerns than
married ones. Without spouse or family to worry about, it's assumed
that late marriers have accumulated a comfortable sum and are coast-
ing on easy street when they find a mate. That may be true for some,
but life isn't quite that carefree for most. In many cases, and especially

in urban environments, it takes two hefty incomes to live the good life—or just a middle-class one. Thus, many late-marrying men and women were relieved that they were finally sharing financial burdens with a partner.

Ivan is a cabinetmaker who has always believed that men and women should have equal financial opportunities *and* responsibilities. Some of the women he dated over the years felt otherwise and, according to Ivan, were specifically looking for wealthy men to support them. Ivan obviously didn't fit the bill. But seven years ago, at the age of fifty-four, he met and fell in love with Emily, a physical therapist with a child from a previous marriage. They married four years later. Ivan told us about his financial arrangements with Emily, who earns slightly less than he does.

> *I always wanted someone who would contribute financially. Pulling equally on the wagon is important to me. I'm not interested in someone who is just an adornment. Even if, hypothetically, my wife made ten percent of what I did, it wouldn't matter as long as she contributed according to her ability.*

When Ivan and Emily first started living together, they came up with an equitable plan. Since the house is in his name, and since he earns more, Ivan makes the house payments and Emily pays for the food and other expenses. As for Ivan's stepdaughter:

> *Emily gets child support, so she takes care of Veronica's expenses. Sometimes I'll pay for certain things for Veronica—like her soccer camp—and that's fine with me. When we go on vacations, we split it, and because I make a bit more money, I'll chip in more.*

Ivan's belief in a kind of "domestic socialism"—each contributing according to his or her ability—runs counter to certain conventional values propagated by our culture. Those values mandate that a man must be the financial head of the household. Although it's now necessary for most wives to work, many middle-aged husbands who grew up with these values are threatened by having to share the breadwinner role. They feel diminished in their identities when their wives work, and while they may acknowledge the need for the extra income, they still find it hard to admit that their wife's work is as important as their own.

Late-marrying men as a group don't feel this way. Remaining single for so long has given them less-traditional attitudes toward sex roles. Prolonged single status means that they come in contact with more independent women and reach middle age having experienced equality between the sexes firsthand. Also, having been going it alone for the first twenty years of their adult lives, they especially appreciate the relief a second paycheck affords them.

Men who marry for the first time after age forty seem to have more in common with younger husbands than with middle-aged ones who have twenty years of marriage under their belts. Sharing financial responsibilities with a wife whose job may be every bit as lucrative as their own is taken for granted by late-marrying men. But that's not to say they don't appreciate their wives' joint contribution to the household. Eric is grateful that his wife can meet him halfway with the expenses. Their combined incomes make for a quality of life neither could afford on their own:

I pay the mortgage, and she pays for the food and other expenses. It sort of balances out. She's got her job, and I have mine. Sometimes she makes more money than I do, sometimes I make more than she does. But we kid about it, and it's not an issue. She pays her own way, and I pay my own way, and together we have a kind of synergy. Certainly, two incomes have given us a bit more horsepower.

Joining forces in midlife with spouses who can hold their own financially has meant improved living conditions for quite a few mature marriers. In Henry's case, the transformation from single to spouse brought enormous economic benefits. A draftsman with a modest income, he never thought he'd be able to save enough to become a homeowner.

Marriage has changed everything. I never imagined us being this well off financially. Before we got married, Shawna and I were both renting. One of the first things we did once we were

*married was borrow money to buy a condo, and now we own
it, as well as some other property. With each of these things, we
thought we couldn't afford it, that we'd be in debt forever. But
we've never been so rich in all our lives. Part of it, I'm sure, was
the joint-venture part of it. Shawna makes pretty good money
as a therapist and might have been able to pull together a lot of
things on her own. But before I got married I had somewhat
resigned myself to a life of tasteful poverty.*

Some experts say a man's ego can become easily bruised when
his wife earns as much as he does, or more. Late-marrying men attest,
however, to the advantages of financial equality. They value the
crucial role their wives play in the economic well-being of their
families, and find that an equal financial partnership solidifies their
bond as a married couple. Mutual respect and a sense of teamwork
develop when both partners "pull equally on the wagon" by assuming
financial responsibility for their shared lives.

WE'RE NOT GETTING ANY YOUNGER—OR NECESSARILY ANY RICHER!

Every stage in our life brings specific financial concerns, from how
much allowance we feel we deserve, to financing a home, to providing
for our retirement. Most middle-aged, middle-class married couples
have dealt with housing needs and raising kids. They've most likely
set up college funds for their children and retirement accounts for
themselves. Those who marry for the first time in midlife, however,
have lived their lives according to a different timetable. Children may
enter the picture when parents are in their forties, and childcare
expenses, money for schools, and life-insurance payments have to be
faced for the first time. Buying a first home may also have been
postponed until marriage, and thus becomes a new responsibility.

Yet mature marriers share with others their age certain unavoidable realities: retirement is drawing nearer, peak earning years are on
the wane, and economic priorities have to be reassessed. However,
their unique circumstances create financial conflicts unknown to other
midlifers. Supporting a new family at age forty-plus—especially if

you've never planned for one—is one concern unique to late marriers. And taking on the responsibility for a family frequently commences at the same time aging parents also need assistance. Thus, quite a few midlife marriers are confronted with the multiple financial demands of young children, elderly parents, and their own impending retirement.

Fifty years old and married six years, Duncan faced just such a dilemma:

> *One of the reasons I married Annie was that I loved how openhearted she is, not just with me, but with other people. When her father became ill four years ago, she wanted us to pay for this very nice nursing home, so that he wouldn't have to suffer the indignities of most care facilities. I wanted to help him, but it meant diverting the limited amount we had just started putting away for our first kid's college and our retirement. I felt cheated, and resentful of this sick old man. Here I'd waited until my forties to get married and have babies, and I was faced with having to share our nest egg with another person. I know we're at an age when we sometimes have to parent our parents, but it just didn't seem fair.*

Often, older first-marrieds get the sense that they've gotten off to a late start on financial planning. Since their family life didn't begin until their forties, they frequently didn't start accumulating assets until then either. Again, their prolonged single life may have required less of them economically than a married one would have. So they find themselves having to catch up in their later years. That was the position Alice found herself in:

> *I went back to work last year full-time for the express purpose of making extra money. I'd been out of the job market since I had my two kids, but now that they're teenagers, we need to make sure they have enough for college. I'm fifty-eight, and Greg and I would love to retire soon, but we can't because we want to provide for our kids' education.*

There were other first-marrieds over forty for whom money was *not* a problem. They'd been earning healthy incomes, investing and saving throughout their single years, and in fact were grateful that children entered the picture later rather than sooner, because they were that much further along economically. But for those like Alice, for whom financial burdens seemed overwhelming, the richness of their lives still outweighed the economic hurdles of marrying late. Alice put it this way:

> *I was happy to devote my forties and fifties to my kids, since I'd spent my twenties and thirties doing lots of traveling, going to grad school, working, and meeting fascinating people. I may be paying a certain economic price now, but I've enjoyed every part of my life. So it's definitely been worth it.*

CHOOSING THE RELATIONSHIP OVER WORK

First-marrieds over forty agreed, nearly unanimously, that they put more emphasis on their relationships and families than on their work. This probably results from two interrelated factors, one relating to marrying late and one relating more broadly to middle age. Late marriers have experienced so many years without a permanent relationship that they tend to appreciate and value their newfound togetherness and intimacy once they marry. And since middle age is a time when people in general tend to involve themselves with the nurturing aspects of life, those who marry for the first time after forty are usually relationship-centered as opposed to work-centered. Although women in general are more likely than men to put their relationships before work, as men get older and more secure in their vocation, their desire for time with their partners increases.[9]

For late-marrying men and women, making marriage and family a priority is a welcome but often jarring transition. Prior to marriage they may have used work to fill the void of not having a mate or family. Or perhaps they were professionally "driven" in their twenties and thirties, only to find themselves wanting something more in midlife. Tess revealed how her number-one commitment to her architectural career gave way to a change in priorities:

> *Both my husband and I had to learn to make our relationship at least as important as our work. I married [a man who was]*

just as much of a workaholic as I am, and so, for both of us, our careers had always taken precedence. But I want this relationship to be different than other ones I've had. I want it to be important. Otherwise, why did we do it? Why did we get married?

Late marriers are especially dedicated to their marriages and families. Even those who spent their twenties and thirties crazed with ambition and drive find that in their forties what's closer to home takes on a meaning as great as, or greater than, the far-reaching dreams and schemes of career life. Ray's professional outlook has changed drastically since the creation of his new family. Even the glitz and excitement of the music business pales in comparison to the satisfaction he derives from being with his wife and two young sons:

I don't have nearly the ambition I had when I was twenty, and it's not because I'm tired. It's because it doesn't mean the same thing to me anymore. Now I really like being at home with the kids. I was recently away on business for a week, and coming back on the plane I was looking through some photos of the family playing together. The business trip just evaporated— even though I've got a lot of money on the line up there. I couldn't wait to get home! My marriage and my kids have created a new priority for me. And the quality of this priority feels a lot deeper than the quality of any priority having to do with my career.

Middle age is a time when many of us begin turning from professional pursuits to interpersonal relationships for a sense of fulfillment. Ray, Tess, Ned (in chapter 5), and others reflected on that transition and found themselves looking forward to the unique rewards of marriage and family life.

As for the professional and economic outlook for late marriers in general, we've seen that not everyone experiences the same pitfalls or gains. Some face burdensome financial conflicts, others receive windfall benefits. Certain late marriers are concerned with holding on to what they accumulated over the many years of being single adults, others consider themselves late bloomers who don't really get going economically until they marry. Some women continue to make as much as or more money than their husbands, while others take time out from the job market to have babies. A few look upon the new responsibilities of marriage and family as an infringement on their freedom, yet others credit their career success to the state of matrimony. With all their differences, however, most women and men who marry after forty agree with Ray that their relationships with their spouses and children have become the most valued part of their lives.

THE FULL NEST: FIRST-TIME PARENTS OVER FORTY

I have a friend who is in his early fifties and just had his third grandchild—his child-rearing days are long *gone! It's scary to think that I'm forty-six and we're about to have our first baby. From now on, I will essentially have* children forever.

—GLEN, age forty-six, married one year,
planning to have a baby next year

I'm a big believer in brothers and sisters. So, if we're doing well enough financially and I'm healthy and strong enough, we'll try for two. I figure I'm forty-two now; if I get pregnant soon, I'd be forty-three when the baby's born. Then I could have another one when I'm forty-four. Otherwise, I'd consider adopting. It just depends on [whether] we're lucky enough to get pregnant soon.

—JACKIE, age forty-two, married two years,
trying to get pregnant

Ben and I never dreamed we'd have children. Thirty-four years ago it was unheard of for a forty-three-year-old woman to have her first baby. I hadn't

*been feeling very well and thought I was going through menopause. When
the doctor told me I was pregnant, I nearly fell off the table. "I don't think
it's possible!" I blurted out. And then I began to cry. I told the doctor I was
too old to have a baby. And he said, "God must not have thought so."*
　　　　　—EDNA, age seventy-seven, married thirty-seven years,
　　　　　mother of a thirty-three-year-old daughter

Most parents in their forties are at the stage when their children are
leaving home to begin college or lives of their own. Late marriers, on
the other hand, are years away from facing an "empty nest." They're
either just beginning their families or still deciding whether or not to
fill the nest at all. As we learned in chapter 5, having children is, for
many people, the essential motivation to marry. For them, marriage
means family. But for others, deciding to have children at age forty-
plus isn't as clear-cut.

Unlike younger marrieds, middle-aged couples must consider a
great many factors that are beyond their control. The two most
important of these are their biological ability to have children, and the
willingness of their spouses to have children together. A number of
women we interviewed, for example, married men who already had
children and didn't necessarily want any more. Some of these men had
had vasectomies, virtually eliminating the possibility of having biological children with their new wives. (Although vasectomies are
reversible, the reversal procedure involves risks.)

Then there are the risks related to having a baby after forty. First
of all, due to a significant decline in fertility, a woman's chances of
conceiving after forty are about half those of a woman thirty-five or
under. When women over forty do get pregnant, those bearing their
first babies are significantly more likely to experience complications
such as hypertension, diabetes, and kidney disease during pregnancy.
Miscarriages are also much more common, occurring nearly four
times as frequently in forty-plus pregnancies during the first trimester
as in younger women. And the incidence of chromosomal abnormali-
ties escalates appreciably. A Down's syndrome baby is likely in one
out of every thirty-nine births to women past forty.[1]

Nevertheless, more women than ever are having their first children later in life. In 1987 the number of first babies born to women
forty and older was triple that reported seven years earlier.[2] And as

later-life pregnancies become even more prevalent, more attention is being given to innovative techniques for monitoring fetal complications and genetic defects. In addition, current reproductive technology is making it possible for infertile or postmenopausal women to bear children by employing "embryo donation," a method in which an egg is removed from a fertile woman, fertilized with sperm in the laboratory, and then transferred to the uterus of the infertile woman. As researchers perfect the ability to freeze unfertilized eggs, young women may someday be able to "bank" their own eggs until they're ready to start a family—perhaps after age forty.[3]

For those women in our sample who wanted their own biological children, there was a further consideration imposed by their age. Being forced to have children as soon as possible meant they didn't have the luxury that younger newlyweds do of spending exclusive time with their mates before starting a family. Late-marrying women and late-marrying men married to women over forty had to forgo the "honeymoon" phase of their marriage if they wanted to have children.

In contrast, several late-marrying men avoided both the reproductive risks of over-forty mothers-to-be *and* the pressure to commence parenthood immediately by marrying younger women. (We'll discuss the inherent inequities between late-marrying men and women later in this chapter.)

And then there were those men and women who simply felt the appropriate time to have children had passed. They had wanted a family when they were in their twenties or thirties, but now felt otherwise. They either didn't have the stamina to begin raising children or else wanted to enjoy the freedom to travel and live unencumbered at this stage in their lives.

At the same time that each of these factors represented narrowing parenting options, late marriers also found that new choices opened up. Those who married spouses who already had children became stepparents with ready-made families to love and nurture. Others who feared the biological risks of childbearing, or who had been unable to have a biological child, either adopted or were considering it. And finally, fifteen of the forty people we sampled—nine men and six women—had their own biological children after the age of forty.

In this chapter we'll consider the process that midlife marriers go through before deciding whether or not to have children, and learn from the experiences of those who became first-time parents and stepparents after forty. We'll see how the family structure changes when parenthood begins at middle age, and we'll hear from the "veterans" in our sample—those women and men now in their late fifties, sixties, and seventies who are parents of teenagers and young adults.

DECIDING TO HAVE A BABY

A generation ago, few women waited past thirty to have their first children. Although women have always been biologically capable of bearing children until menopause, most were afraid of the risks. But reproductive technology and cultural mores have changed. Middle-aged women now feel medically secure and socially more comfortable about delayed motherhood. Still, there are significant personal considerations that go beyond biology or social expectations. When first marriage is delayed beyond forty, the decision whether or not to have a child takes on weighty proportions. The longer we've lived, the more complex our lives have become, and making room for baby is often a pressing and confounding dilemma.

Deciding to have a child is never a straightforward matter. As most of our mothers and grandmothers have advised us, "There's never a right time to have a baby." But by the time we've reached forty, our life history tends to complicate our existence to a greater extent than it would a twenty-five-year-old's. Thus, determining whether or not to have a baby may not be as simple a matter as younger couples might find it. Simply adjusting to marriage after twenty-some years of singlehood is a significant enough emotional task. Additionally, late-marrying women don't have much time left to make one of the most important decisions of their life.

Faith is a case in point. At forty-one years old, she has been married only a year. Eight weeks after she met her husband, Mark, she became pregnant. Mark wanted the child, but Faith felt she was just getting to know him and that a baby would bring them together for the wrong reasons. Although she thought she might want children someday, she wanted to marry Mark for Mark—not because she had to. So Faith decided to terminate the pregnancy, and Mark was ultimately supportive of her decision to have an abortion.

Twenty years of adult life preceded Faith and Mark's new marriage. What went on during those years complicated their decision whether or not to have a baby right away. Mark already had two children from a previous marriage: a twenty-year-old daughter, and a son who died nine years ago in an automobile accident. Faith believes that part of Mark's desire to have a baby stems from the loss of his son. She senses that his wish to bring a new life into the world is partly an attempt to ease some of his pain.

But Faith has her own personal history to contend with. She has only recently made the transition from a lesbian lifestyle to a heterosexual marriage. For ten years she confined her friendships and love affairs to women, and only discovered her attraction for men a few years before she met Mark. The changes she's made just to get married in the first place have been profound. Now, a year into her marriage, she's adjusting to her new life as a heterosexual woman, a wife, and a stepmother. Still reeling from all these adjustments, Faith is being pressed biologically to make a decision that will further alter her life:

> For a long time I didn't know how to have a healthy relationship with a man. I felt that men trivialized my feelings, and I repeatedly got hurt. Getting involved with women provided the acceptance and sense of belonging I needed at the time.
>
> I finally feel comfortable with a man; Mark is someone I can work things through with, someone who totally accepts me. But I need to feel more stable in our relationship before deciding to have a child. Not only has it been an adjustment for me, learning to do things as a couple, but there have also been difficulties with Mark's twenty-year-old daughter, my stepdaughter. Six weeks before Mark and I got married, she wanted to move in with us! The timing couldn't have been worse. Mark has a hard time setting limits, so it was a struggle saying no to her. The experience was traumatic for me, so while I'm contemplating having our own child, I worry that becoming a mother might be one change too many right now.

The issues Faith is attempting to resolve are not simple ones. She's concerned that her relationship with Mark is too new to withstand the upheaval a baby would create. She questions her ability to deal with the demands of an infant while simultaneously learning to be a stepmother to Mark's daughter, a troubled young adult. And, finally, she's worried that adjusting to so many new roles might ultimately prove overwhelming. None of these issues are necessarily age-related. But the fact that Faith has only a year or so in which to make her decision is.

Every prospective parent has doubts, but late-marrying would-be parents have unique uncertainties: If I'm only able to have one child, will he or she suffer in not having siblings? Will I have enough energy ten years down the line when my baby becomes a Little Leaguer, has slumber parties, is ready for rugged camping trips? Will I *ever* have time with my spouse, time to travel, time to myself? How will my child adapt to elderly parents at a time in his life when he's barely an adult? The overriding question becomes, "Is now the right time to have a baby?" Some of the women who answered no would definitely have answered yes earlier in their lives. But circumstances had passed them by; their time and fertility had run out. When Maxine married at forty-seven, bearing children was no longer an issue, but there were some residual regrets:

> *My husband had a vasectomy years ago. But even if he hadn't, I don't think I'd want to have kids at this point in my life. I would have enjoyed having them when I was younger, and I think I would have been a good mother. But at this stage it's not a priority. A couple of my friends had children in their forties, and when I look at their lives, it's not what I'd want now. Hugh and I like the freedom to take off whenever we want and travel. Plus, his kids are grown now, so what does he need it for?*

Like Maxine, Diana also values the freedom she and her new husband are afforded as a result of not having had children together. (He has two from a previous marriage, who live with their mother.) She acknowledges their unencumbered lifestyle as the "up side" of an otherwise sad reality: time made the parenting decision for her. If she'd had the opportunity earlier, she would have welcomed mother-hood. But for her, midlife isn't the appropriate time to start a family:

> *At thirty-six I would have had a child, but now, at forty-three, I just don't think I'm ready to begin such a huge commitment. Fifteen years from now I'd still be driving car pools! And I don't think my patience is what it once was. I love to play with my sister-in-law's twin babies, but I also love it when they go home.*
>
> *There are some things that you do at a particular time in your life. If you don't do them then, you can't make them happen later on. Going to Europe as a hippie and crashing in youth hostels was great. But if I tried to do that now, I'd be a fool. Having babies was one passage I missed, and I'll have to live with that fact. I also know that I got to experience certain things others missed.*

There was a certain sadness in both Maxine and Diana, which wasn't communicated verbally. They've each had to make peace with the fact that they'll never have their own children. Something they always expected to be present in their lives will be missing, and there is a poignancy in that recognition. And yet they're both stepmoth-ers—in fact, Maxine is a stepgrandmother! And filling those roles serves as a kind of substitute for both of them.

Kate's role as a stepmother figures prominently in her ultimate decision not to have children of her own. When she first got married nine years ago, she moved into her husband's house and became instant live-in stepmom to his three young sons—aged nine, ten, and twelve. She was forty-two then, and considering having a baby of her own:

> *Joel had had a vasectomy, but, bless his heart, he said that if I wanted to get artificial insemination, we could raise the child as our own. I would have loved to raise a baby; in fact, when I was younger I fantasized about having a dozen. I would have settled for six if I'd gotten married earlier. But a baby cries a lot, demands a lot of attention. Most of all, I didn't want to jeopardize the relationship with these three little boys. The five*

of us together had such a good family life already—why put
that happiness at risk?

If the baby would have been the boys' real brother, I don't
think it would have been such a serious problem. But for the
child not to be related would have placed too great a strain on
the family. It would have been too hard for the boys to adjust.
Children aren't always as accepting as adults, and it might have
ended up being a case of three against one.

Kate's ultimate decision was based not only on how a new baby
would affect her three stepsons but on the fact that Joel's vasectomy
meant they couldn't have their own biological child. Younger women
might also face a similar predicament, but marrying later in life
increases a woman's chances of pairing up with a man who has
already completed his babymaking. Maxine, Diana, and Kate all had
to accept the fact that circumstances and timing meant they couldn't
have children of their own.

We all have to acknowledge life's givens. And often when we
do, life offers us something else in return. Kate and Diana have
wonderful relationships with their stepchildren, which provide them
both with an opportunity to "mother." We'll learn more about late
marriers' experience of being stepparents later on in this chapter.

"IT'S A MAN'S WORLD"

I remember complaining to my ninety-year-old grandmother that it wasn't
fair men didn't have to worry about their biological clocks. Like Charlie
Chaplin and others, they could father kids forever. She just looked at me in
her all-knowing way over the tops of her glasses and said, "Honey, it's a
man's world."

—LILLY

Theoretically, men do have time on their side when it comes to
fathering a child biologically. Even though they may worry about
having enough stamina to keep up with a young child, at least age
doesn't seriously hamper their chances of producing one. Of course,
it all depends on how old their mates are.

Of the twenty men we interviewed, only six were married to women the same age as themselves or slightly older. Fourteen were married to younger women. This is in keeping with our culture, in which men generally marry women younger than themselves.

Late-marrying men who married younger women often made it clear that they had specifically sought women who had a number of fertile years on this side of menopause: the younger the wife, the less pressure to get on with the familial agenda. Robert, forty-seven, is married to Penny, twenty-six, and is not the least bit worried about age or time. They plan to have three kids, and Robert smiled radiantly as he predicted, "I'm going to be young at seventy-five or eighty, so I'm not concerned about my age. After all, didn't General McArthur have his first child at fifty-seven?"

When men want children, some resort to "age screening." Late-marrying women couldn't help resenting being written off simply on the basis of their age. As with Faith, being told by a prospective partner that they were too old to be mothers was a painful experience, but one they faced realistically. Faith told us she had once dated a very nice man for about two weeks and had looked forward to seeing more of him. Then one day he called her up and told her point-blank that he didn't want to continue seeing her because of her age:

> *His calculations went like this: He was forty-two and I was thirty-eight. He wouldn't be finishing up his Ph.D. for a couple of years yet, and then wanted to become more established in his new career before getting married and starting a family. By the time he'd be ready for kids, I'd be too old to have them. Hearing that cold reality was upsetting, but I appreciated his honesty. Later I developed the attitude, "I am me—take it or leave it."*

Late-marrying men who wanted to postpone having children for a few years all had younger wives. Unlike late-marrying women, they had the luxury of time alone with their mates before taking on the demands of child-rearing. They planned to delay fatherhood until their new marriages were on solid ground. And since their younger wives weren't yet up against the biological clock, they could take their time getting to know each other, enjoying life as a couple, and working out the kinks.

Andy brought up an additional reason to postpone parenthood. Neither he nor his wife had any experience being responsible for anyone but themselves. They'd each led independent lives and had been primarily concerned with their respective careers. They definitely had no expertise when it came to the caretaking role. So Andy appreciated his ability to put off parenthood until he and Carol had the chance to practice their "parenting" skills on a less vulnerable creature than a baby:

> We wanted to get a puppy before we had a baby, and figured it would be good training for us. Carol and I experienced a bit of role reversal since I'd be home working and training the puppy, and she'd be off at the office. The puppy would act up all day, and then, when Carol got home, he'd be this angelic little dog. She couldn't understand why I was so frazzled. But we did get through the dry run with the puppy, so we're finally at the stage where we might possibly be ready to have kids.

Late-marrying women and late-marrying men married to women around forty or older can't afford to be as relaxed about timing as Andy or Robert. Owing to increased risks for biological mothers over forty—and the expense of high-tech procedures— many felt they had to have a baby much sooner than they would have liked. They regretted not having four or five years to spend alone with their spouses, learning about each other as husband and wife. For them, parenthood was a now-or-never proposition.

"MY DADDY HAS WHITE HAIR"

The rewards and hardships of becoming a parent are present from day one. Infants wreak havoc upon their parents' well-ordered lives, demanding attention around the clock. But for most new mothers and fathers, that's a small price to pay for cradling a newborn in their arms and glimpsing their first smiles. Toddlers and young children continue to turn the house upside down, run their moms and dads ragged, require discipline, and need answers to endless questions. But what could be more wonderful than spending Saturday at the zoo with your three-year-old, witnessing her first friendships with other children, hearing him sing to himself in the mornings?

Most parents appreciate the priceless gifts their children give them, just as they also acknowledge the struggles along the way. But what of the unique pressures and benefits of becoming a parent after forty? How do the experiences of middle-aged first-time parents differ from those of younger mothers and fathers? In this section we'll hear from those midlife marriers who presently have young children. Their feelings and insights should be validating to other late-marrying parents and helpful to those contemplating first-time parenthood in their forties.

As we learned in chapter 3, although Luke had never been married before, he has a son from a previous relationship and, for the past four years, has shared custody of that four-year-old child. However, when he married Sally and they had their own baby, Luke became a father on a daily basis. He was unprepared for how completely the infant monopolized their lives. Luke knows the sleepless nights will taper off in the near future, but at the moment his fatigue and the daily sacrifices are foremost in his mind:

> [Our] life as newlyweds has ceased to exist. Sally and I used to be able to drop everything at a moment's notice and go to San Francisco for the weekend. Or we could take off and go skiing for three days during the week. Not anymore! I know there's a light at the end of the tunnel—that the baby will become less dependent as he grows. He gives such joy to us, and that outweighs the circles under the eyes and the feeling that we're permanently grounded.

Being older and more established means Luke and Sally can afford a live-in housekeeper. And with professional seniority, Luke sets his own work hours, so he has more time to spend with his children than a younger father might. But he's also keenly aware of the handicaps older parents face:

> I used to think older parents were better because they're more mature, more together, more patient. They have the self-knowledge and the financial ability to provide a much more complete

home for a child, as opposed to some eighteen-year-old who doesn't have the awareness to handle a child. All that is true, but on the downside, my wife and I aren't eighteen anymore. The energy I expend with my four-and-a-half-year-old is incredible. I'm in excellent shape, and yet my older son is constantly on the go. "Let's run, Daddy! Let's play, Daddy! Hold me upside down, Daddy!" It's nonstop. I work very, very hard, so when I come home to my infant son's intense dependency, I have nothing left for Sally or myself!

The issues Luke raises concerning less energy versus more maturity are on the minds of other older parents as well as experts in the field of delayed parenting. Although there are certainly exceptions, it's generally true that most forty-something parents don't have the physical stamina of parents ten to twenty years their junior. Nor can fifty- or sixty-year-olds keep up with their older children as energetically as thirty- or forty-year-olds can. According to the sociologist Monica Morris, author of *Last Chance Children*, children of older parents complain that older moms and dads are less able to be physically active with their kids.

Most of our interviewees corroborated this shortcoming. Vicki, forty-five-year-old mother of a two-year-old and a four-year-old, confessed, "I went out to dinner and movies with a friend the other night, and at the end of the evening she asked me if I was depressed. It wasn't depression, it was fatigue! I'm really exhausted most of the time." Yet in the next breath she added, "But I don't mind, because my kids are worth it. In fact, I would love to have more."

Vicki's husband, Oliver, is fifty-two and even more concerned about declining physical vigor:

My son is two. When he's ten, I'll be sixty. Vicki's father was a robust, potentially athletic guy when he was my age. Not too much further down the line he got Lou Gehrig's disease. Even if I were the healthiest sixty-year-old guy in America, no one knows what will be. At this point, my kids have no idea what my being fifty-two means. I can still put them on my back, horse around with them, take them on a hike—and it's wonderful. But it's down the road that concerns me.

Several men in our sample who had yet to have children worried about their physical fitness as they looked ahead to fatherhood. Like many of us in these health-conscious times, they maintained healthy diets and exercise regimes, confident that they could stave off some of the effects of aging. Still, they wondered how they'd keep up with young children as they approached forty-five or fifty. But like Derek and his wife Jackie, both in their early forties and currently trying to have a child, they take comfort in the fact that they're not alone. "Almost everyone we know is an older parent," Derek remarked optimistically. "The men talk about balding and heart attacks in the same breath as Batman and Barbie. If they can handle it, so can we."

If younger parents have more endurance, first-marrieds over forty may have the edge when it comes to emotional maturity. Erik Erikson describes the "generativity" stage of adult development as the period when we concern ourselves with being intimate with others and guiding the next generation. While he doesn't specify the age at which these inclinations commence, what he does make clear is that before we get to the generativity stage, we must first form our own identities.[4] We need to know who we ourselves are before we can truly be intimate or giving with someone else.

Chances are a forty-year-old's sense of self is stronger than a twenty- or thirty-year-old's. And that secure identity significantly affects our role as parents. For one thing, we can more easily separate ourselves emotionally from our children because we're clear about where we end and our children begin. Thus, when we give guidance to them, we're not as likely to project our own needs or fears. And our priorities tend to clarify as we mature. We value the opportunity to nurture instead of being completely wrapped up in our own agendas. Having reached a level of success in our careers, we're more confident—and probably less anxious about forgoing an evening board meeting in favor of a preschool art show. More likely still, more-mature parents tend to value their child's art show over a board meeting. They *want* to participate in their child's growth at least as much as, if not more than, ego-building activities of their own.

The psychiatrists Steven A. Frankel and Myra J. Wise found that older mothers and fathers were more aware than younger parents of the finiteness of time, and therefore appreciated the creative and pleasurable aspects of parenthood. They felt less resentful about sacrificing career plans or social life. Older parents "valued the inner resources and sense of competence that come with age, . . . expressed enjoyment in parenting, . . . and were more able to integrate work commitments and family responsibilities."[5]

We also found that late-marrying parents seemed more willing than younger parents might to trade some of their freedom for parenting chores, or to forgo some degree of career involvement in order to become an integral part of their child's life. And they didn't regard those changes as sacrifices since they'd had ample time to enjoy their independence prior to marriage. Oliver explains:

At this point in my life I'm happy to stay home every night and play with the kids, read to them, give them their baths. I don't have much desire to go out and whoop and holler until late at night. I'm not pining away to be out there on the streets. I'm sure people who didn't get a chance to bounce around like I did would miss that. But I don't.

Duncan, father of three-year-old Christina, spoke of happily accepting the trade-offs inherent in being a parent:

I don't mind setting my own life aside for a while to be with my daughter. I love being a part of her world every day. My wife and I have our own small business, so we take turns watching Christina in the afternoons—and it's great! Our profits may be down a little at the end of the year, but this experience of participating in our daughter's life on a day-to-day basis won't come again. It's more than worth it.

Children enrich our lives, and being able to acknowledge that fact is a function of maturity. So is the willingness to balance one's own pursuits with giving time to a child. In that sense, first-marrieds over forty seem to be better prepared to handle parenthood. Not only are they more "ready" to parent in terms of self-awareness and psychological development, but they are more thankful for the opportunity. Many of those we interviewed had feared they might not marry in time to have kids. When you want children and marry in your twenties or thirties, you assume they'll be part of the package.

Late marriers, who've spent twenty-odd years without a mate, haven't banked on that assumption. So when they finally become moms or dads at the age of forty-plus, they tend to be that much more involved with their children, that much more patient, and that much more grateful for the parenting experience. Vicki told us:

I wanted kids desperately and was so happy to have them! I'm grateful and humble, because I know how hard it is for some women just to get pregnant at my age. At twenty-one I may have felt that children were an imposition; at forty-five I feel gratitude.

A DIFFERENT KIND OF FAMILY

Although the rewards of delayed parenting seem to outweigh the burdens, it would be inaccurate to paint an idealized picture. Along with complaints that "energy is wasted on the young," over-forty parents spoke of additional drawbacks. Chief among them was the gnawing possibility that they might not live long enough to see their children into middle age. "If I'd had my children at twenty, I'd live to see more of their lives than I will now," one late-marrying mom remarked sadly. And Duncan told us there isn't a day that goes by that he doesn't wish for an extra twenty years:

Watching my daughter grow up is the most miraculous experience I've ever had. But if I live to be seventy-five, she'll still only be twenty-eight. Will she be married and have kids by then? Not if she takes after me or her mom. I may never meet her husband or get to see my grandchildren. I certainly don't regret the decision to have her, but I feel shortchanged that I won't get to see much of her future.

Not only is it more unlikely that late marriers will enjoy *becoming* grandparents, but they also face the more immediate possibility of their children being grandparentless. Even if their parents are alive, first-marrieds over forty wonder how much longer their children will know and be able to learn from such elderly grandparents. Although nowadays seventy-year-olds run 10K races, take adult education classes, and travel to India, even the fittest among them don't survive forever. Our interviewees often regretted that their parents were less able to do the kinds of things younger grandparents might. Vicki reflected:

> *My grandfather taught me how to ride a bike, and my dad would have done the same with my children, I know. When he was alive he used to tell me how he looked forward to having grandchildren. But he died before my kids were born, so my children will miss having him in their lives. My mom is still alive—and she's great. She takes the kids to the movies and has them over to her house a lot. But she can't do a lot of running around with them—she doesn't have the vitality she had ten years ago.*

In addition to possibly missing out on having grandparents altogether, children of older parents are more often only children. Unless a forty-plus woman immediately gets pregnant with twins (and the likelihood of twins *is* more likely if infertility drugs are taken), has several children in a row, or adopts, chances of her having more than one child are slim. Several of the women in our sample wanted but couldn't have more than one child. In each case, physical problems related to age held them back: multiple miscarriages, gynecological problems, or simple fatigue. Rita was theoretically willing but physically drained:

> *After Melissa, I just didn't feel up to having another baby. I thought about it when I was forty-two or forty-three, but I didn't feel comfortable taking all that on a second time. I think even if I had started having kids at thirty-five, my energy level would have been higher, but unfortunately, at forty-two I was just too tired out.*

When marriage and childbearing are postponed past forty, a new kind of family is formed—one in which siblings are rare, first cousins are twenty years older, children may grow up not knowing their grandparents, and parents may not live long enough to *become* grandparents. Mature marriers were saddened by these inadvertent consequences of late parenthood, but seemed determined to compensate for the drawbacks. Rita makes up for her daughter's lack of siblings by helping her foster close friendships with children her own age. Vicki takes advantage of the fact that her mother is still active enough to spend time with her children. Toby has enrolled her son, Jason, in a "foster grandparent" program to make up for the fact that his own grandparents are no longer alive. And *every* parent with whom we spoke seemed to cherish each moment with their child. They're deeply aware that the special relationship they now enjoy got off to a late start. And they intend to make the most of every remaining day and year.

A DOUBLE GENERATION GAP?

But even with the best intentions, how easy is it to parent a child forty-odd years your junior? Late-life families differ from the norm in that the age spread between parent and child represents a kind of double generation gap. Being forty or so years older than their children sometimes made it difficult for the parents in our study to relate wholeheartedly to their children's interests. Can a middle-aged dad be expected to lose himself in a water-pistol fight? How many times can a forty-six-year-old mom sit through *Teenage Mutant Ninja Turtles* with her five-year-old daughter? First-marrieds over forty mean well; they bring as much dedication and love to parenting as anyone else does. But, as Ray explains, sometimes the more years that separate parent and child, the wider the schism between their worlds:

> *I like to be able to grow with my kids, to discover things with them for the first time. That's part of the joy, I think. And I do a lot with my two little boys. But it may be easier as a younger parent, because I get bored with some of the things my kids want to do. If I'm going to Disneyland with them for the third time, that's two times too many.*

Suffering through yet another Mickey Mouse parade is only the beginning. The more profound attitudinal clashes between parent and offspring tend to surface when children reach puberty. In the next section we'll hear from the "veterans" in our study: those older late marriers who now have teenaged and adult children. Their stories foretell what lies in store for over-forty parents who are only just commencing their lifelong careers as fathers and mothers.

THE "VETERANS"

ALICE AND GREG

Alice met her husband, Greg, while hitchhiking through Europe in the summer of 1956. She was twenty-six and he was twenty-eight. When they returned to their separate universities the following fall, they wrote to and visited each other while they busied themselves with their own academic degrees and careers. Alice was an inveterate traveler. She kept her passport current and took off for anywhere, anytime. By 1970, after a fourteen-year friendship, she and Greg married. She was forty and he was forty-two. Why, we asked Alice, after all those years?

> *I finally thought, gee whiz, here I am in graduate school, in my late thirties, maybe it's time to think about settling down. I had always loved being my own wild self, but I knew that with Greg I'd never have to give up my independence or my spirit of adventure.*

Alice and Greg decided to have kids right away. When we asked Alice how it felt to have babies so late in life at a time when very few others did, she responded:

> *Don't forget, I hitchhiked through Europe in the fifties, long before kids started doing that. I backpacked and slept on beaches when people weren't doing that, and everyone thought I was crazy. I didn't do those things in order to be different; I did them because I wanted to. And at forty I wanted to have kids.*

And so she did. Soon after her first baby, Jane, was born, Alice asked her doctor when she should have the next one. Because of her age, he recommended she get pregnant again as soon as possible. Her son, Adam, was born eighteen months after Jane and eleven months after Alice completed her Ph.D. She jokes now about how she was changing diapers with one hand and typing her dissertation with the other.

Like many parents, especially older ones who have focused on their careers for a long time before having children, Alice felt a profound contrast between her professional competence and her parental naïveté. "I'd say to Greg, 'Here we are, world travelers with three advanced degrees between us, and we're terrorized by this tiny infant!' "

But Alice caught on quickly. Once she completed her dissertation, she decided to stay home full-time to raise her children. Her decision to put her career on the back burner puzzled some of her friends. It was the height of the women's movement, and Alice, as intrepid as always, was going against the grain. But she figured she had already gotten years of satisfaction from her profession, and now she wanted to devote full time to enjoying her children.

Alice is now fifty-eight and Greg is sixty. Their children are sixteen and eighteen. Like other teenagers, they are pushing limits and struggling to define themselves. We wondered how their parents' ages affected Jane and Adam, if at all. Alice replied:

> Both my children have brought up the age thing. Adam was laid back, but Jane still isn't comfortable with it. A few years back, when she was about ten or eleven, she asked me, "How come you're so old?" I told her, "Because I got married when I was older." "I don't want to be like you," she said, "I'm gonna get married when I'm twenty-three!" And I answered, "Well, we all have different timing. My timing is different from my sister's, and your timing will probably be different from mine."

Jane is also concerned that Alice looks older than the other mothers. She encourages Alice to "dress younger" to try to bridge that gap. Unoffended by Jane's critique of her fashion sense, Alice takes it in stride. After all, she *is* considerably older than most mothers of teenagers, since late parenting wasn't as prevalent when she started her family as it is today. But she knows that when it comes to more serious matters, she more than makes the grade as a good mom. With her years of life experience, she brings an added wisdom to her role as a parent. She has led a full life and wants the same for her children. And she knows how to listen.

But what about the double generation gap—the forty years that separate Alice and Greg from their teenagers? Alice doesn't believe in generation gaps:

> *I don't know if there is such a thing as a generation gap. I think it's more an "empathy gap" or an "understanding gap." Greg and I try to be very open to listening to our kids. I remember when they were young and learning to read, they'd read "Dear Abby" and come to us with things like, "What's a homosexual?" or "What's adultery?" Both Greg and I come from a generation when our parents didn't talk openly about such things. But we realized we had to be open with our own children. Being forty-some years older than your kids doesn't mean your mind is dead or that you can't think back to when you were growing up. Empathy is what it means to be a parent, and we've got twenty extra years of it to go around.*

It takes more than superficial rapport for a child to feel comfortable enough to open up with an adult. It requires the adult's ability to truly listen and to understand the child's feelings. Although these skills don't necessarily come with age, Alice and Greg have proven they have what it takes to foster a healthy communication with their teenaged son and daughter, even in the midst of their children's adolescent struggles. As Alice so wisely put it, empathy is the key.

If they had it to do all over again, Alice and Greg would do it exactly the same way. They'd have their adventures, travel, go to graduate school, sample a variety of interesting jobs and cities—and *then* get married and settle down. Alice insists she wouldn't trade parenting at forty for parenting at twenty:

> *I couldn't imagine being twenty-three and having a child! I couldn't imagine missing all that I did, all the things I enjoyed. I would recommend having a baby at forty. By then you're*

ready. Ready to be tired—but also ready to appreciate your children.

Simone and Stuart represent a little-known population of first-time late marriers: ex-nuns and ex-priests who marry each other later in life. They first met in a small village in Mexico. Their respective religious orders ran an orphanage and a cooperative farm nearby. Both were on church assignments, she as a teacher, he as an administrator, and they became acquainted briefly. Midway through her tenure, Simone decided to leave the order. And it was Stuart who, in his official capacity as priest, signed the documents releasing Simone from her duties.

Some years later, Simone went to Germany to visit relatives and found out Stuart was studying at a seminary in the adjacent town. They began seeing each other as friends, catching up on old times. But the more time they spent together, the more their common values, enthusiasm for life, and "chemistry" brought them together. Stuart eventually left the priesthood, and the two married. They were both forty one.

They remained in Germany, where they were social activists in a multiethnic working-class community. During this time Simone had three miscarriages, after which they decided to adopt a baby. Simone recalls the life-changing telephone call from the adoption agency:

We were giving a big party when we got the call. There we were, at this interracial gathering, and Stuart yells out, "Simone, do you mind if we have a mixed-race baby?" But of course it didn't make any difference to us.

Simone was forty-five when they adopted Gary. Nine months later the adoption agency called again, asking if they could handle another baby. Overwhelmed as she was, Simone couldn't say no. So she and Stuart became the parents of two babies only eleven months apart. It was a difficult time because they had several community projects going, their tiny apartment was always full of people, and although Simone found the atmosphere stimulating, she was over-whelmed with her new responsibilities. How did an active woman in her mid-forties deal with two infants?

I had no idea what was going on, since I'd never been around babies before. We used to call it "baby shock" in Germany—women having babies after thirty-five and being confronted with a child who makes demands on you which go far beyond any demands connected with a job. A baby doesn't go away at the end of a workday. But I had all these young mothers from the neighborhood telling me what to do, so that was a life-saver.

After years of being on her own, tending to the unending needs of two babies was a tremendous adjustment for Simone. The transformation she was called upon to make was a profound one—and aptly labeled "baby shock" by her German friends. As dedicated and involved as she'd been in her professional life, Simone was indeed shocked to discover that motherhood was a career that left her little time for "R-and-R." And while mothers (and fathers) of all ages cope with this reality, late-marrying parents often find it even more jarring—since they've lived independently for that many more of their adult years.

Energy, or the lack of it, didn't initially seem to be as big a problem for Simone and Stuart as it was for other late-marrying parents of young children. They'd both led very active lives, lived in rugged conditions at times, and were extremely athletic. So chasing around after two tiny children was something they both took in stride. But as the years went on, they began to feel their age. Simone recounted how their endurance was tested as their children became teenagers:

When I look at pictures of the kids when they were babies, I look like I'm about twenty-five—and I felt that young, too. No big deal, I just had to do the work and keep everything going. But as we got into it—because we were already forty-five when we got the babies, and that's already a whole hunk into forty—I found that parenting required more and more exertion and energy.

As teenagers, our kids are especially active. They constantly want to get out and do things, and I'm really not into such high-powered activity anymore. So when they say they want to go skiing, I tell them to go ahead—without me. Ten or fifteen years ago, I would have said, "Oh, great, let's go!"

Stuart agreed with his wife on the subject of declining energy levels. For example, he enjoys taking his sports-minded son to the track, but he doesn't run *with* him. Still, if Stuart and Simone have slowed down a bit over the years, their devotion to their kids hasn't diminished one iota. They do their best to provide their children, now aged thirteen and fourteen, with a vigorous and interesting lifestyle. Simone explains:

While we can't do everything with them that we once could have, we don't want to deny the kids any worthwhile experiences. So, for example, last year we went camping in Yosemite. We did it for them. Whereas younger parents might want the experience for themselves and might go into it with an altogether different spirit, Stuart and I have passed that stage. But we make sure the kids have a full life. When there's some activity that's too much for us, we try to come up with an alternative solution. For instance, we'll go to the park to play tennis and we'll suggest that Gary and Miranda bring two of their friends along. That way Stuart and I will be well matched, and the kids will get to play with someone their own speed.

Like most parents of young teenagers, Simone and Stuart have recently experienced their children's desire to become more independent. Whereas the family used to set aside Friday night for "game night," Gary and Miranda now prefer to hang out with their friends. Unlike younger parents, who might be worried or hurt by their teenagers' emerging emotional distance, Simone and Stuart feel somewhat relieved to be off the hook. Stuart confesses:

Even as recently as a few years ago I was much better at relating to teenagers than I am now. Energy is one factor, but it's also that the things teenagers are interested in don't have any appeal for me. Simone and I often look at one another and joke, "Can't we make them skip a grade or something?"

If Stuart doesn't find the latest rock video or junior-high gossip as fascinating as some younger parents might, he also has the wisdom to know that each stage in a child's life is only temporary. He acknowledges that it won't be too much longer before he'll have more in common with his fast-maturing teenage children.

Both Stuart and Simone are very young and healthy-looking fifty-nine-year-olds. Simone is a natural beauty who doesn't need blush to make her cheeks rosy, and Stuart is trim and attractive. Yet one of the key issues Simone raised in connection with being an older parent of a teenager was one Alice also addressed. It had to do with her daughter's anxiety about having older parents. It seems Miranda is quite concerned about her mother's appearance:

It's especially important for Miranda to have young-looking parents. She doesn't like us being or looking old. Since I don't wear any makeup at all, and she's very into it, for my birthday she gave me a tube of lipstick and some mascara. I was touched by that. I also knew she was upset about my gray hair, so I used a little hair coloring to brown it up a bit. Now, whenever I use makeup, Miranda will come to me and say, "Oh, Mom, it makes you look so much younger!" I don't place much impor-tance on things like that, but she definitely does.

Like Alice's teenage son, Simone's son, Gary, is less concerned than his sister about physical appearance and the whole age question. Perhaps it's because our culture still teaches girls that beauty and looks are essential to a woman's worth. On this count, our society's unspoken message remains virtually unchanged: when women age, they become less beautiful, less lovable, and less powerful. Looking to their mothers for a glimpse into their own futures, teenage girls hope to see an image that in some way resembles what the media validates. And that image is always a youthful one.

The stigma of having an older parent doesn't apply solely to mothers, however. A teenage daughter may dread showing up at a father-daughter dance with her sixty-year-old father, and a ten-year-old Boy Scout might feel embarrassed that his fifty-five-year-old dad is so much older than the other fathers on the camping trip. As the trend of older parenting grows, children of older mothers and fathers may find they feel less stigmatized. But among today's preteens and teenagers, having older parents is simply *not* the norm.

Miranda and Gary have had to field questions from their friends about why their parents are so old. Coming up with the answers can be a burden or an embarrassment, but being part of a "different" family is also a learning experience. You learn who your real friends are, for one thing. And as a child of older parents you're the recipient of the wisdom of their additional years. Simone and Stuart have led rich lives and share that experience with their son and daughter.

From their point of view, though, Simone and Stuart have learned at least as much as their children. Even all their years in humanitarian professions didn't yield the same lessons parenthood has. The day-to-day trials and rewards have taught them what it means to truly share yourself with another human being. And this process has helped them both grow as individuals. Stuart summed up his feelings about becoming a parent later in life:

> *We would have been happy without the children; we were both very involved in our community work and with each other. But the children bring such a different dimension, such a demand to continue growing. And that would have been lost to us. Without them, we wouldn't have been challenged from crisis to crisis and from each sorrow to each joy.*

BEN AND EDNA

Married thirty-seven years, Ben and Edna have the longest marriage of any in our sample. Both are now seventy-seven years old and were forty when they first married, right after World War II. Ben feels the primary reason he waited so long to marry was economics. Until then, he was working his way out of the Depression and through graduate school. Supporting a wife was out of the question. It wasn't until after the war that he finally felt he was earning enough to get married.

Ben first caught sight of Edna performing a solo in his church choir. They met through the pastor, who referred to Edna as his

"unclaimed blessing." Edna was a beautiful, college-educated professional singer. No one could understand why she was still single, but
she wasn't at all bothered by her unmarried status. Her spunky
attitude was uncharacteristic of the times:

> *Many times people would say to me, "What's the matter with
> you that you can't get married?" And I'd reply, "There's noth-
> ing the matter with me." The fact of the matter was that I
> wouldn't have married any of the men they had married! I
> wanted someone who was well educated, who came from the
> same background I did, who suited me! Even the pastor got after
> me. I would tell him, "You don't need to find me a man. I'm
> perfectly able. Lay off!"*

But when the introductions were made, Ben and Edna clicked
and were married soon thereafter. Four years into their marriage, Edna
discovered she was pregnant. Because she had assumed she was past
the age of childbearing, her pregnancy came as a complete surprise—
but a happy one. Although she would have fit right in with the
growing number of older moms of the nineties, in the mid-fifties she
was an anomaly.

> *When my youngest sister, who's eleven years my junior, would
> wheel the baby around the block with me, people would assume
> she was the mother and I was the grandmother. I'd feel bad for
> my sister, because here she was much younger, married many
> years but unable to have children. And there I was: this old
> woman with a brand-new baby!*

But Edna and Ben's advanced ages proved to be mostly benefi-
cial, according to them. They both felt that what they'd learned over
the course of their lives served them well as parents. They were
relaxed with their daughter, and claimed that the normal aggravations
and conflicts of raising a child didn't bother them. And their worlds
opened up to include unforeseen realms, as Ben explained:

> *It was the greatest thing that could have happened to us. It put
> us with younger people! Our daughter's friends' parents were all*

twenty years younger than we were, and we associated with them on a regular basis. She kept us young. We got involved with different activities at church, I participated on the softball team with her, we went to school functions. We had a lot of fun!

Along with the pleasures of parenthood, the couple also experienced certain difficulties associated with delayed parenting. Many had to do with Edna's health. For example, just when they considered adopting a second child, which would have thrilled their four-year-old daughter, Edna had a serious gallbladder operation that left her weak for nearly a year. Then she started going through menopause, which further depleted her and permanently dashed any hopes of enlarging their family. She wasn't physically up to adopting a second child.

Like Edna, women who have postponed childbirth frequently experience the stresses of menopause at the same time they're raising young children or teenagers. Irregular periods, irritability, depression, and hot flashes are a lot to contend with when you have young ones underfoot—or older children with hormone problems of their own. According to Dr. Cynthia A. Stuenkel, director of the University of California at San Diego's menopause program, "When you have a fifty-year-old mom and a twelve-year-old daughter, the little girl is going through puberty while mom is going through menopause. Consequently, there are all these raging hormones within the household."[6]

Edna's daughter, Camille, had no specific problems as a teenager. She was a well-adjusted girl and a conscientious student. But did she feel limited with a mother who often felt too under the weather to do much with her? One of the handicaps of having older parents is that they're more likely to become ill. Did this affect Camille adversely? Not really, because Ben and Edna came up with specific solutions to their parenting dilemmas. If Edna's health problems kept her and Ben housebound at times, they saw to it that Camille didn't suffer as a consequence. Ben talked about how they worked things out:

We wanted our daughter to get out and have a good time, regardless. So when we weren't able to get out of the house as much as she wanted us to, we called on friends to help out. One of her friends' families took her camping every year, and we were

*elated. Of course we would have wanted to go had we been up
to it, but Camille had a great time, and we always looked
forward to hearing all about it when she got back.*

One of the final questions we put to Ben and Edna concerned
Camille's feelings about having older parents. She's now thirty-three;
what did they think *her* thoughts were on the subject? Edna answered:

*Camille has never said anything to us directly about being older
parents, although that doesn't mean it hasn't crossed her mind.
Undoubtedly it does now, because we are both seventy-seven.
Had we met and married earlier, she could have had us longer.
And we would have had her longer.*

One of the chief disadvantages of beginning a family later in life
is simply that there's less time left. The "life span" of the family is
shorter, and both parents and children are saddened by this. Children
of older parents begin to worry early on about losing their mother or
father. The novelist Ellen Currie is forty-nine years younger than her
mother. She recalls, "There was always the unvoiced threat and
accusation, burden, pang, reality: She'll die soon. This mundane dread
illuminated and clouded life's ordinary rough transactions."[7]

If the threat of death occurring sooner rather than later weren't
enough, there's also the concern about taking care of one's elderly
parents. Children of older parents must also face *that* challenge prematurely. Ironically, as longevity increases, so does the burden of caring
for the elderly. Typically, adult children of parents forty or more years
older than they are must shoulder that responsibility just when
they're getting their own lives off the ground.[8]

Camille is a case in point. She married a few years ago and just
recently had her first child. Chances are her life as a new wife and
mother will be complicated by concern for her aging parents. Although Ben and Edna live independently and have no serious health
problems at the moment, Camille may soon find herself attending to
their needs at the same time she's busy raising young children. It'll be
a tough balancing act.

The "veterans" in our sample attested to the hardships, trade-
offs, and tough times older parents often endure. Age slowed them

down as their children became teenagers and young adults. Retirement was postponed so there'd be enough in their kids' college fund. And facing their own mortality took on a unique poignancy because of their much younger offspring. But what these couples mostly communicated was their gratefulness. Parenthood was a gift they never expected to receive, and they expressed their thanks: "It kept us young, forced us to grow, added a new dimension to our lives."

STEPPARENTING INSTEAD

Stepparenting usually doesn't take the place of being a parent, and children generally don't *want* or *need* two mothers or fathers. But for many late marriers, being stepparents is a way to participate in a child's or a younger person's life in the event they can't have one of their own. It's also a relationship fraught with complexities and the potential for conflict. In many cases stepparents represent the person who has disrupted a child's family: Daddy or Mommy went off and married this "other" person. Regardless of the age of the child, this is a traumatic situation. The level of anger a son or daughter of divorce feels can be overwhelming, and stepparents often bear the brunt of it. Boundaries must be established between stepparent and stepchild, and establishing them is a hit-or-miss process.

Tess found this out when she first met her seven-month-old stepdaughter, Rachel. Having recently had a miscarriage, Tess wanted a child and was looking forward to being with and loving baby Rachel:

> *Being Rachel's stepmother was going to be a wonderful chance for me to be with a baby. But the first time she set eyes on me, she started to scream. From then on, she hated me. Over the next two years I tried everything: talking to her sweetly, talking to her while she slept—kind of like subliminal brainwashing—I even tried bribery. She'd like me for about three or four minutes, she'd really like me, and then she'd despise me again. Mel felt guilty for having left her and her mother, Rachel felt angry and powerful, and I felt lousy. I was cast as the wicked stepmother, and Mel was the fabulous daddy. No one could stand it any-*

more, so we decided to see a shrink. He pointed out that Rachel was going through a divorce too, that she had a lot to be angry and confused about, and that her only vocabulary was her emotions. He advised me not to set my expectations too high.

At that point I was just beginning to face not being able to have my own child. And although I wasn't consciously trying to mother Rachel, I was bringing all my desire to be a mother to her. I knew I was never going to be her mother, but I don't think I was behaving as if I knew that.

Becoming aware of the distinction between parent and stepparent can be a tricky proposition for those who expect stepparenting to be a substitute for parenting. Knowing that being a stepparent is the closest one will get to having a child of one's own makes crossing that boundary between stepparent and parent a temptation. But once stepparents accept their own special role in a child's life, they can learn to enjoy it. Diana's straight talk clarified her relationship with her stepdaughter from the beginning:

I had a great relationship with my nine-year-old stepdaughter right away. I remember one of the first times we were together. We were in the supermarket squeezing the tomatoes, teasing each other, being silly. When we got to the checkout stand, a lady in line said, "It's so nice to see a mother and daughter laughing together." Rebecca's smile became a frown. When we got to the car, I said to her, "It's important that you know that I know you love your mother very much. I don't want to be your mother, and I don't want you to forget that you have someone called 'mother' who will be with you forever. But I hope you and I will have something separate and different." Rebecca needed to hear that.

For both Diana and Tess, stepparenting is a part-time undertaking. Their stepchildren live with their husband's ex-wives most of the time. However, in Ivan's case, being a stepfather is a round-the-clock commitment. His stepdaughter, Veronica, lives with him and his wife full-time. Ivan's involvement with this little girl would have shocked even him eight years ago, before his wife and her child came into his life. Ivan is now sixty-one, his wife, Emily, is forty-one, and Veronica is ten.

Veronica was four when Ivan and Emily started living together. Ivan had never considered having children of his own because he never wanted to relinquish his independence. But with Veronica, it was instant fatherhood:

> I liked Veronica right away, even before I thought about marrying Emily. I used to go to their house and spend a few hours at a time there. But once they both became part of the household, I got to see all of Veronica's behaviors—up and down—on a twenty-four-hour basis.
>
> At first Emily and I fought a lot about child-rearing. I was too much of a disciplinarian, but Emily was patient with me. She guided me and I took her advice. I changed my behavior so that I could become the kind of father Veronica could accept.

Ivan's role as stepparent is clearly different from either Tess's or Diana's. Since Veronica's real father sees her only on occasion, Ivan has filled a void in the child's life and has become her primary father figure. He listens to her daily concerns, soothes her hurt feelings, makes sure she does her homework, gives her pointers on her soccer game, and shares an ice cream cone with her after practice. Their lives are connected in the most essential ways.

Owing to their work schedules, Emily and Ivan decided that he should take sole responsibility for Veronica at particular times during the week. Ivan doesn't seem to mind his parental duties one bit, and now that he is financially secure and works less, he has the time to be with Veronica:

> I take care of Veronica two full days a week. I love it! I'll be out in the garden working, and she'll be nearby playing with her dolls. At some point she'll come over and try to persuade me to stop working so I can take her out for an ice cream cone. Who could resist? Certainly not me!

The relationship Ivan has with his stepdaughter attests to the claim that biological ties aren't necessarily the strongest. As with adoptive parents, when stepparents are there for their kids in a primary way, the connection becomes a vital one. Unlike Tess's or Diana's stepdaughters, Veronica *needs* Ivan. And he has grown to need her as well:

> *In the beginning, Veronica called me Ivan, not to detract from her real father. Emily thought it would be nice if she would call me "papa," so she did for a while. Now "papa" has disappeared and she calls me dad. I wanted that very much. I'm very proud of her. I think she's a part of me, even though biologically she's not my child.*
>
> *As she gets older, we have more meaningful conversations—and arguments—but I love it! Sometimes people think that marriage to someone without kids would be easier. But I wouldn't have missed my relationship with Veronica for the world!*

THE CHILD WITHIN

Making a child a permanent part of your life is always an enormous adjustment. Doing so in midlife brings unique pleasures, sorrows, stresses, and surprises. Many late-marrying parents and stepparents claim they have less physical energy but much greater patience and perspective. Some regret not being able to have more than one child, yet they're grateful for the maturity that enables them to appreciate and enjoy the child they've been blessed with. Many feel the strain of the "double caretaker" role: caring for children at the same stage in life when they must look after aging parents. Yet the unanticipated delights children bring to a family always seem to make the hardships worthwhile. Children wear out their older parents, test their limits, inhibit their freedom; they also rejuvenate them, open them up to reexperience their own childhoods, broaden their worlds.

Parents strive to give their children wisdom, guidance, nurturance, love. What children give back is a certain purity of spirit. There is in all children something divine. They keep us in touch with what we most value in human nature: curiosity, creativity, truthfulness, spontaneity, authenticity, humor. They help us find again the child within ourselves. Being a constant companion during a son or a daughter's childhood enables parents to relive their own. Often it's an opportunity to remember and resolve unpleasant childhood experiences. Sometimes it shakes us out of our old routines and habits, allowing us to reinvent ourselves.

The eminent child psychologist Bruno Bettelheim encouraged parents to reexplore their own childhoods through their children:

> *Only by exploring and reexploring the steps we made in becoming ourselves can we truly know what our childhood experiences were and what they signified in our lives. . . . Separation from one's childhood is temporarily necessary, but if it is permanently maintained it deprives us of inner experiences which, when restored to us, can keep us young in spirit and also permit greater closeness to our children.*[9]

There are both advantages and disadvantages to delaying parenthood. When we asked our late-life parents to weigh the pros and cons of becoming a first-time parent after forty, most said they wished they'd started a family at around thirty-five. With that slight margin of time, they would have had the best of both worlds: the wisdom *and* a bit more energy, the financial security *and* the opportunity to have more than one child. Mostly, though, they were thrilled to have finally become parents. Ray's words can only begin to describe how special that experience has been for him:

> *I discovered intimacy through my child, my firstborn. When I'd walk in the door and he'd come running up to me with his tiny arms opened up, waiting for my big hug, he'd scream for joy, "Daddy! Daddy!" That completely unblocked feeling that comes from inside me when I'm hugging him—it's a feeling that makes me whole, makes me feel like nothing can touch me, like nothing else matters. I could die in that moment and it would be all right.*

10

You Can't Hurry Love

In the last nine chapters we've explored the minds and marriages of men and women who bettered the odds and married for the first time after age forty. We've discovered that marrying later is a great deal more *possible* than all the deflating statistics would lead us to believe. We've also come to understand how the unique weave of each woman and man's life contributed to delaying and influencing their first marriage after twenty odd years of adult singlehood.

If you've never married so far, there's probably a part of you that feels as though you've never grown up. That's because marriage bestows the mantle of maturity and serves as an initiation into adulthood. Once a woman or man has passed through this social ritual, irrespective of age or emotional development, their social status automatically shifts. Ironically, even those who have had brief, unhappy marriages enjoy a privileged position denied to others who may have had long satisfying relationships outside of wedlock. Late marriers of both sexes will tell you there is an insidious stigma attached to never having been married—one that is far greater than being divorced.

Because we live in a society that is so pro-marriage, images of the sour spinster and the carefree, don't-give-a-damn bachelor cling to our collective consciousness. These images are reflected in the inferences people make about the lives and personalities of never-marrieds. Even though more people are marrying later in life for the *first* time, negative stereotypes and assumptions about who they are and why they haven't married still abound. When someone asks the not-so-innocent question, "Why hasn't a nice person like you ever been married?" they may also be silently assuming part of the reason is that you are

1. overinvolved in your career
2. too attached to your parents
3. troubled psychologically
4. too picky, cold, or standoffish
5. dodging commitment or unable to love
6. too independent and not "womanly" enough (if you are a woman) or not "manly" enough (if you're a man)
7. all or any combination of the above

Undoubtedly you've heard other barbs, but we'll stop here. Knowing that these same attributes may describe aspects of married and divorced people as well, doesn't take the sting out of these judgments. Nor does knowing that they are simply prejudices help to immunize us against self-doubt if we are among those who have yet to wed. No matter how secure or optimistic about our future we may be, in our vulnerable moments these generalizations seep into our perceptions of self-worth and undermine our confidence.

It's our hope that this book has dispelled some of the myths about delayed marriers. Their stories illustrate that the reasons for staying single are highly individual and can't be reduced to a list of shared traits. It is important to remember that many men and women in our sample remained unmarried because they *chose* to. Either they eventually wanted to marry but were in no rush, they were biased against marriage and didn't want any part of it, or they didn't feel strongly about matrimony one way or the other. A good number had spent their twenties and thirties enjoying, not mourning, their single-hood. They hadn't put off their lives or intimate relationships just because they had put off marriage. Some preferred to live together with their intimate partners instead of marrying them. Some would have remained single if children and family hadn't become a pressing concern. Only a few had *always* wanted to be married earlier in their lives. Marriage had eluded them because likely opportunities hadn't come along or none of their special relationships had worked out.

All late marriers have been where many of us still are: single and (sometimes) scared we're going to stay that way—forever. They've listened to the same well-meaning counsel of countless others and have worn out ways of meeting "the one." When these schemes failed, they did exactly what we all do—wallowed in self-pity, trashed the opposite sex, lamented lost loves—anything and everything before bracing themselves to go out and try again. "There are no formulas for finding love," cautioned Toby, "just a lot of lucky guesses and even more endurance!"

As we listened to late marriers recount their life histories, one truth stood out: much of what happens depends on chance—especially in love. Fewer rules govern our fate than we like to think. On the one hand, this makes things a lot more unpredictable than many of us feel comfortable with. On the other, it leaves room for a great many unanticipated events to happen. Contrary to formula books that purport to tell you how to meet someone and marry him or her, our stories reveal that *no one set of conditions* need be satisfied in order to find someone we love and marry that person.

Late marriers were in every imaginable state of mind when they met their spouses-to-be. Many felt better about themselves than they ever had in their lives; several had never felt worse. Some had given up completely and resigned themselves to a life of singlehood; a few lucky ones were absolutely resolute and primed to meet their match. Some had other relationships going; others had been alone for years. Some strategized like generals—joining dating services, placing personal ads, accepting every date, blind and otherwise. Others quietly surrendered to the fates.

Ultimately, however, every one of our midlife marriers *did* meet someone. Judging from their stories, their encounters have something in common with snowflakes: no two are the same. And when late marriers did meet their spouses-to-be, it was usually in an unlikely place when they least expected it: in a hospital emergency room, in an office elevator, in an alley while taking out the garbage, in a video store, in the backwoods of the Sierras, in a church choir, in a ballroom dancing class, in an airport lounge, backstage at a music club, at an adoption fair, at a political fundraiser . . . the possibilities are endless.

So were the styles of their courtships. Many late marriers said they "knew" as soon as they met their future spouses that he or she was *the* person, and they didn't waste any time; others were sure about the person but not as sure about marriage. Kate moved in with Joel five days after they met, and married him three months later; Eric wed Sheila during their ninth year of living together. In other instances, midlife courtships were as much about tying up the loose ends of previous relationships as they were about new-found romance. Tess's courtship limped through Mel's messy indecision to leave his first wife. Nancy's with Dennis required a similar degree of fortitude and faith. The nature and length of courtships were also shaped by the exigencies of life. Ned's three-week courtship was short and practical, driven by the impending death of his father. Andreas's was impatient and passionate, propelled by his desire to make a marriage so he could make babies.

Delayed marriers met and married every which way. But all of them share at least one key characteristic that sets them apart from *anyone* else who marries: at midlife they are embarking on a rite of passage most typically completed in early adulthood. By taking tardy vows, they are also challenging the accepted sequence and timing of life events and are radically redefining the role of marriage in adult development.

FORTY ISN'T WHAT IT USED TO BE

Traditionally, the age of forty has symbolized the end of youth and the beginning of life's decline. Even Shakespeare wrote that old age begins after "forty Winters . . . besiege thy brow." Of course, back then, when life expectancy hovered somewhere around fifty, forty *was* old![1] But in today's world, women and men are healthier and more physically fit and living longer than ever before. Now that the average life span is 69.9 years for a man and 77.8 for a woman, the age of forty has taken on a whole new physiological and social meaning.[2]

Contemporary midlifers seem to be younger than their parents were when they were forty, or at least many see themselves that way. In the space of one generation, middle age has gone from representing a predictable and settled stage of life to one that invites personal reexamination and change. Whereas the progression of our parents' lives appeared to unfold through a fixed set of milestones, ours often seem less predictable. We have more freedom to choose and order our major life events (marriage being one of these), independent of strict social conventions. Our choices are often based on the question, "What might enhance the quality of my life and promote my personal well-being?" rather than "What is expected of me now that I've reached this age?"

We all know women and men who are getting started on second and third careers by midlife or who are just settling down and buying their first homes. And, yes, we can probably think of one or two others who are marrying for the first time and becoming new parents! Given the unique timing of their passages, late marriers can teach us something about how little chronological age has come to matter.

Unlike some long-time marrieds the same age who wearily complain that they are used up and ground down, late marriers feel as though they are "at the beginning"—a phrase they used repeatedly in their conversations with us. Even though their last birthday cake might have been ablaze with candles, they frequently identified with younger adults in their twenties. "My chronological age has nothing to do with my social age," Cheryl explained, looking as though she was getting away with something and enjoying every minute of it. "I did it all ass-backwards, so I figure that now I'm actually about twenty-six!"

First-time newlyweds who'd recently become parents after forty felt they'd turned back the clock as well. Marrying and conceiving babies had a powerful regenerative influence on their self-image: they'd finally come into their own, their lives were flowering, and their dreams were being realized. But with their dreams came the reminders that they weren't always as young as they felt. Tending newborns and toddlers saps energy at any age, and being older put them at a slight disadvantage. Rebounding from a string of sleepless nights wasn't as easy for them as it might be for a twenty-five-year-old.

Even so, later-life parents thought of themselves as being considerably younger in spirit, if not in body, than their own parents in their forties. Victor made the comparison this way: "At forty-four my dad had ulcers and a twenty-year-old son, and here I'm just about to have my first child. Of course I'm getting older, but overall I feel so good that 'middle age' seems a long time off."

Later-life parents continued to feel they'd skipped down a generation even as their children grew up. They found themselves smack dab in the middle of preschools and day-care centers alongside younger parents whose children were the same age as theirs. Shared parenting concerns bridged their age differences and forged unlikely friendships. Later-life parents discovered they often had more in common with a woman of twenty-nine who was toilet-training her three-year-old than with their best friend from graduate school whose college-bound teenagers were gearing up to take the SATs. These kind of encounters further supported their beliefs about the relative meaninglessness of absolute age.

Late marriers stormed the age barrier another way: by marrying husbands or wives ten to twenty years their junior. They claimed that living with someone younger kept them in touch with the younger sides of themselves. As a bonus, by keeping company with a younger spouse's friends they were exposed to more than just an outsider's glimpse of the next generation or two behind their own, since most of us cue our behavior relative to those who are younger and older than we are. So when Rita spends time with Rick's friends, most of whom are in their early to middle thirties, she subtracts years from her age. "I'm cheating," she told us. "When I'm around them, I feel like I'm not quite into my forties even though I'm closer to fifty!"

It is not as though late marriers are denying they're forty plus, plus, plus; many are simply *experiencing* aging contrary to their own expectations. Because of their special circumstances, they find themselves straddling conventional age-related roles and boundaries. Having extended their single status into their middle years, they're novices at marriage and child-rearing at a time when most people are weary veterans. By engaging in life events that were atypical for their age group, midlife marriers often found they had more in common with those younger than themselves than with their own peers. They surprised themselves at how easy it was to break ranks with conceptions of what "middle age" was supposed to be.

But not only do over-forty marriers claim to *feel* younger, many also think they *look* younger than their long-term married friends. In theory, they've been spared the years of daily annoyances, problems and pressures of married and family life, so they've had fewer worries and more time to take care of themselves. But can it really be true that late marriers have really staved off the ravages of time? We can't say that staying single for a sizable portion of one's adult life can make a person look younger—even though we'd like to!

What's more likely is that love itself is responsible for their generous self-perceptions. The aura of youth that so many of them experience may be due to the combination of their prolonged freedom as singles *and* the invigorating thrill of new-found intimacy, for intimacy enlivens us and rekindles hope and expectancy at *any* age. However, it would be misleading to draw too sugary a portrait of first marriages after forty. They aren't, after all, simply wine and roses. Like everything else in life, they have their disadvantages as well.

THE BITTER AND THE SWEET

It is no surprise that first marriages over forty share a great many of the same challenges and rewards that other marriages face. We expected as much. But late marriers in our sample were also quick to point out that small but significant differences set their marriages apart. Owing to their timing, these marriages are underscored by bittersweet ironies, many of which, strangely enough, heighten the intensity of midlife love and late marriers' commitment to it.

Years of faltering hopes, endless experimentation, and emotional limbo provided our late marriers with a well-defined vantage point from which to view and appreciate their marriages. "If Emily and I had started when we were twenty-five, we would have had much more time to take advantage of our happiness," Ivan said with a twinge of sadness in his voice. "That's why something inside me pulls to make up for all the time we haven't had."

Mindful of this poignancy, late marriers don't take their marriages for granted. When they realize this time can never be recovered, they're even more aware of what they *almost* missed entirely. This is precisely why they work harder to make their marriages count for something in the here and now.

Depending on how you look at them, these drawbacks may be blessings in disguise—gentle incentives that remind late marriers to value what they have. Finally having someone to cherish and belong with are gifts that nearly erase the cumulative loneliness and longing of so many years! Jackie expresses this sentiment perfectly:

> *Some nights if I've been out, Derek is already asleep when I come home. As soon as I get into bed and our bodies touch, it's just like linking logs. I'm not talking about physically, but emotionally. I spent so many years not having what I instinctively knew I needed, that finding it makes an enormous difference. No matter what has gone on before, I belong here with him.*

But certain joys *are* lost forever when one marries later in life; bearing biological children is one of these. Although adopted children or stepchildren are close substitutes, and often just as satisfying, some couples would have loved to create life together had they had the chance. So it was for Kate, who, by the time she married Joel, couldn't have even one baby, let alone the six she'd always fantasized about. While her marriage hasn't suffered, this missed opportunity will always remain a small regret. It is not an uncommon predicament among later marriers.

There is another downside specific to late marriages: less shared history. All couples build one from scratch, but when these couples meet and marry, huge chunks of their lives are already lived. Unlike married couples who have known each other for years, midlife marriers will never be part of their spouses' earlier lives. There are bigger gaps, more to catch up on, and fewer common references to the past that can be telegraphed by a word or a glance. Many told us there had been moments when their spouses would suddenly feel like strangers who had lived separate and distinct lives. And you know what? They had.

Diana explained, "When I see photos of Jim ten years back, I think to myself, 'I barely recognize this person. Who is he? What would it have been like to have known him?' " Perhaps Diana can meet some of the important people who shaped Jim's life, but she will only hear, secondhand, about the seminal events that influenced him.

The same holds true for the lives of Jim's children. She continued, "I would have liked to have seen my stepkids growing up. I will never know who they were when they were little. I just wasn't around." Diana, like so many late marriers, must fill in the blanks for herself.

But having had a lengthy independent life that preceded marriage was also perceived as a plus that added immeasurably to later marriages. Prolonged unmarried life had provided midlife marriers free rein to follow their hearts and libidos. They were more ready than ever to "settle in" and enjoy the cozy comforts of companionship. Lilly is one who can't ever imagine herself whining about having "missed out." She didn't, and knows her commitment to her marriage is stronger for it:

> I've done it all. So it's great to be at home in front of the TV on a Saturday night eating delivered pizza with my honey. If I were younger, I'd want to be out in the world raving. Friends of mine say, "I have never done this or that." Well, I did all those things, and this is exactly where I want to be.

First-time late marriers come to their marriages with a lifetime of experience, inside and out. They are self-aware, equipped with strong identities and well-developed personalities. This is not to say they are necessarily rigid or "set in their ways." Now that their personal boundaries are well defined, they feel *more* capable of being more flexible and selfless in a marriage because they have fewer fears of losing themselves in it. Convinced that having a solid sense of themselves is a prime ingredient of a marriage based on mutuality and partnership, late marriers have no regrets that they did it *their* way. Faith recalled how her own personal evolution has enhanced the viability of her new marriage:

> Twenty years ago, all my intimate relationships were built around my fears of not knowing who I was or what I wanted.

Even when I did know, I wasn't able to ask for it. I expected the
other person to read my mind. When they tried and got it wrong,
I'd feel angry and disregarded. Who could ever have a happy
marriage with a person like that?

Once Faith got to know herself better, she was better prepared
for marriage. And this is just the point: choosing a marriage partner
during young adulthood means you *grow up* with your spouse; choosing a marriage partner at midlife means you've got enough of yourself just to *grow with* your spouse. This is a subtle but important
distinction.

It takes time to create one's individuality and autonomy. The
interval between being dependent on parents and getting married is
best used for self-exploration and interaction with the world, and
marrying too early can potentially dilute this process. However,
midlife marriers enter into matrimony as full-fledged adults. They
know themselves better than they have at any time before in their
lives. They've had the luxury, either by design or default, of becoming a "me" before they became a "we." Now that they know the
dividends of maturity, most wouldn't go back in time and do it any
other way. Neither would Ray:

After twenty years of kicking around and doing everything I
wanted to do as an adult, I don't mind compromising some of
my own needs for the sake of my wife. I was ready for a healthy
kind of dependency—the kind that's critical for a good marriage.

There is no doubt that an established identity counts for a great
deal in a relationship; without one, the possibility of a vital, healthy
connection with another human being is severely hampered. Hind-
sight helps too, especially during marital conflicts. When unresolved
psychological issues surface, as they do in every marriage, late marriers feel they can short-circuit problems that might prove disastrous to
younger, less experienced couples. With so many past relationships
under their belts and much of their psychic baggage sorted out,
they've done their emotional homework. Either they've resolved
personal stumbling blocks or know what to do when they trip over
them. From practical experience, they're alert to those behaviors that

work in relationships and those that don't. Some say they're better at honoring individual differences and accepting their own and their spouse's frailties.

But does this mean that midlife marriages are divorce-proof? After all, late marriers *begin* their marriages long after the period of highest divorce risk is past—between the ages of twenty-five and twenty-nine for both men and women.[3] In addition to statistics, one can speculate ad infinitum on why divorce might be less likely for men and women who marry later in life for the first time: they've searched long and hard for a mate, and truly appreciate having found one; they've logged less time with their spouses and aren't bored or disinterested yet; or they're creating a family when most other married couples who have stayed together for the sake of their now-grown children are splitting up.

Most late marriers thought it would be sheer folly to believe their marriages were immune from divorce just because they were beyond the critical danger zone. Nor are they pinning their hopes exclusively on the popular notion that later marriages are "smarter." While late marriers do bring considerable determination and wisdom to their new unions, they aren't the least bit overconfident that these advantages alone qualify as "divorce insurance."

Characteristically, most have well-grounded expectations when it comes to the challenge of marriage. They've witnessed the pain of close friends and family who have gone through breakups. They're familiar with the staggering divorce statistics. And since it's rare for two older never-marrieds to marry each other, it's likely one's own spouse has been divorced at least once. Other people's unhappy endings have provided late marriers with valuable examples of what not to do. Determined to make the best of their own hard-won relationships, many take preventive measures by consciously nurturing their marriages with care and attention. Andy believes this is the "real stuff" of commitment:

> *People say the longer you wait, the more chance you'll have of having a happy marriage. To deny the possibility of getting divorced is ridiculous. Carol and I had to let go of the fantasy that marriage is forever, because it's not. The bottom line is that you get divorced unless you choose not to.*

*We're committed to staying out of a destructive loop, so we
talk about how our individual behavior affects the relationship
all the time. A year after our wedding we renewed our vows, and
we're going to do it again—the commitment has to be vital and
real to be worth it.*

When warning signs indicated their relationships were heading
toward trouble, most of our group of late marriers didn't hesitate to
confront the problem head-on themselves or see a marriage counselor. Anticipating and working through marital problems was an area
where many had high confidence. They knew that solving marital
problems took guts: guts to put themselves on the line; guts to be
honest about their hurts and weaknesses; guts to vent their anger and
frustrations. And they also knew that once those risks had been taken,
they'd have to risk sticking around to work the issues through to
mutual satisfaction. They credited maturity for these indispensable
skills. Maxine commented:

*I really know what I have in this marriage and don't want to
blow it. I just want to make it better. Maybe some younger
people feel that way too, but I never felt that before. I've been
around, had a lot of boyfriends, so I know how to communicate
with Hugh—experience has been my teacher. I no longer have
the foolish sense that I have all the answers, which sometimes
drives younger people to say, "This problem is uncomfortable—
I'm leaving." That attitude is gone now and it's been replaced
by a feeling that there is nothing we can't overcome if we want
to.*

Sometimes, however, the will to overcome problems isn't
enough. There is some evidence that late marriers feel less morally
obligated to marriage *because* they've been unmarried for so long.[4]
This idea is based on the notion that since they haven't conformed or
caved in to the social pressure to get married earlier, they might not
be as intimidated by divorce. None among those we interviewed felt
they would remain in a troubled marriage simply to avoid the threat
of aloneness. And while actually divorcing was the furthest thing
from their minds, many were confident they'd be prepared to pick up

the emotional and financial pieces in the event of a breakup. Accustomed as midlife marriers are to long-term singleness, they are no strangers to solitude: they would survive matelessness again *if* they had to because they already have done so for so long. Their lives would go on. Cheryl spoke to these very sobering issues:

> *I'd hate to get a divorce. But there have been moments when I've started thinking about where I was going to live and who was going to take the dog. What's astonishing is that it's only since I've been married that I've felt it would be okay for me to be alone again.*
>
> *I can now say, "If this marriage is only eighty percent the way I want it, I can handle it; maybe I could even handle seventy percent." But there is a point past which it isn't okay for me to stay in this marriage any longer. And if that were to happen, I'd be a wreck, but I also know I'd get through it and be okay.*

Unfortunately, neither age nor wisdom provides an ironclad guarantee that any marriage will endure. With all the advantages that later marriages seem to have, some of them may not last. If someone has simply married out of desperation or with a singleminded agenda such as having children, he or she may be overlooking less obvious issues of compatibility that will inevitably surface. And when problems do erupt, late marriages are just as vulnerable to divorce as any other.

On the positive side, the majority of our midlife marriers regarded their marriages as a precious resource—to be protected and treasured with all the body, heart, and soul they could muster. At every turn of the way they drew on their considerable life experience to support and breathe life into their unions. In darker moments they marshaled the difficult lessons they'd learned from their past heartbreaks and vowed to keep their vows. They'd accepted the inherent consequences of marrying for the first time after forty. They were committed to turning the minuses into pluses. And, above all, they were optimistic: this time they were starting way ahead of the game—they were married!

YOU CAN'T HURRY LOVE

If there is one lesson we'd like to leave you with, it is that finding someone to love and marry *can* happen at *any* age—this is the magic of life. Try not to forget this!

Leave the notion of "the right time" behind you. Remember— the proper time to find lasting love is *anytime.* Each of our lives unfolds differently; each of us has his or her own timetable and unique rhythm. Try not to devalue yours.

These simple truths may be especially relevant to you if you've come to midlife with fixed expectations about what should have happened to you by now—love, marriage, babies, grandchildren, and all the rest. Since your life may not be the way you thought it was going to be, maybe you've sealed your fate and locked down your future. If you have, perhaps some of the lives you've read about will inspire your faith, reinstate your resolve, and stir your confidence that something you've almost ruled out might actually happen. Try believing you may actually get what you want; many midlife marriers have!

Loving and being loved taps into our primary human instinct: to live in a state of emotional relatedness and physical warmth so that we may thrive and grow. As human beings we are drawn toward the magnetic pull of marriage, for it promises to provide us this opportunity and symbolizes this challenge. In our search for love and marriage, we all experience the depths of loneliness, disappointment, and despair. These are the difficult parts of the journey.

There are scary parts too, and those parts involve risk and uncertainty: Dating. More dating. Living your own life to the fullest—single or married. Letting yourself off the hook that strips you of self-worth just because you've never been married. Breaking through your self-doubt and bucking ageist attitudes that make you feel like you've missed the boat or that you're "too old" to attract someone you really want. Sitting down and clarifying what you really think you want, and then committing yourself to action. And, last of all, knowing and accepting that you can't hurry love!

NOTES

1. Choice vs. Chance

1. JOSEPH CAMPBELL, *The Power of Myth*, edited by Sue Flowers (New York: Doubleday, 1988), 200–201.

2. GALLUP POLL 54, no. 1 (May 1, 1989).

3. ARTHUR J. NORTON AND JEANNE E. MOORMAN, "Current Trends in Marriage and Divorce Among American Women," *Journal of Marriage and the Family* 49, no. 1 (February 1987): 3–14.

4. U.S. CENSUS BUREAU, *Current Population Reports* series P-20, no. 418 (Washington, D.C.: U.S. Government Printing Office, 1986).

5. ANDREW CHERLIN, "Postponing Marriage: The Influence of Young Women's Work Expectations," *Journal of Marriage and the Family* 42, no. 2 (May 1980): 363–64.

6. FRANCIS KOBRIN GOLDSCHEIDER AND LINDA WAITE, "Sex Differences in the Entry into Marriage," *American Journal of Sociology* 92, no. 1 (July 1986): 106.

7. Ibid.

8. PAUL C. GLICK, "Updating the Life Cycle of the Family," *Journal of Marriage and the Family* 39, no. 1 (February 1977): 5–13.

9. Ibid.

10. JESSE BERNARD, *Future of Marriage* (New York: World Publishing, 1972).

11. MARY BARBERIS, "Women and Marriage: Choice or Chance?" *The American Woman, 1988–1989: A Status Report*, edited by Sara E. Rix (New York: Norton, 1988): 272.

12. JEANNE E. MOORMAN, "The History and the Future of the Relationship between Education and Marriage," Miscellaneous Publications, Census Bureau of the United

States (Washington, D.C.: U.S. Government Printing Office, 1987).

13. "Advance Report of Final Marriage Statistics, 1986," National Center for Health Statistics vol. 38, no. 3 supplement 2: 5 (July 13, 1989).

14. THOMAS EXTER, "How to Figure Your Chances of Getting Married," *American Demographics* 9 (June 1987): 50–52.

15. ROLLO MAY, *Love and Will* (New York: Dell, 1969), 91.

16. JEAN SHINODA BOLEN, *The Tao of Psychology* (San Francisco: Harper & Row, 1979), 59.

2. Marriage Meant Growing Up, and Growing Up Meant Dying

1. JACK KEROUAC, *On the Road* (New York: New American Library, 1957), 161.

2. BARBARA EHRENREICH, *The Hearts of Men* (Garden City, New York: Anchor/Doubleday, 1983). In the beginning of her book, Ehrenreich discusses how *Playboy*, the beat writers, and certain media rebels contributed to the American male revolt against the traditional breadwinner role.

3. WILLARD L. RODGERS AND ARLAND THORNTON, "Changing Patterns of First Marriage in the United States," *Demography* 22, no. 2 (May 1985): 271.

4. National Center for Health Statistics, Monthly Vital Statistics Report 38, no. 3, supplement 2 (1989): 3.

5. ANNIE GOTTLIEB, *Do You Believe in Magic: The Second Coming of the Sixties Generation* (New York: Times Books/Random House, 1987), 251.

6. CHERYL MERSER, *Grown-ups: A Generation in Search of Adulthood* (New York: G. P. Putnam's Sons, 1987), 64–68.

7. PAUL LIGHT, *Baby Boomers* (New York: Norton, 1988), 21.

8. ASHLEY MONTAGU, *Growing Young* (New York: Bergin & Garvey, 1989), excerpted from *UTNE Reader*, January–February 1990.

3. Living Together Instead

1. MARTHA FRANSWORTH RICHE, "Post-Marital Society," *American Demographics*, November 1988, 26.

2. LARRY BUMPASS, JAMES A. SWEET, AND ANDREW CHERLIN, "The Role of Marriage in Declining Rates of Marriage," *NSFH Working Paper* no. 5 (Madison: Center for Demography and Ecology, University of Wisconsin, August 1989), 11.

3. E. GRANT, "Marriage: Practice Makes Perfect," *Psychology Today*, March 1988, 14.

4. H. HALL, "Marriage: Practice Makes Imperfect?" *Psychology Today*, July–August 1988, 15.

5. JEAN MARBELLA, "Heartbreak of Cohabitation Ends in Divorce," *Los Angeles Times*, 16 November 1989.

6. ADOLF GUGGENBUHL-CRAIG, *Marriage: Dead or Alive?* (Dallas: Spring Publications, 1977).

7. JO McGOWAN, "Marriage Versus Just Living Together," *Commonweal*, 13 March 1981, 143.

4. Psychic Baggage

1. ROBIN NORWOOD, *Women Who Love Too Much* (Los Angeles: Tarcher, 1985), 77–78.

2. LINDA LEONARD, *On the Way to the Wedding: Transforming the Love Relationship* (Boston: Shambhala, 1986), 19.

5. Why Get Married Unless You Want Kids?

1. National Center for Health Statistics, *Trends and Variations in First Births to Older Women, 1970–1986*, National Center for Health Statistics, Hyattsville, Md., series 21, no. 47: 8.

2. "Mid-Life Moms," feature on ABC television network series "20/20," 6 April 1990.

3. DANIEL LEVINSON, *Seasons of a Man's Life* (New York: Ballantine Books, 1980), 286–87.

6. From Me to We

1. ERIC FROMM, *The Art of Loving* (New York: Harper, 1956), 20–21.

2. ———, *The Art of Loving*, 22–24.

3. CARL ROGERS, *Becoming Partners: Marriage and Its Alternatives* (New York: Dell, 1972), 201.

4. ROGER FISHER AND WILLIAM URY, "Getting to Yes," excerpted from JUDITH SILLS, *A Fine Romance* (New York: Ballantine Books, 1987), 199.

5. W. ROBERT BEAVERS, *Successful Marriage: A Family Systems Approach to Couples Therapy* (New York: Norton, 1985), 70–82.

6. LINDA LEONARD, *On the Way to the Wedding: Transforming the Love Relationship* (Boston: Shambhala, 1986), 248.

7. W. ROBERT BEAVERS, *Successful Marriage*, 79.

8. CARL ROGERS, *Becoming Partners*, 204.

7. Monogamy? After All These Years?

1. ANDREA SACHS, "America's New Fad," *Time*, 19 February 1990.

2. Ibid.

3. HELEN FISHER, "The Four-Year Itch," *Natural History*, October 1987, 28.

4. Ibid.

5. ANN SWINDLER, "Love and Adulthood in American Culture," in *Themes of Work and Love in Adulthood*, edited by N. J. Smelser and Eric Erikson (Cambridge: Harvard University Press, 1980), 139.

6. ROBERT A. JOHNSON, *We: The Psychology of Romantic Love* (San Francisco: Harper & Row, 1983), 102.

7. Phillip Blumstein and Pepper Schwartz, *American Couples* (New York: Morrow, 1983), 219–23.

8. Ibid.
9. ADOLF GUGGENBUHL-CRAIG, *Marriage: Dead or Alive?* (Dallas: Spring Publications, 1977), 101.
10. ROBIN MARANTZ HENIG, et al., *How a Woman Ages* (New York: Ballantine Books, 1985), 11.
11. SAUL H. ROSENTHAL, M.D., *Sex Over 40* (Los Angeles: Tarcher, 1987).

8. Money and Careers: Yours, Mine, and Ours

1. GRACE WEINSTEIN, *Men, Women and Money: New Roles, New Rules* (New York: New American Library, 1986), 3.
2. Ibid., 125.
3. KENNETH CLOKE. Attorney and mediator. Personal communication with the authors.
4. WEINSTEIN, *Men, Women and Money*, 73.
5. KATY BUTLER, "The Great Boomer Bust," *Mother Jones*, June 1989, 35.
6. CAROL COLMAN, *Love and Money: What Your Finances Say About Your Personal Relationships* (New York: Coward, McCann & Geoghegan, 1983), 63.
7. PHYLLIS FURDELL, National Commission on Working Women, Washington, D.C. Personal communication with the authors.
8. WEINSTEIN, *Men, Women and Money*, 39.
9. PHILLIP BLUMSTEIN AND PEPPER SCHWARTZ, *American Couples* (New York: Morrow, 1983), 164–77.

9. The Full Nest: First-Time Parents Over Forty

1. ROBIN MARANTZ HENIG, *How a Woman Ages* (New York: Ballantine Books, 1985), 98–106.
2. "Mid-Life Moms," feature on ABC television network series "20/20," 6 April 1990.
3. ROBERT STEINBROOK, "Technique Aids Pregnancy in Women Over 40," *Los Angeles Times*, 25 October 1990.
4. SUSAN ISAACS AND MARTI KELLER, *The Inner Parent: Raising Ourselves, Raising Our Children* (New York: Harcourt Brace Jovanovich, 1979), 92.
5. STEVEN A. FRANKEL AND MYRA J. WISE, "A View of Delayed Parenting: Some Implications of a New Trend," *Psychiatry* 45 (1982): 223–25.
6. LINDA ROACH MONROE, "Menopause: Baby Boomers' Next Step," *Los Angeles Times*, 5 December 1989.
7. ELLEN CURRIE, "One Chick," *Lear's*, September–October 1988, 118.
8. JANE MENKEN, "Age and Fertility: How Late Can You Wait?" *Demography* 22, no. 4 (November 1985).
9. BRUNO BETTELHEIM, "A Good Enough Parent," in *Reclaiming the Inner Child*, edited by Jeremiah Abrams (Los Angeles: Tarcher, 1990), 285–86.

10. You Can't Hurry Love

1. STANLEY BRANDES, *Forty: The Age and the Symbol* (Knoxville: University of Tennessee Press, 1985), 99.

2. Bureau of the Census, *Statistical Abstract of the United States* (Washington, D.C.: U.S. Government Printing Office, 1981).

3. HELEN FISHER, "The Four-Year Itch," *Natural History*, October 1987.

4. ALAN BOOTH AND JOHN EDWARDS, "Age at Marriage and Marital Instability," *Journal of Marriage and the Family* 47, no. 1 (February 1985): 69.

BIBLIOGRAPHY

ALLEN, SUZANNE M., AND RICHARD A. KALISH. "Professional Women and Marriage." *Journal of Marriage and the Family* 46, no. 2 (May 1984).

BARBERIS, MARY. "Women and Marriage: Choice or Chance?" In *The American Woman: 1988–1989: A Status Report,* edited by Sara E. Rix. New York: Norton, 1988.

BEAVERS, W. ROBERT. *Successful Marriage: A Family Systems Approach to Couples Therapy.* New York: Norton, 1985.

BERNARD, JESSE. *The Future of Marriage.* New York: World, 1972.

BETTELHEIM, BRUNO. "A Good Enough Parent." In *Reclaiming the Inner Child,* edited by Jeremiah Abrams. Los Angeles: Tarcher, 1990.

BITTER, ROBERT G. "Late Marriage and Marital Instability: The Effects of Heterogeneity and Inflexibility." *Journal of Marriage and the Family* 48, no. 3 (August 1986).

BLUMSTEIN, PHILLIP, AND PEPPER SCHWARTZ. *American Couples.* New York: Morrow, 1983.

BOLEN, JEAN SHINODA. *The Tao of Psychology.* San Francisco: Harper & Row, 1979.

BOOTH, ALAN, AND JOHN EDWARDS. "Age at Marriage and Marital Instability." *Journal of Marriage and the Family* 47, no. 1 (February 1985).

————, AND DAVID JOHNSON. "Premarital Cohabitation and Marital Success." *Journal of Family Issues* 9, no. 2 (June 1988).

BRANDES, STANLEY. *Forty: The Age and the Symbol.* Knoxville: University of Tennessee Press, 1985.

BRUBAKER, TIMOTHY. *Later Life Families.* Beverly Hills: Sage Publications, 1985.

BUMPASS, LARRY, JAMES A. SWEET, AND ANDREW CHERLIN. "The Role of Cohabitation in Declining Rates of Marriage." *NSFH Working Paper* no. 5 (August 1989). Madison: Center for Demography and Ecology, University of Wisconsin.

BUREAU OF THE CENSUS. *Statistical Abstract of the United States.* Washington, D.C.: U.S. Government Printing Office, 1981.

BUREAU OF THE CENSUS. *Current Population Reports.* Series P–20, no. 418. Washington, D.C.: U.S. Government Printing Office, 1986.

BUTLER, KATY. "The Great Boomer Bust." *Mother Jones,* June 1989.

CAMPBELL, JOSEPH. *The Power of Myth.* New York: Doubleday, 1988.

CHERLIN, A. "Postponing Marriage: The Influence of Young Women's Work Expectations." *Journal of Marriage and the Family* 2, no. 2 (May 1980).

COLMAN, CAROL. *Love and Money: What Your Finances Say About Your Personal Relationships.* New York: Coward, McCann & Geoghegan, 1983.

CURRIE, ELLEN. "One Chick." *Lear's,* September–October 1988.

DARLING, JON. "Late-Marrying Bachelors." In *Single Life: Unmarried Adults in Social Context,* edited by Peter J. Stein. New York: St. Martin's Press, 1981.

DOUDNA, CHRISTINE. "Where Are the Men for the Women at the Top?" In *Single Life: Unmarried Adults in Social Context,* edited by Peter J. Stein. New York: St. Martin's Press, 1981.

EHRENREICH, BARBARA. *The Hearts of Men.* Garden City, New York: Anchor/Doubleday, 1983.

ETZKOWITZ, HENRY, AND P. STEIN. "The Life Spiral." *Alternative Lifestyles* 1 (1978).

EXTER, THOMAS. "How to Figure Your Chances of Getting Married." *American Demographics* 9 (June 1987).

FABE, MARYLIN. *Up Against the Clock.* New York: Random House, 1979.

FISHER, HELEN. "The Four-Year Itch." *Natural History,* October 1987.

FLEMING, ANNE TAYLOR. "Babies Over 40." *Lear's,* September–October 1988.

FRANKEL, STEVEN A., AND MYRA J. WISE. "A View of Delayed Parenting: Some Implications of a New Trend." *Psychiatry* 45 (August 1982).

FROMM, ERIC. *The Art of Loving.* New York: Harper, 1956.

GLICK, PAUL C. "Marriage, Divorce and Living Arrangements: Prospective Changes." *Journal of Family Issues* 5, no. 1 (March 1984).

GLICK, PAUL C. "Updating the Life Cycle of the Family." *Journal of Marriage and the Family* 39, no. 1 (February 1977).

GOLDSCHEIDER, FRANCES KOBRIN, AND LINDA J. WAITE. "Sex Differences in the Entry into Marriage." *American Journal of Sociology* 92, no. 1 (July 1986).

GOTTLIEB, ANNIE. *Do You Believe in Magic: The Second Coming of the Sixties Generation.* New York: Times Books/Random House, 1987.

GRANT, E. "Marriage: Practice Makes Perfect." *Psychology Today,* March 1988.

GREENGLASS, ESTHER R. AND REVA DEVINS. "Factors Related to Marriage and Career Plans in Unmarried Women." *Sex Roles* 8, no. 1 (1982).

GUGGENBUHL-CRAIG, ADOLF. *Marriage Dead or Alive?* Dallas: Spring Publications, 1977.

GUNSBERG, LINDA. "A Cold Look at Motherhood Over 40." *Lear's,* September–October 1988.

GURIN, JOEL. "Tick, Tick, Tick . . . Do Men Have a Biological Clock?" *Ms.,* September 1986.

HALL, H. "Marriage: Practice Makes Imperfect?" *Psychology Today,* July–August 1988.

HANSEN, RON. "The Male Clock." *Esquire,* April 1985.

HENIG, ROBIN MARANTZ, ET AL. *How a Woman Ages.* New York: Ballantine Books/Esquire Press, 1985.

ISAACS, SUSAN, AND MARTI KELLER. *The Inner Parent: Raising Ourselves, Raising Our Children.* New York: Harcourt Brace Jovanovich, 1979.

JOHNSON, ROBERT A. *We: Understanding the Psychology of Romantic Love.* San Francisco: Harper and Row, 1983.

KIMMEL, MICHAEL (ed.). *Changing Men.* Beverly Hills: Sage Publications, 1987.

LASCH, CHRISTOPHER. *The Culture of Narcissism: American Life in an Age of Diminishing Expectations.* New York: Warner Books, 1979.

LASSWELL, MARCIA E., AND NORMAN M. LOBSENZ. *Equal Time.* Garden City, New York: Doubleday, 1983.

LEONARD, LINDA SCHIERSE. *On the Way to the Wedding: Transforming the Love Relationship.* Boston: Shambhala, 1986.

LEVINSON, DANIEL. *Seasons of a Man's Life.* New York: Ballantine Books, 1980.

LIGHT, PAUL C. *Baby Boomers.* New York: Norton, 1988.

MANEKER, J., AND ROBERT P. RANKIN. "Education, Age at Marriage and Marital Duration: Is There a Relationship?" *Journal of Marriage and the Family* 47 (August 1985).

MAY, ROLLO. *Love and Will.* New York: Norton, 1969.

MARBELLA, JEAN. "Heartbreak of Cohabitation Ends in Divorce." *Los Angeles Times,* 16 November 1989.

MCGOWAN, JO. "Marriage Versus Just Living Together." *Commonweal,* 13 March 1981.

MENKEN, JANE. "Age and Fertility: How Late Can You Wait?" *Demography* 22 (November 1985).

MERSER, CHERYL. *Grown-Ups: A Generation in Search of Adulthood.* New York: G. P. Putnam's Sons, 1987.

MONROE, LINDA ROACH. "Menopause: Baby Boomers' Next Step." *Los Angeles Times,* 5 December 1989.

MOORMAN, JEANNE E. "The History and the Future of the Relationship between Education and Marriage." Miscellaneous Publications, Census Bureau of the United States. Washington, D.C.: U.S. Government Printing Office, 1987.

MORRIS, MONICA. *Last Chance Children: Growing Up with Older Parents.* New York: Columbia University Press, 1988.

NADELSON, CAROL, AND MALKAH NOTMAN. "To Marry or Not to Marry." In *Concepts of Femininity and the Life Cycle,* edited by Carol C. Nadelson and Malkah T. Notman. New York: Plenum Press, 1982.

National Center for Health Statistics. *Advance Report of Final Marriage Statistics.* 38, no. 8, supplement 2 (July 13, 1989) Hyattsville, Md.

National Center for Health Statistics. *Trends and Variations in First Births to Older Women, 1970–1986.* Vital and Health Statistics, series 21, no. 47.

NICHOLS, MICHAEL P. *Turning 40 in the 80's.* New York: Simon and Schuster, 1986.

NORTON, ARTHUR J., AND JEANNE E. MOORMAN. "Current Trends in Marriage and Divorce among American Women." *Journal of Marriage and the Family* 49, no. 1 (February 1987).

NORWOOD, ROBIN. *Women Who Love Too Much.* Los Angeles: Tarcher, 1985.

OPPENHEIMER, V. K. "A Theory of Marriage Timing." *American Journal of Sociology* 94 (November 1988).

RICHE, MARTHA FARNSWORTH. "Post-Marital Society." *American Demographics,* November 1988.

RODGERS, WILLARD L., AND ARLAND THORNTON. "Changing Patterns of First Marriage in the United States." *Demography* 22, no. 2 (May 1985).

ROGERS, CARL R. *Becoming Partners: Marriage and Its Alternatives.* New York: Dell, 1972.

ROSENTHAL, SAUL H., M.D. *Sex Over 40.* Los Angeles: Tarcher, 1987.

SACHS, ANDREA. "America's New Fad." *Time,* 19 February 1990.

SCHOEN, ROBERT. "The Continuing Retreat from Marriage: Figures from 1983 U.S. Marital Status Life Tables." *Sociology and Social Research* 71 (June 1987).

SHEEHY, GAIL. *Passages.* New York: E. P. Dutton, 1976.

SILLS, JUDITH. *A Fine Romance.* New York: Ballantine Books, 1987.

SMELSER, NEIL J., AND ERIK H. ERIKSON, EDS. *Themes of Work and Love in Adulthood.* Cambridge: Harvard University Press, 1980.

SMITH, JAMES R., AND LYNN G. SMITH. *Beyond Monogamy: Recent Studies of Sexual Alternatives in Marriage.* Baltimore: Johns Hopkins University Press, 1974.

SOLOMON, MARION F. *Narcissism and Intimacy: Love and Marriage in the Age of Confusion.* London: Norton, 1989.

STEIN, PETER. "The Lifestyles and Life Chances of the Never-Married." *Marriage and Family Review,* vol. 1, no. 4 (1978).

STEINBROOK, ROBERT. "Technique Aids Pregnancy in Women Over 40." *Los Angeles Times,* 25 October 1990.

TANFER, KORAY. "Patterns of Premarital Co-habitation among Never-

Married Women in the United States." *Journal of Marriage and the Family* 49 (1987).

THORNTON, ARLAND. "Cohabitation and Marriage in the 1980s." *Demography* 25, no. 4 (November 1988).

THORNTON, ARLAND, AND DEBORAH FREEDMAN. "Changing Attitudes Toward Marriage and Single Life." *Family Planning Perspectives* 14, no. 6 (December 1982).

VAUGHAN, PEGGY. *The Monogamy Myth.* New York: Newmarket Press, 1989.

WALTER, CAROL AMBLER. "Babies Over 40." *Lear's,* September–October 1988.

WATSON, ROY E. L., AND PETER W. MEMEO. "Premarital Cohabitation vs. Traditional Courtship and Subsequent Marital Adjustment: A Replication and Follow-up." *Family Relations* 39 (1987).

WEINSTEIN, GRACE. *Men, Women and Money: New Roles, New Rules.* New York: New American Library, 1986.

WIERSMA, G. E. *Cohabitation: An Alternative to Marriage?* Boston: Martinus Nijhoff, 1983.